Janet S. Steinw[...]

The Golden Key to Executive Coaching

...and One Treasure Chest Every Coach Needs to Explore

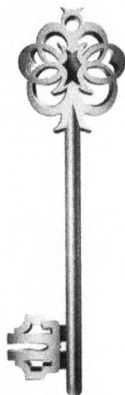

BOOK 1 OF
THE STEINWEDEL RED BOOK SERIES

CHIRON PUBLICATIONS • ASHEVILLE, NORTH CAROLINA

www.ChironPublicatons.com
ISBN 978-1-63051-351-1 paperback
ISBN 978-1-63051-352-8 hardcover
ISBN 978-1-63051-353-5 electronic

Book and cover design by Nelly Murariu
Cover artwork by Mariá Eva Trajterová
Printed in the United States of America.

Library of Congress Cataloging-in-Publication Data
Steinwedel, Janet S., author.
 The golden key to executive coaching : ...and one treasure chest every coach needs to explore / Janet S. Steinwedel.
    pages cm
 Includes bibliographical references.
  ISBN 978-1-63051-351-1 (pbk.) -- ISBN 978-1-63051-352-8 (hardcover) -- ISBN 978-1-63051-353-5 (electronic)
 1. Executive coaching. I. Title.
 HD30.4.S736 2015
 658.4'07124--dc23
                    2015032299

"Dr. Steinwedel's approach to coaching is tremendously helpful in the real world—full of wisdom and balance, made possible by years of practice and experience. This erudite book, a small tour de force of modern psychological thought as applied to a business environment, gives us insight into why she is so effective. Highly recommended, even for those who are not coaches but just interested in learning more about the general subjects related to growth and development."

DR. CHARLIE REESE
Department Chair, Healthcare System

"*The Golden Key* offers a thought-provoking perspective on the external forces that shape our persona through midlife along with rich and proven techniques for increasing self-awareness and getting back to "who you really are". While directed towards forming authentic relationships between executive coaches and their clients, Steinwedel's book provides a structure everyone will find useful for enhancing emotional and social intelligence, building trusted relationships and defining/embracing their own individuality. If you are interested in increasing your own personal effectiveness, I encourage you to read this book."

ARMAND GIRARD, Vice President
Corporate Development, GlycoMimetics, Inc.

"Janet Steinwedel guides us on an illuminating journey back to our true selves in "The Golden Key." She explains how and why we get away from our authentic selves early in life, and then shows us a path that, when undertaken with courage, will lead us beyond self-awareness to genuinely conscious and authentic living. With humility, grace, and humor, Janet inspires us to build the best lives that we can for ourselves and to unlock the potential in those whom we coach. No book has ever had a more powerful impact on my personal and professional growth as "The Golden Key.""

JILL HEWITT
Senior Organizational Excellence Consultant

"I have worked with Janet as not only my personal coach but also as the coach of our company's leadership team. Reading this book takes me back to my journey with Janet on a personal level as she coached me to continue developing as a leader. Janet's book guides you to becoming an authentic leader versus the leader you thought you needed to be. Being a strong leader does not only apply to the workplace but to life in total. Developing your authentic self makes you a better leader, family member, community servant and overall person. I strongly encourage you to read this book and begin this journey."

MIKE SWIDERSKI
President, ConMet

The Golden Key to Executive Coaching is not just for executive coaches in the business world. It holds the *key* to authentic leadership for all those who manage staff in religious institutions as well. Janet Steinwedel not only helps coaches and leaders understand the necessity of engaging their own inner process, she provides a clear, accessible road map for that journey. The book is written in a conversational style that is authentic and engaging, but never elementary. Steinwedel goes deep and the reader goes with her willingly. I will return to this valuable book time and again. It has earned a place of honor alongside selected others in my own canon for leadership and personal growth resources."

SUSAN D. MOSELEY, D.Ed.Min.,
Certified Educator in the Presbyterian Church, U.S.A.

"Dr. Steinwedel's interest and understanding of Carl Jung's work and her integration of his concepts into the profession of coaching are genuine and deeply insightful. I found the questions posed and exercises provided to be challenging, thought provoking and growth producing. The book is well-organized and well-researched, offering readers levels of insight into the evolving field of Leadership Coaching. The numerous quotations and additional references provided add to the breadth and depth of the material being presented. I believe it will be an excellent resource for therapists as well and truly anyone who wants to understand themselves more deeply."

FRITZ HAAS, Director of Wellness Counseling
Neumann University

"Steinwedel's book takes foundational psychological theories and provides testable and practical ways to incorporate them into coaching practice. Incorporating psychological principles into coaching practice, as Steinwedel suggests, will allow for greater reflection and self-knowledge with regard to one's coaching style and behaviors, enhancing client experiences and increasing future avenues for improving leadership."

KATINA SAWYER, PhD
Assistant Professor of Psychology
Graduate Programs in Human Resource Development
Villanova University

Professional Dedication

This book is dedicated to Carl Gustav Jung and the many analysts who have followed him into the world of analytical psychology. I am grateful for their research, writings, and commitment to the analytical process.

Their personal individuation efforts and their interest in guiding others on the personal growth path have enabled me to dig into and work toward my own individuation. It has also allowed me to support organizational and leader development in deep and conscious ways.

Fifty-four years after Jung's death, and six years after the publication of Jung's *Red Book*, Liber Novus, this is the Introduction to The Steinwedel Red Book Series. It starts with *The Golden Key to Executive Coaching...and One Treasure Chest Every Coach Needs to Explore.*

Personal Dedication

For the Wildgrubes, Lederers, Waculas, Nemethys and Steinwedels who laid the foundation for me and are important figures in the collective energy that brought me to this work. They each showed leadership in their careers, with their families and in their lives. They were teachers, tradesmen, musicians, artists, athletes, business leaders and politicians. They took risks to make better lives for their families and communities and I'm grateful for their contributions, values and commitments.

Table of Contents

Acknowledgements

Thank you, everyone! When you take on a project like this you find so many people you appreciate because the smallest bit of encouragement on a tough day can mean a great deal and just a little piece of information can save you a lot of time. And, with the world-wide-web at our disposal, where literally everyone contributes information, everything is possible.

I am grateful that there were those individuals who read the manuscript front to back and provided me with excellent feedback from their areas of expertise, most especially, Irina Filippova, Cindy Stengle-Paris and Steve Steinwedel. And, for those who read the manuscript to provide endorsements I am humbled by your kind and generous support. Many thanks to my editor, Melanie Votaw, for her suggestions and perseverance; to Chiron Publications for the many ways they enhanced the book, especially Len Cruz, Steve Buser, Jennifer Fitzgerald and Nelly Murariu. For reading and rallying and daily encouragement, thank you Susan Moseley. In the end, the opinions expressed are my own and don't necessarily represent those who have helped and supported me.

There were those that gave freely from their experiences the advice for getting a book published and I'm especially grateful for Wendy Axelrod, Bob Barner, Mary Benedetto, Charles Decker, Mindy Hall, James Hollis and Cheryl Rice.

What a wonderful joy it was for me to meet my cousin, Mariá Eva Trajterová in Bratislava in 2012 and to discover Jung's Red Book (in Slovak) sitting in her living room. She is an artist and author and together with her daughter, Luci, created the cover art for the book. My Mother, who has maintained and developed her ability to speak the language over her lifetime provided the many translations that enabled us all to work together. Quite a synchronistic treat!

There is no way to adequately thank clients who risked and trusted and shared and challenged – enabling me to keep growing as we worked honestly together. It is an honor and a privilege to do this work.

For so many kind and generous mentors and teachers, Charlie Seashore (posthumously), Jeremy Taylor, Jean Hauser, Cliff Smith, Sallie Bell, Alden Josey, Ph.D., the PAJA organization – the many analysts that provided greater understanding through Jung seminars (www.cgjung philadelphia.org). For bountiful pilgrimages with David Whyte and Marcus Borg (posthumously). Additionally, I have greatly appreciated and benefitted from a long membership (and many friendships) with the Philadelphia Society for People and Strategy (formerly PHRPG & PHRPS), and the Delaware Valley Association for Psychological Type, an MBTI® network (www.dvapt.org).

I'll say it once and try to put it aside: Forgive me for any mistakes, miscommunications, or any unconscious liberties taken. This is the nerve-racking part, but as Marion Woodman noted so spot on in the preface of one of her books, "The book is about a beheading. It has been hewn out of the hard rock of an addiction to perfection. Repeatedly, I have done battle with the black crow sitting on my left shoulder croaking, 'It isn't good enough. You haven't anything new to say. You don't say it well enough.' Repeatedly, I have had to stop trying to perfect a sentence here, a paragraph there, while the rest of the book remained unwritten" (Woodman 1982). Thank you, Marion and all who face and dance with the shadow.

Many thanks to my husband, Steve – a seeker who ensures we have exciting and interesting travel and learning opportunities. I am grateful for your daily challenge and support of my individuation journey – more than you know!

About This Book and its Context in the Series

While there are many books on leadership and executive coaching, I have not found one that tackles the issues and development of the coach from a depth psychology perspective. That is the focus of this book – it looks at the psychic development of the individual coach and their client from personal, reflective experience. In this series, the experiences shared are of my thirty plus years in the organizational and corporate worlds, including becoming a leader, working with leaders, and, at the same time, connecting with *Self* in a deep and conscious way.

Cognitive development has been an important part of the journey, but it isn't the golden key. Behavioral learning has played a part in my development, but it isn't the golden key. And that's where the series starts. We all hold a golden key to the door behind which lie all the answers to our questions and challenges, we just need to figure out which door. We must find the lock that this particular key fits.

So, this is a book and the beginning of a series of books primarily for coaches – for their personal growth, as well as the work they do with leaders. It recognizes that the coach benefits as much from ongoing development as any leader. Experienced coaches will be the largest benefactors as they will be challenged to enlarge themselves by living in relationship with the Self. In this way they will increase their effectiveness and personal insights. These are likely professionals nearing or in midlife[2]. If you are not yet in midlife, the book will help you plan for a conscious approach to growth and development toward midlife. New coaches will gain insights to guide their thoughtful beginnings and set the stage for necessary growth beyond classroom learning. Talent Management, Organizational Development,

---

1   Self – The capital "S" self that Jung referred to when he spoke of the whole and unified personality. There will be much more said on this throughout the book.
2   From an analytical frame, midlife is not seen as an age but a level of maturity, a shift in interests from how we establish ourselves in the world to what is meaningful. It typically doesn't show up before our 40s, and some people never get there.

Change, and Leadership Development professionals who utilize coaching skills to influence leaders and teach them how to be influential will benefit greatly from journeying through the *Red Book* Series, as will leaders who have been coached, have been changed by the experience, and wish to coach others. And, finally, therapists, social workers, and staff members of faith-based communities have expressed the value of the messages contained within for their increased effectiveness in their work.

Our busy lives stimulate unconscious desires for a quick fix; yet, as coaches we come to realize that there is no silver bullet, whether a tool, a process, or a particular approach. We are all challenged by situations that arise: Should I take this coaching assignment even though the manager has a clear desire to fix this person? If I work with this manager, will that preclude me from working with the leader of the department later? The executive I'm working with isn't really interested in doing this work, so should I continue? It's a good client, so I can't say no even though I'm at capacity already – what should I do? Living more consciously enables us to make better decisions. If these are the kinds of issues you're grappling with and you want to take responsibility for continuous improvement, you will find a lot of value in the pages ahead.

There is only one prerequisite – you must be curious and interested in learning without parameters. So, if you see yourself as an insatiable and continuous learner, you've come to the right place – drink up!

Why Red Book Series?

Since my first brush with the Myers-Briggs Type Indicator® assessment (MBTI®, see myersbriggs.org for more information), an instrument based on Jung's theory of personality, I have been intrigued by the work and life of Carl Gustav Jung (1875-1961). Recently, his *Red Book* was published, which is made up of his own notes of self-observation. It is the evidence of a truly and painfully examined interior life, an exploration that enabled the man to live his destiny. He was intent on learning about his emotions – his highs and lows and his fears and joys. I marvel at his efforts to live a meaningful authentic life – a life lived with integrity.

Granted, that kind of self-examination isn't for everyone. We mostly live our lives from our own subjectivity, lucky if every once in a while we see clearly without projecting. But if you want to learn at a deeper level and assist others in deep learning, this book and series will assist you in that endeavor.

While you may have become briefly acquainted with Jung in a psychology class in university and may have brushed up against a remnant of his work through taking the MBTI® Assessment, it is unlikely you really got to know his genius in understanding the human experience.

I study Jung's work and Jungian literature because the insights resonate so deeply with my experience of being human and being able to access a meaningful life. I study Jung because of the lack of rigidity of his theories. There is room in his ideas for the differences and nuances that make up our days and lives.

This makes sense to me because I've seen such a range of diversity from one person I meet to the next. I'm often disappointed by theorists who defend a very tight and organized approach to the human experience. In contrast, Jung himself did not believe there should or could be "Jungians," but that only *he* could be Jungian. He fought the idea of a Jungian Institute, although he relented in the end. At the risk of sounding "new age-y," I find true *wisdom* in Jung's approach. I believe this is due to the breadth of his studies – cultural, religious, spiritual, philosophical, historical, psychological, medical, and his insistence on considering the individual experience in the theoretical paradigm.

The *Red Book Series* has come about because, like C. G. Jung, we all have an exploration in front of us and a "Red Book" to write. Yet, when the idea of a *Steinwedel Red Book Series* was first suggested to me, I couldn't imagine it. The concept felt too arrogant and lofty. And while it still feels like mighty large shoes to fill, as I was writing over the last several years, I realized that this thread of integrity, truth, and life experience that Jung emphasized was at the heart of my work and my life.

The Golden Key to Executive Coaching...and One Treasure Chest Every Coach Needs to Explore

I've learned that it is only in doing my own work that I can be of value to others. I can only reach out and assist others to the degree that I have gained insight through my own internal exploration. My doctoral research led me in this direction of the purity and integrity of the "instrument" – the instrument in this case being the coach. (Note that "purity" is a word that has negative connotations, and there are good reasons for that. The purity system and the idea of being clean or unclean is not what I mean here; rather, it is right intention, a driving toward integrity, a developmental work that helps us see ourselves clearly.)

As coaches, we learn a fair amount about the emotions of our clients, but how much time do we give to our own emotions? Jung set the example, and I concur with his insights – we must all explore our inner world, gaining access to the *Self* – our curiosities, our needs, our reactions, and our ways of being in the world. I believe if we give more time to our intra-psychic world, we will have greater satisfaction in our relationships and more success in our coaching efforts.

Coaching provides a great opportunity for leaders to have more of this personal learning experience, too. Unfortunately, however, our society tends to meet the idea of therapy with its defenses up, referring to it as navel-gazing and seeing it as some twisted excuse to blame our parents for our problems. Some still hold a skeptical perception of coaching, although that has largely dissipated. Many in the coaching field like to say that we have to separate ourselves from psychology. But people *are* psychological, so it is impossible to separate psychology from coaching if we hope to assist others in gaining insights and making meaningful and lasting change. The psyche is the totality of who we are – both the unconscious and the conscious aspects of our minds. This cannot be denied...at least not forever. As Jung put it:

> During my first years at the university I made the discovery that while science opened the door to enormous quantities of knowledge, it provided genuine insights very sparingly, and these in the main were of a specialized nature. I knew from my philosophical reading that the existence of the psyche was

18

responsible for this situation. Without the psyche there would be neither knowledge nor insight. Yet nothing was ever said about the psyche. (Jaffé, 1989)

In my studies of human and organizational systems, there has always been a lot of crossover with psychology and sociology. In the last ten years, while studying Jungian analytical psychology, I have come up with some satisfying answers to the questions I started with. How do we learn at a transformative level? Why are some people more interested in learning than others? How can we raise the allure of personal learning and gain greater value through conscious living? I explore those questions and potential answers in this book.

The Organization of the Book

This first book is organized in three parts. In Part I, we'll dig into the question, "Why Leadership Coaching?" It is important to know this for when the going gets tough. Guidance is provided for answering this question, and I give some of my personal reasons for getting into coaching. A comparative look at aspiration and inspiration, as well as the four phases of the Analytical Coaching Process that evolved from my experiences and studies, are also discussed.

In Part II, "Authenticity is a Gem," we'll work on finding out who we are at our core, the importance of self-awareness, and our fallibility and humanness. The work of coaching is not for the weak and fragile – we must each strengthen our own core. We'll review some assessments and theorists, and we'll discuss how to differentiate ourselves in the marketplace with a framework that expresses why we do the work and a flexible process for how we believe the work gets done. In closing Part II, we'll take what we've learned about our own authenticity and discover how to inculcate this knowing to become authentic leaders and developers of authentic leaders.

Finally, in Part III, "The Price of Admission: One Gold Key," we bring all the pieces together, and you will discover very clearly how to unlock your future success by bringing the treasure chest up from the depths and studying all of its contents.

The upcoming books will build on ideas of projection, metaphor, archetype, character, challenges from psyche, and other aspects that have surfaced in this book but need further expansion.

The chapters that make up the parts of these books will illuminate my personal journey because it is the only one I can speak to with any authority. It will also provide activities for securing the next steps in your journey. There are case studies, stories, poetry, and some foundational theory in order to clarify the ideas and the practice. No real names are used in the cases, and situations are appropriately altered to protect clients[3] and colleagues.

At the end of each chapter, you will find three key areas for sustaining insights – Introduction to Jung; Reader's Notes ("Your Notes"); and Additional Readings and Resources. Here, I will introduce or reinforce some of Carl Jung's ideas and theories; those of other theorists that are important and which reinforce the main message; and make connections to coaching.

The Reader's Notes section is for you. I encourage my readers to engage by writing in their books and making them useful for years to come. I hope you will note your insights, your questions, and your connections. Also, consider songs, poems, or movies that surface and resonate with you, and note them in this section with a short explanation about the connection.

"Additional Readings and Resources" provides a variety of resources to connect you deeper to the ideas presented. Some suggestions will come

---

3   Clients can be HR, project leaders, other executives, or sponsors of those being coached. Sometimes, those being coached are referred to as "coachee," so as not to be confused with the person who might actually hire a coach into the organization and sponsor the process. I will typically use "client" unless clarification is needed.

from popular literature and some from academic literature. You will see both fiction and non-fiction, organizational and leader-focused, and myth and depth-focused works. Choose as you feel appropriate. For those who do well with poetry or songs, there are some listed that might be effective for reflection and use with your notes section. This is meant to provide a way to continue your exploration and insights beyond what happens in your experience with this book.

* * *

Leadership is challenging, and yet, it is required from all of us in some way at some time. I anticipate you will meet and resolve some of those challenges in your exploration of the *Red Book* Series. Balancing curiosity and a hunger for insight with a reverence for ambiguity and a willingness to sit with paradox will provide you with amazing possibilities.

Preface

Leadership coaching has been on the rise over the last several decades. Coaches have become quite a force, and programs to develop coaches, for better or for worse, abound. Today, Executive Coaching is primarily focused on the high potential leader with the goal of strengthening the leader to be more resilient, agile, relationship-focused, even more successful, and an even greater asset to the organization. The effort entails guiding successful individuals to a next level by ridding them of any derailing qualities. Often, the contracting of coaching is focused on "deliverables," "key takeaways," and "return on investment (ROI)." Typically, many of these items are relationship-oriented, i.e., "Joan is not working well with her peer group;" "Jim can't delegate effectively;" "Sue doesn't manage up well;" "Tom must learn that the key to selling is building relationships;" "the EVP can't relate to the line;" "the COO has no emotional intelligence;" "the CEO is personable but not personal;" and so on.

Rarely, however, does the boss inquire about the intra-personal focus, requesting emphasis on the individual's intra-personal insight (who am I; what do I want; what will really get me jazzed; am I finding meaning in my work?) and asserting the need for a primary deliverable from this category. And rarely does he or she realize that they themselves might benefit from such an experience or that their organization might benefit *greatly* from such an experience.

In a Wall Street Journal article on October 21, 2011, former Tyco chief executive officer, Dennis Kozlowski, noted, "My sentence was far too drastic." In 2005, he was found guilty "on 22 of 23 counts, including grand larceny, conspiracy and securities fraud" and sentenced to up to 25 years in jail. In terms of pay (in 2000 he took home a pay package of over $105 million), Kozlowski noted, "When you're... trying to have the best possible company on the planet, being the competitive person I am, I think my compensation was a way of showing how well I was doing."

We only need to look back on the last 10-15 years to the Enron, Tyco, and WorldCom corporate scandals and then to the Bear Stearns, Lehman Brothers, and Merrill Lynch debacles and the fall of the financial markets in 2008 to realize this is an understatement.

I don't think just any coaching will help us steer clear of these types of disasters. Many of the executives who found themselves in trouble were probably considered high potential. Any one of them may have had a coach. If the coach was only focused on the client's goals and business, the coach might have missed some important shadow[4] issues. In contrast, the coach with an analytical frame is looking for consciousness[5] and encouraging consciousness around issues of integrity and authenticity for internal and external alignment and overall effectiveness.

> "I'll bet most of the companies that are in life-or-death battles got into that kind of trouble because they didn't pay enough attention to developing their leaders."
>
> WAYNE CALLOWAY
> Former Chairman, Pepsico, Inc.

Our experiences in life enable us to "individuate,"[6] to become our fullest, truest, best selves – that which we are meant to be and which the whole life journey is directed toward. We can take the challenge or look away, focus on this aspect of our lives or give in to distraction. If we don't know that we are getting side-tracked or that we are ignoring our innate dreams, are we then doomed to a life of dissatisfaction – an incomplete life? Carl Jung (and many other psychologists and development experts) would say that we will likely end up feeling we didn't get some deeper meaning from our lives, some deeper connection with ourselves. Yet,

---

4   Here I am referring to aspects that are unconscious, out of alignment with our true integrity.

5   Consciousness is the highest value of analytical psychology according to Jung (CW 16, *Practical Use of Dream Analysis,* as noted in Zoja, *Ethics,* pp. 55-56). It is how we bring our shadow out into the light of day and explore it.

6   To Individuate is C. G. Jung's term for becoming whole. Individuation is the basis of his theory of personality. It is the accessing of knowledge from within that enables us to find our true path in life. The entire book and series revolves around the clarification and importance of individuation.

research shows that meaning-making is at the top of the list of what really motivates us. Is it a highly unconscious motivation or one that scares us?

It seems to me that if our work and our lives are meaningful, we are living authentically. But how do we get there when we receive so many mixed messages and the many people in our lives all have their own personal expectations of us? One avenue is to continue working to understand our own emotions and needs.

Yet, frequently, even the people at the forefront of emotional intelligence seem to avoid doing just that. I attended several workshops and conferences in the late 1990's and 2000 in order to stay up on the emotional intelligence and neuroscience research. It was good to hear from the leading EI gurus and the sessions were all quite good and stimulating. In one instance, a question was posed to a panel from an audience member: "What have you each done to develop *your* emotional intelligence?" This was obviously difficult to answer as only one panelist responded to the exact question and told us about actions he'd taken to help develop his own emotional intelligence.

In that moment, I knew that one of the areas of focus for me personally and with clients would be how to actually do the work, make the change, and mature for the sake of individuation as well as to contribute to the community and thereby, the world. *Knowing about* EI was not enough. It is e-m-o-t-i-o-n-a-l intelligence we're after – building emotional understanding and strength. It is the emotionally intelligent leader who is resilient, agile, authentic, and globally effective.

Like many of you, I want to incorporate good "use of self" – often thought of in the OD and Change Management worlds as the skills and understanding one has developed. But additionally, I want to use what James Hollis, Jungian Analyst, refers to as Self, "the superordinate wisdom and purposive energy" (Hollis, 2013) – to assist in the transformation of others. In the '90 s, we learned not to just *train* or *teach* for mere activity, hoping someone would pick up a new trick, but for impact. It has been made clear by a century of psychologists that we cannot motivate others but that we can only create a motivating environment. We have to begin to understand where we are, where the individual we're coaching is. When we get some piece of this understanding – i.e., where the psyche has been and where it is today – we can assist in the process of defining internal motivation and raison d'être.

And so we seek further insights and commit to continuous learning. And still, with all our "knowing," we will make some mistakes. It is too easy to project our own experiences, insights, and beliefs onto another person. It's an *unconscious* activity. Coaches are *only* human, and to reach for perfection is arrogance. It doesn't exist. There are too many variables. But I find I am much more aware of it now because of my immersion in Jungian psychology, including personal time in analysis. More often, I can adjust, apologize, and course correct.

Journaling certainly helps me with my personal learning, and yet it would be impossible to journal about everything or after every client meeting. So, this book is for my personal and ongoing growth and development, as well as any insights it might provide for you.

Additionally, this book is an effort to assist all who make a life of slugging it out in the corporations and various industries and workplaces of the 21st century to find meaning in their lives through opening to the Self, their choice of work, and the human experience. Thoreau said that most of us are living lives of "quiet desperation," but I don't think it has to be that way. I'm not necessarily a proponent of the happiness movement, however. I believe it is valuable to entertain the full spectrum of our emotional responses. I don't think we need to stay stuck in any one situation or emotion. Yet, where we are in a given moment is where the work begins. Rumi wrote a poem that expresses it particularly well.

> This being human is a guest house.
>
> Every morning a new arrival.
>
> A joy, a depression, a meanness,
>
> some momentary awareness comes
>
> as an unexpected visitor.

Welcome and entertain them all!

Even if they're a crowd of sorrows,

who violently sweep your house

empty of its furniture,

still, treat each guest honorably.

He may be clearing you out

for some new delight.

The dark thought, the shame, the malice,

meet them at the door laughing,

and invite them in.

Be grateful for whoever comes,

Because each has been sent

As a guide from beyond.[7]

I hope that you will want to step up to this maturing along with me, for we need it as individuals. Our communities and organizations need it, and our country and our world need *you* – the best of you – *all* of you. I invite you to join me on this journey through the *Red Books of Executive Coaching*. And I invite you to make this your book by writing in the margins and the boxes provided. (If you just can't write in the book, please use *sticky notes*, but don't use that as an excuse not to engage.) Life is short, and you've stumbled on an opportunity to make yours a little more robust, a little richer, and dare I say, a veritable treasure chest!

---

7   Rumi, from the *Essential Rumi*. I was introduced to this poem by David Whyte. David has been very influential to my thinking, feeling, reflection, and integration of ideas. As well as reading David's books and incorporating him personally in leadership development programs, my husband and I have taken three of David's tours to the Burren Region and Galway Bay areas of western Ireland, to the Lake District in Northern England, and to the Galapagos Islands of Ecuador. See www.davidwhyte.com.

Foreword

This above all: to thine own self be true,

And it must follow, as the night the day,

Thou canst not then be false to any man.

Shakespeare
[Hamlet Act 1, scene 3, 78–82]

When C. G. Jung said that "Everything human is psychic", he might almost have been providing an epigraph for Dr. Janet Steinwedel's new book *"The Golden Key to Executive Coaching, And One Treasure Chest Every Coach Needs to Explore"*. In his spare comment, Jung meant to express that any genuinely significant understanding of the human phenomenon must rest upon the knowledge of the human psyche, in both its individual and collective aspects. The same psyche is the engine and the dynamism of all our being and doing, past, present and future.

Similarly, Alexander Pope advised men and women that they should "Seek not the ways of God to span; the proper study of mankind is man." Wisdom would seem to be the reward of the seeker with "eyes to see and ears to hear" who would examine man to the fullest extent of his outer physical and inner psychic life. It would appear that to accomplish the first goal may mean to take to heart these philosophers and psychologists.

The contemporary corporate culture wants, out of its own interests, to cultivate effectiveness and efficiency in its leadership corps within the narrowest spectrum of time and expense. Dr. Steinwedel here shares her deep conviction that it augments and deepens this work immensely when the executive has grasped that the process works best as he or she becomes a firmly committed partner in the endeavor to understand the roots of behavior and its transformation in the play between external and internal psychic factors.

This new book makes a bold leap toward a model and a process for Executive Coaching grounded in the depth psychology of Carl Jung. It was Jung's profound researches into the nature and the wellsprings of his own character that gave life to his development of ideas of the unconscious and its role in shaping personality and behavior. The living "organ" of the unconscious owed its personal aspect to the dynamic emotional responses of the individual to the world and to others, and its deeper and more ancient collective archetypal aspects to the gathered experience of humanity across the span of Time.

Jung made his own personal 20th century journey into deep reservoirs of psychic life, and found this "descent" both risky and dangerous, but also the source of genuine healing and of psychological and spiritual well-being. Some of this early and ground-breaking experience has recently appeared for the first time in the publication of Jung's famous "Red Book", a stunning collection of words and images that form a roadmap of this inward journey.

It is no accident that the book you are holding is the first of a series, the Steinwedel Red Book Series, in which the author outlines her own discoveries from the marriage of depth psychology principles with those of executive coaching practice. The basic premise of this marriage is that there can be no genuine understanding and transformation of human behavior without awareness of the influence of unconscious contents into the dramas of conscious life.

The author is well-equipped for this task through her past membership in the Advanced Seminar for Jungian Studies of the C. G. Jung Institute of Philadelphia as well as through an extended period of her own personal analytical work. This approach of "do as I do, not as I say" along with her many years of professional work as an executive coach within major corporate bodies has made her an effective proponent of the application of depth psychological principles to this field.

The new model, christened Coaching with an Analytic Frame (CAF), develops the premise that Jungian psychoanalytic ideas and principles can be brought smoothly and integrated fully into executive coaching practice. Further, these Jungian principals can contribute significantly to the development of personal and professional skills of executive-level leaders in any organization. The reader unfamiliar with Jungian terminology will find a useful glossary that defines terms like "persona", "shadow", "complex", "projection", "archetype", and the like.

Dr. Steinwedel is clear that this kind of coaching relationship does not constitute a psychoanalytic working relationship as one might find between the professional psychoanalyst and the client/patient. It is essential that these two modes of working with psychic material be differentiated in theory, but especially in practice. For example, coaches will not work analytically with the dream material of their clients since this work requires extensive supervised training and experience.

The coach's direct experience with personal analysis will be invaluable, but not required. However, it can be helpful if coaches are knowledgeable about depth psychoanalytic resources to which referrals can be made. Coaches working in the CAF mode must be specially trained to stay clear of such interventions, while at the same time helping the executive client to become aware and knowledgeable of internal psychic factors at work in themselves respecting their relationship to their own work as well as factors affecting the work of those they supervise.

Dr. Steinwedel's book is accessible to the reader interested in understanding and modifying his or her experience at work or in any other activity. The book's language is frequently conversational, even jaunty at times, and is clearly the voice of an enthusiastic seeker. The book is welcomed as a venture toward a general cultural goal in which psychodynamic principles will be seen to lie like a "Golden Key" at the heart of every kind of human activity and which demand our diligent and careful awareness if we are to survive and prosper as a human community.

ALDEN JOSEY, PhD, Jungian Analyst, Wilmington, DE

PART I

Compelling Purpose on a Silver Platter: Why Leadership Coaching?

Coming to know the true Self through exploring our aspirations and inspirations, and in dialogue about the integration of both for our effective individuation and skilled work in the world...

Chapter 1

Introduction

To accomplish great things we must not only act,
but also dream, not only plan, but also believe.

Anatole France

Early in my new life as an executive coach, I was at a meet and greet. You know the kind where you're new in a community (be it work, social, or neighborhood), and you have the opportunity to get to know others and share a bit about yourself. It was all going quite well. I enjoyed the people I met, and the music was at the right level to hear it but still be able to hold a conversation. One gentleman said, "Oh, you're an executive coach. So is another person I met earlier. You should meet Ted! You'd have a lot in common." This guy felt I *really needed* to meet Ted. I responded that I would look out for Ted and thanked the gentleman for letting me know.

But it didn't end there. He walked me over to Ted. At first blush, Ted and I did have something in common. We both work with people in a variety of businesses to assist them in building their leadership skills. That, however, is about where our common ground ended. I quickly realized that we didn't go into the work for the same reasons. Ted had always had his own business in some field or another, and then, it was coaching. After a few minutes of learning how we each got into the work of executive coaching, Ted said, "Well, Janet, all I can say is, 'It's a great gig, isn't it?!'" It wasn't the first time or, unfortunately, the last time I was "dragged" into such a conversation. Lucky for me, we got the call to join our tables for dinner. Saved by the bell!

For me, my livelihood has always been more of a calling than just some way of earning a living. Using the term "gig" seems to minimize the importance of the work and the sincerity in which I come to the labor. These efforts bring personal growth and meaning to my life, and I have always wanted to make a difference for others in some valuable way. Each of us comes to our work uniquely and finding understanding in our commitment to it is of great importance to living our life authentically.

Additionally, the work of coaching from an analytical frame is a relational endeavor. It is about two people coming together, finding the humanity and vulnerability in one another enough to be able to heal old wounds and build new confidence and clarity in one's purpose.

I started my career as an intern in a Training & Development department in a medium-sized organization with enough like-minded co-workers to encourage me onward. A Master's in Training and Organizational Development secured my direction. I was driven to succeed, but I wanted to understand what was driving me and what success meant to me, as well as what made this work compelling to me. These are important questions to ask ourselves as we do this work. What is driving you? What is success for you? What do you want to accomplish as a coach, and how deeply do you wish to work with your clients?

A famous paraphrase from *Alice in Wonderland* reminds us, "If you don't know where you're going, any road will get you there." How can you pick a road when you don't know where you're going? How do you reach a meaningful destination in that way? It is worth contemplating these questions as we explore different approaches to coaching.

Should Coaches Discuss Childhood Experiences?

Coaching and therapy are often differentiated by clarifying that coaching does not deal with childhood experiences; it is future-focused. There are issues that require more expertise and more attention than a coach is qualified to give. In my experience, this is mostly true. As coaches, we don't *deal* with childhood experiences, but it does help us to note them.

There are some things that, once remembered by a client and a connection made, are easy for the client to assimilate. The insight comes from the "aha" moment, when a locked up, stuck place becomes loose and malleable again. But this only happens when one is open to seeing something anew, and the ego[1] is strong enough to accept it.

In one situation, a client let me know that she had been abused as a child, and she'd had a good deal of therapy that was invaluable to her groundedness in adulthood. We did not *deal* with the fact that she'd been abused, but it did help me to know her more completely. And it was very useful to know when she called me a couple of years later with a big issue on her hands.

Today, when I begin a coaching engagement, I often ask about early family life – expectations, messages, parents, and siblings. This is not with any intention to pass the blame to someone else for my client's current situations. It does, however, provide a meaningful look into the early influences on a person. Our values and attitudes are drawn from our very young lives. Whether or not we felt supported in our families of origin has an impact on our behavior. We learn our powerlessness from our experience of being a child – being dependent and needing help to accomplish the simplest of tasks. Our maturing depends on our reflection and connection to certain early experiences that often trouble us if not explored.

No influences in our lives, no grinding of the lens by culture, no newly learned experience plays as large a role as that played by parents in the formative life of the individual. We receive our genetic inheritance from them and with that not only our somatic tendencies, aging patterns, propensity to certain disorders, and lifestyle predilections, but the actual physiological apparatus of

---

1   The ego is an aspect of the psyche. It is "concerned with such matters as personal identity, maintenance of the personality, continuity over time, mediation between conscious and UNCONSCIOUS realm, cognition and reality testing, it also has to be seen as responsive to the demands of something superior. This is the SELF, the ordering principle of the entire personality" (Samuels, Shorter, and Plaut 1986).

our perceiving and processing tools: eyes, ears, brain, et al. But as obvious as this physical inheritance is, and as pervasive an influence, a *Lebenwelt* in itself, the psychological influence is even greater. (Hollis, 2013)

One young woman said to me, "My whole family is made up of accountants. I just knew I'd be one, too.... Now, I'm relieved to know why I'm not happy with that career and that I probably have other options that would be much more satisfying." Our coaching went on in the direction of aligning her with her interests, abilities, experiences, and style. While it took a little time to make the whole transition to another career, her inauthentic accountant personality died off, and her real self began to shine through.

Over the years, I've found that for some, life seems to be completely set up on a silver platter, while for others, making life work is a struggle and a tension. Even when the plans seem quite clear, there are lots of things that can get in the way and muddy the waters.

Some psychologists refer to our "schemas," such as *disconnection* and *rejection* – these are a "reality based representation of the child's environment" (Young, Klosko, and Weishaar 2003). Schemas often give rise to defensiveness or mistrust as patterns of behavior that a person displays when triggered. Similarly, Carl Jung speaks of "complexes" – *a cluster of energy resulting from ideas, memories, beliefs – conscious or unconscious, that get in the way of our effectiveness.* (You'll hear more about these ideas throughout the book.)

There is an important clarification to make here, however. There are many kinds of coaches working with leaders. If I were "Queen of Coaching," I would make it a part of our code of ethics that each coach state the type of coach they are. For example, there are coaches who are very skilled in finance and/or strategy but have no human behavior training and should not be working with issues that relate to human behavior. I would like to suggest that this type of coach be referred to as a "Business Coach," who does not need to know and should not know about a person's childhood experiences. Business Coaches might make a suggestion about an issue that comes up with a boss or colleague, but they would be specific as to how they come by that suggestion, i.e., "in my experience...." But as soon as they begin moving into the relationship management domain, they need to clarify that it is not their area of expertise. The same would be true of a leadership coach with only a human development background who offers advice about strategic business direction. That coach needs to have grounds for why the advice is given. In fact, many coaching schools say our work is not to give advice for this very reason.

The work of coaching is serious work. The coach often has an impact on a person's choices and decisions. As someone who has studied and focused on human development, my experience with clients is that they often note that the time spent together was *therapeutic*. When I've inquired as to what this means for the client, the response has been, "I feel calmer;" "I'm more confident;" "I'm clearer about my next steps;" or "I feel more grounded again." This is one of the ways in which coaching with an analytical frame provides greater opportunity for lasting change in the inter- and intra-personal domains.

One approach to coaching is not better than another; it's just different. There are different features and benefits, but know what you're selling and what the client wants to buy.

A New Ethic in Coaching

Erich Neumann was a German psychologist who was, some say, Jung's most gifted student. Around the time of World War II, he wrote *Depth Psychology and a New Ethic* (Neumann, 1969) to express what he felt was necessary to call out in the way of ramping up the ethical standards of the day. He felt the world needed to demand a new expectation, a "higher and more exacting" set of standards.

In Luigi Zoja's book, *Ethics and Analysis*, he reminds us that the root of integrity comes from both beauty and truth. Aesthetics in the days of the Greek gods were an important part of what was deemed ethical (Zoja, 2007). The two worked hand-in-hand. That seems right to me – that there is a beauty in being, in finding and allowing ourselves to *be* that which we're meant to be. It's quite elegant.

The analytical coaching framework is meant to provide an ethical approach that allows both coach and client to find this elegance, this comfort of being in order to access transformational growth. Ethics are the fibers in the fabric.

What do I really mean by "transformation?" People often use the words "transition" and "transformation" synonymously, but there are important differences. One such difference is that in transition, we know that we are going from one known thing to another known thing. For example, I was the VP of the department, and now I'm going to be the SVP – doing the same basic work with a little more authority and responsibility. Or I was working out of the Philadelphia office, and now I'm going to be in the Houston office.

In transformation, we go from one known thing to an unknown. We journey toward the next iteration of who we're to be. It may be a new vocation, new relationship, or whatever. But we don't know what *it* is. Yet, we know we have to go forward, break new ground, *and see* what's around the corner. Often, we think we are just transitioning, but surprising situations create some remarkable transformations within us. You may have heard yourself or another say, "After that experience, I'll never be the same" or "That tour of duty really changed me." What we're saying in these kinds of comments is that we have been *transformed* in some way. Values have shifted, our way of seeing the world has changed, and something is fundamentally different. But one thing we're sure of is that *we're not in Kansas anymore*[2]!

You can see the threads of integrity in transformational work. I want to emphasize that we can only be acting with integrity when we, as

---

2   The Wizard of Oz – a fantastic story of the human journey of growth and individuation (finding one's true person-hood). "Not in Kansas anymore" has come to be an important metaphor in our language. The story is discussed further in Part 3, Chapter 1, in the closing section of this book.

coaches, are also gaining insight in a partnered and mutual approach to development. As was elucidated in my dissertation study, ongoing development is critical for the coach as the facilitator of development in others. This means continuous observing and reflecting on one's own behavior and working toward one's own individuation. When coaches only focus on skill development or cognitive development (for self or client), they miss the opportunity for meaningful growth that can be sustained and transcended.

This is a maturing process. If we don't mature mentally – psychically, along with our physical maturing – we're always out of step in some way. The emphasis in organizations on emotional intelligence is due to this very fact that the more mature individual makes better decisions in every aspect of their lives.

As midwives of development in others, coaches risk directing clients in inappropriate ways when we aren't expanding our own consciousness and becoming more self-aware in an effort to work with greater and greater integrity. This is what it means to be coaching with an analytical frame and to bring a new ethic to coaching.

Where the Work Begins

Jung was open and curious, and he believed in humankind. He designed his theories around the notion that there are two main phases in life – that of developing the ego in the first half of life (the "morning" of life) and that of connecting with the Self (see footnote 2 on p. 15) in the second half (the "afternoon" of life).

A human being would certainly not grow to be seventy or eighty years old if this longevity had no meaning for the species. The afternoon of human life must also have a significance of its own and cannot be merely a pitiful appendage to life's morning. The significance of the morning undoubtedly lies in the development of the individual, our entrenchment in the outer world, the propagation of our kind, and the care of our children. This is the obvious purpose of nature. But when this purpose has been attained – and more than attained – shall the earning of money, the extension of conquests, and the expansion of life go steadily on beyond the bounds of all reason and sense? Whoever carries over into the afternoon the law of the morning, or the natural aim, must pay for it with damage to his soul, just as surely as a growing youth who tries to carry over his childish egoism into adult life must pay for this mistake with social failure. (Jung, 1960)

As a leadership coach, I am typically working with an executive or with groups of leaders who are approaching midlife and are anticipating or fearing some kind of transition. I recognize this not by their age, but by the questions they ask and their general attitude about their lives. For some, there is a readiness for something new and more meaningful. Some express a longing for new projects, committing to volunteer work, traveling to ancestral homelands, or starting a new career from an old hobby. Others share worries about their mortality and disappointment over dreams not likely to be realized. It can be a devastating time when people feel their lives are not what they signed up for and not meeting some expectation from within. If they are unaware, this time can hit them as crisis, but if they are more conscious of their feelings, they can make adjustments and changes that engage them in a new, satisfying, and fruitful period of life.

These are defining moments. Can we rise to the bigger questions brought about by midlife, as well as the challenges of our families, professions, and communities? With the support of an analytical coach, I have seen people gain strength and clarity about their direction and find greater equilibrium and sense of self once again.

When I found myself in midlife, I entertained these very questions for several years. I needed to understand and make sense of the confusion in organizations, the leaders that make them up, and my own leadership and coaching approach. So, I decided to immerse myself in new learning. With fresh information and insights, I wound up starting my own business and was compelled to write this book.

In midlife, Jung's ideas of individuation, with its connection to personality theory, complex theory, and other areas of analytical psychology, have become much clearer for me. His framework for analysis and working with the challenges of being human dovetailed with my framework for coaching. While there are parts that don't fit with coaching and should not be pursued outside of the analyst-analysand (client) context, there is plenty that has enabled me to be much more effective in my process.

Where Are You?

What about you? What led you to the world of coaching? If you're not yet a coach, what makes you think you might want to be? What unique qualifications or experiences do you have? What draws you to the work? Are you in midlife? If Socrates is right, and the unexamined life is not worth living, how have you examined your own life? If someone were to ask you, "Who are you?" how would you answer? If you think this is a lot of nonsense, you might try to understand why you think so. What defenses are kicking in? (You might choose to make some notes in the space allotted below.)

On Jung

In this first section on Jung, I want to begin to unravel for you the influence that Jung has had on so many and why I think his work is so important to coaching. In an article titled, "The Cosmos, The Psyche and You," editor and journalist Carter Phipps discusses Carl Jung as one of two individuals who has had the greatest influence on hundreds of 20th century "scientists, philosophers, researchers, academics, mystics and others at the leading edge of their fields." They had been individually asked "who had been most prominent in shaping their work and ideas." Phipps notes:

> But as our global society hurtles toward the second decade of this young century, the influence of Carl Jung and Pierre Teilhard de Chardin is arguably more significant than ever. Like stone guardians standing at the gates of the future, Jung and Teilhard continue to subtly and profoundly shape the voices and

perspectives that are defining the leading edge of our contemporary culture. And, these voices are, in turn, influencing our collective perception, understanding, and most important, our response to the challenges of the new century (Phipps, 2008).

Freud was the first to discover the conscious and unconscious realm, but as I once heard a presenter aptly note, "Freud was fishing while sitting on a whale." Jung expanded on the notion of the unconscious to show that within this realm of the psyche, we have both the *personal* unconscious and the *collective* unconscious. The personal unconscious is what we have repressed or suppressed from our own life, and the collective unconscious is information that is available to all of us from the beginning of time. When we begin to realize how much knowledge is available to us within our own psyches, we hunger to make more of it conscious. In fact, we're drawn to exploration.

"He was a scholar of impressive erudition, and read English, French, Latin and Greek fluently as well as his native, German....Physician, psychiatrist, psychoanalyst, professor, scholar, writer, social critic, family man, and citizen—Jung was all of these. First and foremost, however, he was a relentless student of the psyche." (Hall and Nordby 1973)

In the Arthur I. Miller book *Deciphering the Cosmic Number*, on Jung and Wolfgang Pauli, the famed physicist, Miller notes:

For Pauli realized that quantum mechanics—despite its grandeur, and in the face of his distinguished colleagues—lacked the power to explain biological and mental processes, such as consciousness. It was not a complete theory. As he put it, "Though we now have natural sciences we no longer have a total scientific picture of the world. Since the discovery of the quantum of action, physics has gradually been forced to relinquish its proud claim to be able to understand, in principle, the *whole* world." To Pauli the only hope was an amalgam of quantum mechanics and Jung's psychology. (Miller 2009)

Looking back on Pauli's relationship with Jung from a twenty-first-century viewpoint, it is important to remember that Jung, Pauli, and their contemporaries considered Jung's research to be as important as Pauli's work in physics. Jung's exploration of the human psyche was just as serious as quantum mechanics' exploration of the physical world. (Miller, 2009)

The New York Times Magazine dated September 20, 2009 announced Jung's *The Red Book* on the front cover as "The Holy Grail of the Unconscious." Jung began work on *The Red Book* (also referred to as *Liber Novus*) almost 100 years prior, after he split from Freud and experienced his own middle passage. It is a beautiful book with his personal drawings and calligraphy and his most personal reflections and experiences. It had been sequestered in a Swiss bank vault for 25 years. Then, in October of 2009, it was "published by W. W. Norton and billed as the 'most influential unpublished work in the history of psychology' (Corbett, 2009)." Sonu Shamdasani, *The Red Book*'s editor, notes that the message for us is to "value your inner life (Ibid.)."

The work of analytical coaching is also about tapping into the inner life – learning the basic threads of who we are in order to build the best lives we can for ourselves – lives rich with meaning and fulfillment. This allows us to work and live with integrity and to leave a legacy that brings us some inner contentment, if not delight.

Your Notes

Jot down anything that has come to mind for you personally at this time:

——————————————————————————————————————

——————————————————————————————————————

——————————————————————————————————————

——————————————————————————————————————

——————————————————————————————————————

——————————————————————————————————————

——————————————————————————————————————

——————————————————————————————————————

——————————————————————————————————————

——————————————————————————————————————

——————————————————————————————————————

——————————————————————————————————————

——————————————————————————————————————

——————————————————————————————————————

——————————————————————————————————————

——————————————————————————————————————

——————————————————————————————————————

——————————————————————————————————————

——————————————————————————————————————

——————————————————————————————————————

——————————————————————————————————————

What are you feeling right now? What surprises you from your notes? What insights did you get about yourself? Any other thoughts right now? Anything you want to do, communicate or absorb because of this reflection?

Additional Reading and Resources

Poems

- » *The Journey* by Mary Oliver
- » *The Prelude* by William Wordsworth

Read

- » *Beyond Change Management: How to Achieve Breakthrough Results Through Conscious Change Leadership* by Dean Anderson, Linda Ackerman Anderson
- » *Collective Genius: The Art and Practice of Leading Innovation* by Linda A. Hill, Greg Brandeau, Emily Truelove & Kent Lineback
- » *Competing for the Future* by Gary Hamel
- » *Discovering Your Authentic Leadership, HBR article* by Bill George, Peter Sims, Andrew McLean, Diana Mayer
- » *Finding Meaning in the Second Half of Life: How to Finally, Really Grow Up* by James Hollis, Ph.D.
- » *The Heart Aroused* by David Whyte
- » *Leadership: The Inner Side of Greatness* by Peter Koestenbaum
- » *Servant Leadership* by Robert Greenleaf

Songs

- » *Pilgrim* by Enya
- » *Superman* by Five for Fighting

Movies & Television

- » *The Best of Men* (2012)
- » *Middlemarch* (1994)
- » *Vitus* (2006)

Chapter 2

The Heart of the Matter

"The years…when I pursued the inner images were the most important time of my life. Everything else is to be derived from this. It began at that time, and later details hardly matter anymore."

C. G. Jung

The French word for heart is "coeur," which is where we get the word "courage." Coaching and being coached takes courage. As coach or coaching client, we often travel on lonely, sometimes dark and desolate roads, seeking the heart and soul of our life's work. When we're in the day-to-day, "the grind" so to speak, it is hard to figure out how to get more of what we want.

I feel as though I am truly one of the fortunate ones. I thoroughly enjoy my work, and I've said so my whole career. I derive great joy from watching others gain insights into themselves, their lives, their joys, and their frustrations. Now, that doesn't mean I like every situation, but enjoying my work has meant that I can manage more effectively through the white water of life. Currently, I find that not only do I like the work, but I am particularly happy with the freedoms I have as an independent practitioner. It allows me to construct my work in a way that is most satisfying, drawing on hobbies, interests, and new challenges. I have also always delighted in continuous learning and expansion.

Most people who discuss a possible coaching engagement with me are not as clear about what would bring them fulfillment. They inevitably get to a point in the conversation when they note that they'd like to slow life down just enough to be able to consider what it is they *really* want.

In our modern society, we have filled our lives to capacity with kids, dogs, cats, birds, and even pigs, travel, second homes, fast cars, bikes, skis, boats, never mind friends, and blended and extended families. I know many people who live on six hours (and less) of sleep each night. Often, they are the same ones who eat on the run – dashboard dining at its best. All too often, this means coffee, chocolate, snacks, and whatever is quick and manageable with one hand. They arrive in their corporate parking lots with sticky fingers, overloaded minds, and dogged determination to meet the day's challenges. Let's face it: Jobs are demanding and unrelenting in this 21st century. We are so connected that we couldn't get lost if we tried.

It is no surprise, therefore, that the field of coaching is flourishing. Yet, people in business rarely put "personal effectiveness" or "thinking about self" on the calendar, so when they get the message from senior management that they should go to a leadership workshop and work on "X" (X = delegation, conflict resolution, listening, team building, etc.), coaching becomes another "check-the-box" experience. Some potential new clients are not sure they want to engage in self-development, as it presents like just another thing in the schedule to juggle.

Of course, if they're emotionally ready to do the work, they'll make the time, and the coach is there to help them use time well. For example, a senior level client of mine was struggling with his workload and not finding time to meet. When I asked what kept him so busy, he disclosed that he resented some of his tasks because he believed they would be eliminated before long, making the effort and craziness a waste. But he was still working hard on these tasks like the good "A" student he'd always been.

In an effort to guide him inward I asked that he think about just getting a "B" in these questionable areas. He didn't feel like he could put a hold on any of them, but it resonated with him that he could temporarily stop working quite so hard on projects he thought would be cut. I suggested he not make any immediate decision. Obviously, as in all situations in coaching, it was important that the decision was his and not mine. How could I know if it was sound decision-making without being privy to the many other variables that play into such a decision? The client needs to be accountable in the end and ready to say why a decision was made, and the coach needs to be humble enough to realize that some suggestions could be very bad ideas that are not right for the individual, the situation, or the time.

It is typical for me to request that my clients journal during our work together. This is important for the clarification of goals, the notation of feelings, the reinforcement of insights, and the ability to reflect back on where they have come from. Often, the unspoken goals show up in obtuse ways in the journals, already fairly specific and direct but simply unrecognized. It is equally important for the coach to keep a journal, noting and reflecting on frustrations, delights, expectations, and disappointments, as well as our own emotional responses and feelings.

When you coach someone and navigate a path with them, you provide them with both the ballast to keep going and the challenge to make the path worthwhile. You need to do the same in your own life. When is the last time you took a step back to examine your *own* path and to determine what is at the heart of your own contentment, motivation, and joy? What is the work you're meant to be doing? One coach I know continuously announces new specialties, suggesting he has no specialty at all. So, how do you stay innovative, relevant, *and* authentic?

You must also consider your client load as a coach. How many individuals or assignments can you take on and still remain agile and effective? What is too much for your own reflection and life balance? At what point do you lose your ability to be useful to your clients? Have you left time to gain new insights? Sometimes, you get forced breaks when work dries up for a period of time, and you need to have a plan for using those times to your benefit. These are just some of the questions that are important to ask yourself.

Learning how to balance the tension of no work with time to renew, replenish, and reengage with a clearer focus and purpose is difficult, but in the end, quite enriching. Ultimately, it is what allows *you* to stay on the right path as you continue to help others determine their own right paths.

Aspiration and Inspiration

What do "I" want? What's going to get me there?

Building on why I do the work I do, the study of aspiration vs. inspiration helps us to answer the questions: *Who do I want to be? What do I like about me? What do I want to experience more? What do I want out of life, and what does life want out of me? What are my options, and why are they viable? And, of course, what is going to get me there?* This kind of work enables us to get closer to the authentic self.

We get away from this authentic self early in life. It could be the family business, a parent's passion, the armed forces … or just falling into some opportunity. Sometimes, children are told early on, "You'd make a great doctor;" "You're an engineer; all you want to do is build;" or to the contrary, "Don't ever work with people; you wouldn't do well at it;" or "You'll never make a dime in the arts, so do that for a hobby, not a real job." I overheard one father say to his son, "Just get a job…with benefits!" And from that, we begin to design a life for ourselves.

We take in a good many "introjects"[1] by the time we graduate high school. Introjects are the suggestions – or projections – of others that stick. We unconsciously take them in, swallow them whole, and there they lie until something or someone comes along to challenge their being. Typically, it is someone close to us who makes the statements that become introjected. They in some way believe these statements are true, so we believe them, too.

Repetitious comments are other examples of introjects that we take on as if they were truths. These include: You're lazy; you're selfish; you'll never amount to anything; you have big dreams; don't you think you're reaching a bit; try something more attainable; you were never good in math; you're not quick on your feet; you're oblivious to the world around you. The list goes on. By the time we forge out on our own, we have a

---

1   It is unclear who first established this word. Fritz Perls used it as a term in Gestalt psychology, but Jung also uses it in The Collected Works. The etymology dates to 1866 before either of them and suggests it comes from intro and the stem of projection, and the German, introjektion.

sense of our false self[2] and what is "possible" or "best" for us. The opportunity to work with a coach is often the first time individuals confront these old, so-called *character flaws*. As we begin to tap into the authentic self, we feel a desire for greater consciousness, and we evolve. We find our creative self, and we are energized. So, working through aspirations and inspirations helps to unleash a true self.

Aspiration and inspiration are typically words that come up in relation to people's work lives – aspiration perhaps more so in our 21st century organizations. *Funk and Wagnalls* says to *aspire* is "1. to have an earnest desire or ambition, as for something high and good; 2. to long for; seek after." *Aspiration* is defined as "1. the act of aspiring; exalted desire; high ambition." *Inspiration* is said to be "1. the infusion or imparting of an idea, an emotion, or a mental or spiritual influence; 3. an actuating or exalting influence; a stimulus to creativity in thought or action."

While aspiration is having the ambition for something, inspiration includes the root—where the ambition comes from—suggesting that it comes from someplace bigger than my ego self.[3] The definition of inspiration also notes the act of *actuating*. You might remember Maslow's "hierarchy of needs" with *Self-Actualization* at the top (see chart). Maslow posited that, "Self-actualization is not an end state but also the process of actualizing one's potentialities at any time, in any amount…using one's intelligence" (Maslow 1971). I would think this reflects the bigger intelligence – more than just cognitive. Maslow says it's about making the "growth choice rather than the fear choice" (Maslow 1971). There are several ways of going about making the growth choice, or going to the root or depth, to understand what might be self-actuating, moving one toward individuation.[4]

---

2   D. W. Winnicott, a psychoanalyst, introduced the term in 1960 to express what other people's expectations of us create. He also noted the term "true self" for the authentic self.

3   Ego self as opposed to whole "Self." It's important to note that we need ego. The ego in itself is not bad, but when it gets inflated, it can turn against us. In analytic psychology, we talk about the ego-Self axis. This is the process of establishing a connection between the conscious and unconscious that enables us to move toward individuation. We will discuss this with greater depth.

4   Self-actualization is similar to Jung's idea of individuation.

TABLE 1 – MASLOW'S HIERARCHY OF NEEDS

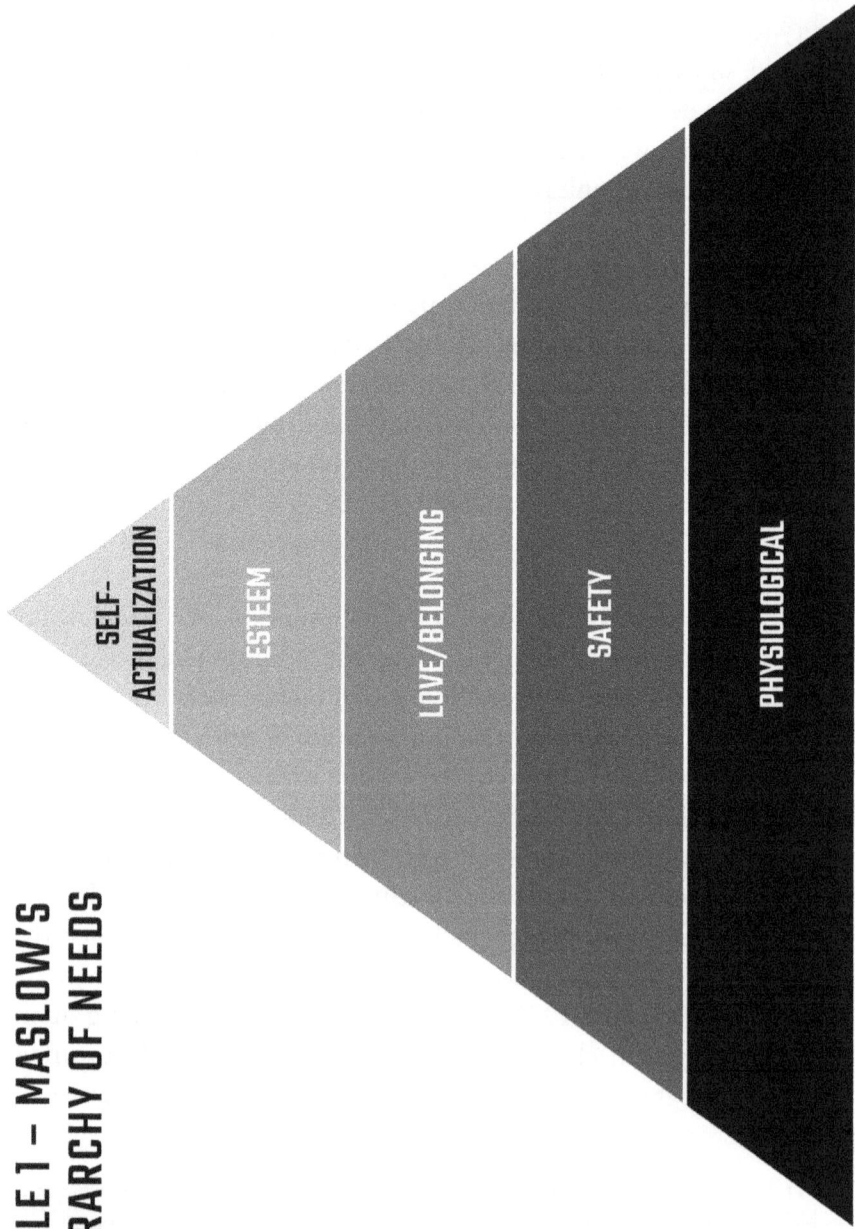

SELF-ACTUALIZATION

ESTEEM

LOVE/BELONGING

SAFETY

PHYSIOLOGICAL

My experience has been that we grow in four major directions—cognitively, emotionally, spiritually, and physically. Howard Gardner, psychologist and Harvard Professor of Neuroscience, introduced the idea of multiple intelligences in 1983. While it was challenging for educators and cognitive scientists at the time, we pretty much take these varied intelligences for granted today.

There are now nine intelligences as Gardner has compiled them: (1) linguistic; (2) logical-mathematical; (3) musical/rhythmic; (4) bodily kinesthetic; (5) spatial; (6) naturalist; (7) interpersonal; (8) intrapersonal; and most recently, (9) existential.

Gardner sees an emotional facet to each of these intelligences rather than separating out emotional intelligence. He believes we all have all of these to some degree, and, of course, the many profiles are infinite.

Early in the new millennium, I was working on an idea I called *emotional mastery and agility*. This came primarily from working with the theories of Gardner, Goleman, Senge, and Lombardo & Eichinger (Lominger tools now part of Korn/Ferry Intl).

"What blows spiritus into the lungs of the bawling infant? That spiritus—ésprit, re-spiration, in-spiration—is energy, a force-field blowing, blowing through eternity into time-bound bodies whose curving trajectory brings them inexorably back to earth. Even as plummet-bound bodies, decaying, dying as we lurch through life, we remain nonetheless force fields of energy, dancing on the grave of history and aflame with eternal fires." (Hollis, 2013)

I had designed a program with colleagues on Senge's ideas in *The Fifth Discipline*, with a particular interest in self-mastery. At the same time, I was using and getting certified in the Lominger tools with a resonance in their work on agility. By mid-2001, I was using a model (see diagram) to express the territory I considered to be important to human development. It made very good sense to me for five or six years. Then, I set it aside for a while.

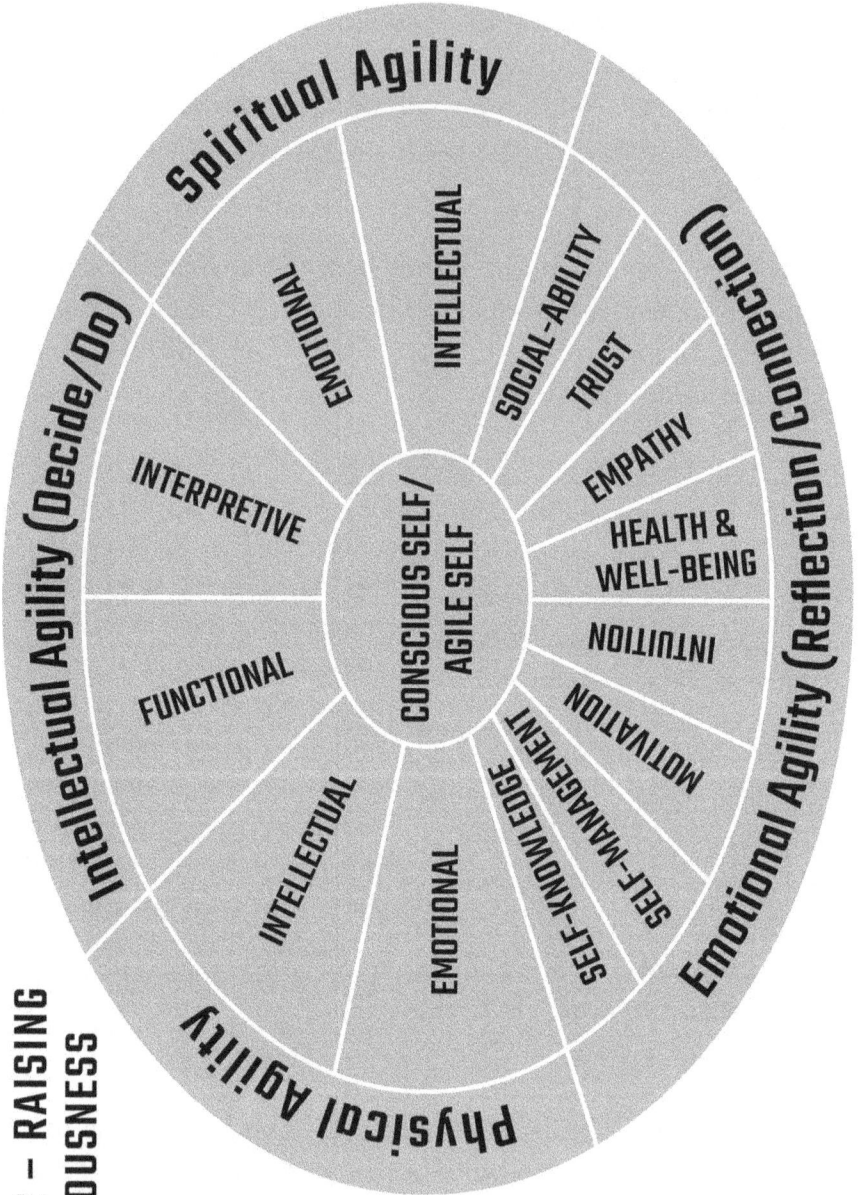

TABLE 2 – RAISING CONSCIOUSNESS

Spiritual Agility

Intellectual Agility (Decide/Do)

Emotional Agility (Reflection/Connection)

Physical Agility

CONSCIOUS SELF / AGILE SELF

EMOTIONAL

INTELLECTUAL

SOCIAL-ABILITY

TRUST

EMPATHY

HEALTH & WELL-BEING

INTUITION

MOTIVATION

SELF-MANAGEMENT

SELF-KNOWLEDGE

EMOTIONAL

INTELLECTUAL

FUNCTIONAL

INTERPRETIVE

During this period, I began studying Jungian psychology and immersed myself in the importance of conscious vs. unconscious being in the world. I no longer had the tolerance for "mastery," as it felt like an ultra masculine[5] word that seemed to describe something in a finite way. We "master" it, and it is done? In our work with emotional and spiritual development, we never *master* it, and it requires a lot of feminine energy. At our best, we become more conscious of how and why we emote – what triggers our emotions; what "complexes" have control over us; what emotions or complexes are showing up in others. And how can we respond rather than react?

One author, psychologist and business advisor puts it this way:

We are composites. We have *both* masculine *and* feminine traits within us. How much we develop and display these traits depends on our social conditioning, life experiences, and deeply held beliefs and assumptions. Healthy, mature individuals are comfortable with both sides of their character.

The Western notion that we possess both masculine and feminine characteristics was developed in depth by psychologist Carl Jung in the first half of the twentieth century (Rosen, 2008).

There comes a point when we must grow up. We must take notice of our "stuff" and call ourselves on it. My husband and I were having dinner with a therapist friend one evening when she suddenly stopped her conversation mid-sentence and said, "judging, judging, judging," in a calm, singular pitch to remind herself that she had noticed her behavior. We all laughed and knew exactly what she was doing with great appreciation for our own *judging* in the world. It was lighthearted but clear, and we moved our conversation on to a more enjoyable one.

---

5   Most of us will benefit from a good mix of masculine and feminine, not to be confused with male and female. Actually, Jung wants us each to project our own sense of what is masculine in the world vs. what is feminine and consider when we're out of balance. Organizations have been out of balance from the beginning with overuse of what most would agree are masculine traits. Designed and structured by men, it has been nearly impossible for women to be fully accepted in business.

There are complexes at work here.

> …but few of us appreciate the importance and the daily utility of this idea [complex], which Jung brought to our attention. A complex is a cluster of energy in the unconscious, charged by historic events, reinforced through repetition, embodying a fragment of our personality, and generating a programmed response and an implicit set of expectations (Hollis 2005).

If we can make the connection to the complex, we gain insight. Jung said it was not about getting rid of our complexes, however. He also made reference to the emotions that tag along with complexes, which help us to see them for what they are:

> We psychologists have learned, through long and painful experience, that you deprive a man of his best resource when you help him to get rid of his complexes. You can only help him to become sufficiently aware of them and to start a conscious conflict within himself. In this way the complex becomes a focus of life. Anything that disappears from your psychological inventory is apt to turn up in the guise of a hostile neighbour [sic], who will inevitably arouse your anger and make you aggressive. It surely is better to know your worst enemy is right there in your own heart (Jung, 1970).

In the work place, as in family life, our complexes can be very useful:

> Some of these programmed, reflexive responses can be helpful, as they defend us and preserve our psychological territory. If we did not have some positively charged clusters of relational experience, we could not trust, could not love, could not make interpersonal commitments, could not operate in the world without divisive distrust and distancing from others. We could not love music, esteem justice, or treasure our values if we had not had deeply felt positive experiences of them (Hollis, 2005).

Back to the diagram, the spiritual development, which includes the existential questions that come and go in their intensity, is not to be mastered either, but to challenge us and take us to another level of understanding. While we definitely become more agile in this consciousness effort, it is not a question of mastery like developing a skill or learning information. My model is now the "Conscious Self / Agile Self" – the more conscious we get, the more adaptable, flexible, and nimble we can be. This is very helpful in life.

Working with complexes is the work of analysis. I have found that some of this work can be done in the coaching relationship, too, but a coach must be skilled and have the benefit of a Jungian analyst and/or supervisor in order to work with it effectively. It has served me well in those instances when I have been able to observe a complex constellating. If I had ignored the pattern, I would have lost an opportunity for both of us.

Nurturing Individuality/Individuation

Interestingly, over the years, I have repeatedly found night dreams to be one of the most important ways to understand the growth or the self-actuating choice. For example, one VP I worked with as an executive coach had been having a dream with a recurring theme for years. Dom described this recurring dream as having a dark, "flying dragon-like presence." It took place in different areas such as a bombed-out cathedral. He wasn't threatened by it, "but it is ominous," he said. This was just the first of many dreams we discussed over the ensuing years, but it proved very important in terms of his inspirations and former aspirations.

Dom had planned to be a priest early in his life, but circumstances took him away from seminary after just one year. He was very good in math and also studied marketing. By the time we met, he'd done quite well for himself financially and socially, but there was this recurring dream theme and an unsettled feeling in his life. It didn't take long to sense his longing for the more spiritual life he'd given up.

As our coaching progressed, and Dom became more courageous about looking wholeheartedly at what he really wanted, he decided that he would go back to school and pursue a Master's in Spiritual Counseling. He began to change his life to meet his earlier inspiration. This wasn't an easy decision, and he struggled with the aspirations he had for his employment at that time. It was a decision that would impact his family, his relationships, and his income, but it was literally *haunting* him and long overdue.

After doing the hard work of announcing his desires to his family and making the adjustments that would help him move toward his dream, he started school and soon told his boss so that they could devise a viable exit strategy. Dom continued to work at the same organization throughout his studies, but he took on a different role, still in an executive capacity. It involved less travel, which allowed him to focus more on his other work. It wasn't an easy transition, but the inspiration was so strong that it outweighed the former aspirations of his job. Our work in coaching centered on this for quite a while.

Dom was also getting spiritual counseling (a requirement of his degree program) and some family counseling to help with the strain on his marriage. He wrestled with the shifting and lessening of executive responsibilities and how that felt personally and for his family. However, he visibly matured through it all. This transition held many transformations for him and for his family, and six months into his new work, he told me he had no doubt that he had done the right thing. Not only is he more fulfilled, but his wife was challenged to take her work more seriously to help with the family income. She, also, is much more fulfilled in her life.

While it is not typical for such a drastic change to be made, I think this case shows that it would be easy to miss the real tension for Dom and try to resolve it within his current work situation. There were times when Dom tried to go back on his intentions and inspirations, reverting to what was comfortable and socially acceptable in his circle of friends and colleagues. It was up to me to hold the space for what his soul ached for, and yet provide enough room for him to go in either direction. The work required a lot of truth telling, fortitude, and patience on both our parts. Had he ignored the promptings, he surely would have had to deal with ghosts of some sort or another.

Much is required of each human being to play their part in the collective scheme of life. In the infamous Dickens story, "A Christmas Carol," Scrooge begs Marley to tell him what is expected of him to pay his debt so that the menacing spirits will stop visiting him at night. Marley replies with a definite and haunting, "m-u-c-h." Much is required of us and our corporate leaders. We have the challenging task of assisting and guiding others to make it through life "successfully" (whether the individual considers success in relation to societal, religious, familial, or personal expectations, or some combination thereof). Of course, success can be defined in many ways, and, ultimately, it is specific to each individual. That is why Jung named the process "individuation." My path is not your path.

When people don't get thoughtful and "planful" around life decisions, the organization or "others" will make plans for them. People find themselves in countries they don't want to be in, doing work they have no interest in doing, every day.

We have mistakenly set up mentors to be *role models* for our own careers and lives. Fifteen years ago, everyone modeled their leadership off of Jack Welch or Anne Mulcahy. Then, Roberto Goizueta, Larry Bossidy, Meg Whitman, Ellen Kullman, and Michael Dell. Today, it's Opray Winfrey, Jeff Bezos, Sheryl Sandberg, Jeff Weiner, Angela Ahrendts and Mark Zuckerberg. It's good to look at what others do well, but we must each do well from the center of our own being.

At times in our lives, we might relate to The Rolling Stones when they sing, "I can't get NO SA-TIS-FAC-TION!" (By the way, the riff from this song came from a dream. Now, that's inspiration!)

The work of the coach is to guide the client through fear, overwhelm, and other emotions, and seek out some of that elusive satisfaction. Coaches need to hold the space [6] for important aspects of consideration—to expand their clients' thinking and the field of their vision. In order to solve the issues that arise, coaches must remind clients how to envision the aspirations of the board of directors, the C-suite, leadership as a collective, as well as their own. This requires an interest in business, in systems, and in individuals.

> "RE: Coaching the CEO: I think that we should look at "gaps" between what is being worked on and what weaknesses are highlighted. For example, 23 percent of CEOs are working on their team-building skills, but only 13 percent of directors believe this is an area that needs improvement."
>
> HBR Blogs, 8/2013

The busyness of organizational life is often a concern. There has to be time for reflection and making sense of effort, as well as time lines, goals, expectations, and changes in the environment. Clients have expressed their frustrations to me relative to work they're doing just to finish something that was started, not because it is still important.

Organizations need a quicker response time to close out projects and work efforts that are no longer of value. Coaches can assist individuals with their emotional responses to these types of conundrums and help create a strategy for proposing change in the organization. When

> "Individuation is a natural necessity... its prevention by a leveling down to collective standards is injurious to the vital activity of the individual."
>
> C.G. JUNG

I first left organizational life, I thought, why would I ever want to be a shareholder of a large company? I know the waste and the lost time and the continuous reworking of strategies and work-arounds. But truly, now I feel I can have a hand in small, but meaningful changes.

---

6   For me, "holding the space" refers to slowing down a moment and highlighting a comment or feeling so you can work with it, literally or symbolically, in order for insight to emerge.

In reality, everyone in organizations knows about some piece of this lost time, and they would like to do something about it. But how do they get started? If a coach values ethical practices and has an interest in the way businesses operate, he or she can be of assistance with these issues.

Serving the Aspirations of Individuals Unlike Ourselves

It was Jung's attestation that we are all "one-sided." We have interests, preferences, and values that make us vigilant and effective in some areas, but not so strong in others. In MBTI® language, this is made clear by the fact that we are one of 16 types. (Within a given type we are still quite unique due to dominant function, innate tendencies, etc.) One-sidedness has its benefits, so the goal is not to find some idyllic, central zone. If Einstein was not fanatical about math, if Gandhi didn't go over the edge caring about the individual human experience, and if Michael Phelps wasn't in the pool 350 days a year … well, you see where I'm going.

It is not a question of *if* we are one-sided but of being *conscious* of that one-sidedness and using it thoughtfully. It is mind-blowing to see how the puzzle pieces we've each been given come together to create a distinctive whole with a reliance on

"Every man takes the limits of his own field of vision for the limits of the world."

ARTHUR SCHOPENHAUER

certain characteristics and capabilities. I do want to challenge the belief that consciousness is about finding some moderation so that you can be "happy." Having an impact, making a difference, feeling fulfilled, and being all we can be is not necessarily about moderation or being happy. And moderation is no sure path to a life of satisfaction (in spite of the moral advice, "everything in moderation.") Success – a life well-lived – probably holds a host of emotions, many of which might seem negative.

Not everyone is aspirational, of course, and that is okay. (Maybe it is better than okay; maybe it is good.) From my experience, aspirations can take their toll, yet I can't imagine my life without them. Is that partially due to my preference for "J" in the MBTI® type code? Maybe. In my world (from my projections) it helps enormously to be Planful, Organized and an Early Starter – behaviors typically aligned with a Judging attitude. The "P" (perceiving) attitude generally shows Adaptable, Emergent and Casual behaviors. But does this mean those individuals are slothful, not ambitious, without aspirations? That might be a "J" projection as we often see the opposite preference in a negative light. They certainly still hold value to society. Is it their role to slow us down a bit, to make us reconsider decisions, and consider the wisdom of our drive for closure? Well, I'm getting a little philosophical, but I think there is a purpose in following these strands of bias far enough to get in touch with the "otherness" in ourselves as well as others. It helps us realize there aren't as many finites as we might think. We take for granted that our paradigm is *the* paradigm. We see life in black and white and forget it is rich with colors. This is a very important insight for coaches who work from an advice-giving or mentoring model. At the end of one off-site I facilitated using the MBTI® and several other assessment instruments, the leader looked at me very seriously and asked, "Wait, so you're telling me not everyone thinks the way I do?"

I will admit that I like having goals. How do I work with a person who is less goal-oriented than I am? How do I keep from pushing my preferences on my client? I have found that life is truly interesting when I don't judge it, and I continuously see that the tapestry each one weaves is rich. What color should it be? How long should it take to weave? Are there clients I should or should not work with? Maybe we try too hard to get it all perfect. Well, when all of our individual preferences, interests and expertise come together, and when aspiration and inspiration surface, it is quite amazing to see what we can accomplish. The congruence of finding a deep knowing of *who* you are and *what* you're meant to be doing is so very satisfying and at the heart of the matter.

Aspiration or Projection?

Sometimes, a coach will find that *they* hold an aspiration for a client. This occurred to me after a session with a smart 40-something woman who had a lot of opportunity in front of her, but from my perspective, could not get off the dime. I left our meeting feeling frustrated as I could envision all kinds of success for her that she was unable to drive toward. I mentioned this to my analyst and experienced a lightning bolt "aha" when she said, "That is a projection." Of course! I was projecting my ideals on to my client and expecting her to follow through. That was an important moment – and it was *my* coach, my analyst who helped me catch it.

While it is right for me to encourage aspirational thinking and discuss the aspirations of the boss with the client, it is not appropriate for me to *have* aspirations for my clients. I say "have" rather than "share" because even if I only *hold* aspirations for a client and don't *share* them, I can still manipulate the client unconsciously. This is not to say I have no aspirations whatsoever. For example, it may be appropriate to hope that my clients will learn to be more assertive, less threatening, less guarded, etc., but I must not have aspirations that clients don't hold for themselves. I must not hope for them to achieve goals that might not be their true path. That would result in pushing people in directions that might not be right for them, or it could just be that the timing isn't right for them. My projections onto clients could mean wasted time, or worse, result in clients making decisions based on *my* hopes and dreams for them and not their own.

Clients often want to please their coaches, but that is not valuable to the real work. Sometimes, a coach will use a projection in order to stir a reaction – to learn where the individual stands, to see what the person has passion for. It takes being very conscious to manage this well, however, and that is the subject of *The Wounded Healer: An Exploration of the Coach-Client Relationship* Book 2 of *The Red Book Series*.

Over these thirty-odd years of experience working in and consulting to organizations, these are some of the things I've learned about aspiration and inspiration as it relates to executives:

Executives talk and think a lot about their aspirations and goals. Most consider it at least yearly at performance review time when they are once again considering the future and what they aspire to achieve. (And, some go through the motions but never *really* think about it.)

Many executives don't know *who* they really are – they haven't taken the time necessary to reflect and make connections to the Self. The fast track executive is smart and quick, but considering self-awareness is often put on the back burner of life. (And many *assume* they do know themselves.)

Executives would benefit from being clearer about what inspires them because it would help them find more meaning from their work. In many job satisfaction surveys, meaning is the number one thing people say they are looking for from their jobs. But is their behavior backing that up?

When a leader's aspirations come out of inspiration, they have more confidence in their decisions and gain more value from their achievements.

Our inspirations lead us to a "vocation" – stemming from the root *vocare*, meaning "to be called." That ties into our personal mission– what we wish to be at our core – what the *Self* wants for us.

Marshall Goldsmith, famed executive coach, noted with the title of his 2007 book, *What Got You Here, Won't Get You There*. When I use that phrase, however, I am thinking of larger, deeper, and usually emotional things that keep clients from moving along. I am thinking of Jung's idea of one-sidedness that must be consciously assessed if we are to be our most effective selves.[7]

---

7   I made an attempt in the body of my writing to allude to the fact that there are some people who should not seek to manage their one-sidedness. They should just go on being and doing as they are. This does not mean that they are not individuating. If it is a person's destiny to be the genius who creates a way to move civilization forward, it may require one-sidedness, or some singularity of focus to do that.

Becoming a Conscious Coach

I hope the examples in this chapter help you start to think about how you lay the bricks that form your framework. How do you learn? When have you gained new insights about yourself and your work?

It was my coach who suggested I use an Appreciative Inquiry framework in designing a client's offsite team building and vision planning session to co-create a shared vision and mission. Recently certified in AI, I was inexperienced in applying it to a strategic planning session and the initial thought of doing this was daunting. After several planning calls with the client it became apparent that he wanted to present his vision and mission without engaging his team in its co-creation. A few days before the session took place he insisted the AI activity be removed. I pushed back several times but to no avail. What happened? Did I get so enamored by the opportunity to use AI in a team planning session that I wouldn't let it go? Did my passion get the best of me? I tend to get passionate - did I overdo it this time? Did my motives somehow change along the way? I intuitively knew that if the client, with his command and control style, presented his vision and mission to his new team without first gaining their input it would disengage them and could have downstream repercussions for him, his team and the organization. My inner voice kept telling me to intervene. So I created a fifteen-minute opening activity rooted in the tenants of AI to provide the team with an opportunity to participate in envisioning the future. I included the client in this activity. I did not share with him my intention behind the design. Should I have? After all, the client is not always right but as coaches we have to do what is right for the client. Ten minutes into the activity, the client comes running up to me at the front of the room. Feeling completely exposed, I immediately told him I would shut down the activity so he can present his vision. He pushed back on me and said he wanted to continue with the activity as his team was coming up with some great ideas! This was the springboard in developing the co-created team vision and was pivotal to the success of the meeting on so many levels. Having a coach's coach to challenge me to bring in an AI framework, to serve as a sounding board for the unexpected challenges and to provide professional and objective support, gave me the extra confidence to stand my ground with the client even while challenging my own thinking. This session wasn't just a breakthrough for the client and his leadership team it was a breakthrough for me.

MARLENE CAROL HARDING,
Coach and Organizational
Development Consultant,
Conscious Coaching in the
Corporate Environment

Are you aspiring to be a coach or to increase your capability as a coach? Is this an inspiration as well? What inspires your clients? We know that "meaning" tops the list of motivational factors – what gets you (and your clients) jumping out of bed before the alarm in the morning?

What is your commitment to the work? What is your interest in understanding the human experience, how people develop, how organizations grow? Have you been giving advice where perhaps you shouldn't have been? Do you think you may have given some bad advice? To say "yes" is a huge leap forward. Once acknowledged, you can make a decision as to what you want to do about it. This is being conscious in one's leadership. This is the beginning of authentic, conscious living.

But what does all of this have to do with excelling in your work as a coach and differentiating yourself in the marketplace, guiding leaders to also differentiate themselves in their workplace? "Much." What about that golden key and the promising treasure chest? Finding your path and moving along it with greater confidence and intention will not only make you better as a coach, but it will lead to more effective outcomes in a multiplicity of ways.

So, what is it you want – *really* want? How do you know? What will it take to get there? Are you passionate about progressing these aspirations and/ or inspirations? Why? How will it benefit the community or industry? At the heart of the matter in leadership coaching is consciousness...conscious conversations, expectations, questions, considerations, explanations, and more.

On Jung

According to Jung, the Self is the major archetype of the psyche. An archetype is an idea, a metaphor, a pattern that people everywhere can clearly associate with. Hillman (1975, p. xiii), defines archetypes as "the deepest patterns of psychic functioning, the roots of the soul governing the perspectives we have of ourselves and the world...which hold whole worlds together and yet can never be pointed to, accounted for, or even adequately circumscribed."

Right from the start Jung wanted to shed light on those deep recesses of the unconscious that were beyond Freud's method, which dealt only with the areas of the unconscious generated by events in one's daily life. Yet Jung was far more than just a psychologist. His interests ranged far and wide across religions, Chinese philosophy, alchemy and UFOs. He saw the same patterns underlying radically different ways of thinking across the world, and he was convinced that these patterns arose from the mind. He called them archetypes, essential elements of the psyche. Thus he developed the concepts of the collective unconscious and of archetypes, which are today taken for granted. (Miller, 2009)

When we begin to come into our own through the individuation process, we have more moments of recognizing the Self. Jung distinguished between big "S" Self and little "s" self to delineate *Self* as wholeness and *self* in just speaking of me, myself, and I – from a standpoint of the ego. We also use words like self-awareness, authenticity, and humility in working with the notion of Self.

An HBR (Harvard Business Review) article that was an introduction to Collins' book, *Good to Great,* referred to *humility* and *will* as what it takes to be a "level 5 leader" (Collins, 2001). I continue to see this book on leaders' desks years after it made its debut. For Jung, however, humility is something we grow toward – it is a maturing. When we open ourselves to understanding *Self,* we can't help but begin to understand that others bring their own amazing individual capabilities to the world. We have new admiration for all around us, if only for a moment.

In the *Collected Works,* volume 5 (of 18), on Psychological Types, Jung writes:

Hence we possess today a highly collective culture which in organization far exceeds anything that has gone before, but which for that very reason has become increasingly injurious to individual culture. There is a deep gulf between what a man is and what he represents, between what he is as an individual and what he is as a collective being. His function is developed at the expense of his individuality. Should he excel, he is merely identical with his collective function; but should he not, then, though he may be esteemed as a function in society, his individuality is wholly on the level of his inferior, undeveloped functions, and he is simply a barbarian, while in the former case he has happily deceived himself as to his actual barbarism. This one-sidedness has undoubtedly brought society advantages that should not be underestimated, and acquisitions that could have been gained in no other way, as Shiller[8] finely observes:

Only by concentrating the whole energy of our spirit in one single focus, and drawing together our whole being into one power, do we attach wings, so to say, to this individual power and lead it by artifice far beyond the bounds which nature seems to have imposed upon it. (Jung, 1956)

We don't often see the word "barbarian" in this day and age, and it reminded me of the famous book, *Barbarians at the Gate: The Fall of RJR Nabisco*, (later made into a movie) which tells the story of the leveraged buyout and the difficulties that ensued. It is a perfect example of how our connection to Self can lose out to the demands of the ego and of the collective culture. I remember the media coverage about this event early in my career. CEO, F. Ross Johnson wanted to buy up the company from the shareholders and discussed this first with Henry Kravis. He later chose to do the deal with Shearson Lehman Hutton, and Kravis' fury erupted. Of course, we've seen this organizational angst repeated in various ways. I am immediately brought back to reflect on the Enron debacle. It wasn't just the CEO, Kenneth Lay, but all those he drew into his corrupt business dealings, following like lemmings right into the barbarian archetype. Most recently, we had the financial fallen – the many perpetrators of the economic downturn or what has become known as the meltdown of the world financial markets – Bear Stearns & Co,

---

8   Johann Cristoph Friedrich von Schiller 1759-1805, German poet, philosopher, historian and dramatist. Jung resonated with Schiller's ideas and built on them. He is referenced in Vols. 5 & 6 of the Collected Works.

Merrill Lynch, Goldman Sachs, Lehman Brothers. The list encompasses many leaders and executives who lost themselves to collective greed at the expense of their humanity and their responsibility to the greater good.

Of course, "barbarianism" needn't be this severe or with horrific outcomes for the organization, the community, and the world. In many cases, this bravado, and what might appear as arrogance, provides good – new inventions, new medicines, great art, and so on. Here, "barbarian" may simply mean, primitive in one's understanding of Self, or one's ability to manage self. Likely these individuals have not taken the time for an inner life.

But this one-sided development must inevitably lead to a reaction, since the suppressed inferior functions cannot be indefinitely excluded from participating in our life and development. The time will come when the division in the inner man must be abolished, in order that the undeveloped may be granted an opportunity to live. (Jung 1971)

Considering this notion of good vs. bad, I will note Jung's thoughts:

What is then meant by "good"? Good for him? Good for me? Good for his relatives? Good for society? Our judgment becomes so hopelessly caught in a tangle of subsidiary considerations and relationships that, unless circumstances compel us to cut through the Gordian knot, we would do better to leave it alone, or content ourselves with offering the sufferer what modest help we can in unravelling [sic] the threads. (Jung, 1989)

How do you relate to these ideas? What does "good" mean to you? How is your moral compass set? How have you connected to your inner life? What do you know about your true self and the transcendent Self? In what ways are you grateful for your one-sidedness? Is it time to develop other aspects of your personality, or is it serving you well just as it is? Where in your efforts to grow do you need more courage?

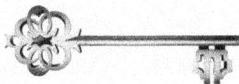

Your Notes

Jot down anything that has come to mind for you personally at this time:

_____

_____

_____

_____

_____

_____

_____

_____

_____

_____

_____

_____

_____

_____

_____

_____

_____

_____

_____

_____

What are you feeling right now? What surprises you from your notes? What insights did you get about yourself? Any other thoughts right now? Anything you want to do, communicate or absorb because of this reflection?

Additional Reading and Resources

Poems

- » *The Self Slaved* by Patrick Kavanaugh
- » *The Summer Day* by Mary Oliver

Read

- » *Female Authority: Empowering Women Through Psychotherapy* by Polly Young-Eisendrath
- » *Level 5 Leadership* by Jim Collins, HBR
- » *Living Your Unlived Life* by Robert Johnson
- » *The Nibble Theory and the Kernel of Power: A book about leadership, self-empowerment, and personal growth* by Kaleel Jamison
- » *The Presence of the Feminine in Film* by Virginia Apperson and John Beebe
- » *The Psychology of Dreaming* by Robert Van de Castle
- » *Why Good People Do Bad Things* by James Hollis, PhD

Songs

- » *Brilliant Disguise* by Bruce Springstein
- » *I Am…I Said* by Neil Diamond

Movies & Television

- » *Barbarians at the Gate* (1993)
- » *House of Cards* (Netflix Series, 2014-2015, BBC series, 1990)
- » *Inside Job* (2010)
- » *Too Big To Fail* (2011)

Chapter 3

A Thoughtful Theoretical Coaching Framework

"Progress has not followed a straight ascending line,
but a spiral with rhythms of progress and retrogressions,
of evolution and dissolution."

Johann Wolfgang von Goethe

In my work assisting organizations in the development of their coaching programs, I have interviewed hundreds of coaches. Roughly 30% of these coaches incorporate a lot of structure (steps, processes, questionnaires, frameworks) in their approach, and about 20% have little to no clear structure. While the majority of coaches fall somewhere in the middle, I think it is important to rethink the extremes – too much structure or a free-for-all approach. It makes sense to me that one will choose to be more or less structured based on the client's needs. Unfortunately, a lot of times our own stuff gets in the way. In the MBTI®, Step II™, you gain further insight into your behaviors through Facet Poles. Some Facets are associated with your MBTI® preference, but not necessarily in every case. This additional information provides greater understanding of who you are and how others might experience you. Considering how preferences and behaviors impact your style may tell you something about your approach to coaching. And, remember our inclination toward one-sidedness – being overly "Planful" – is hubris. On the other hand, if one is continuously Open-Ended most hopes for effective outcomes are lost. There needs to be some direction a fair amount of the time and, certainly, a revisiting of the direction for course correction.

Once a direction is drawn up you might consider these questions over time...

» Is this still the right direction?

» How are we meeting the goals we set?

» Are they still valid? If not, why not?

» What goals replace them? Why?

» Does the sponsoring partner agree?

Often, when an organization contracts a coach, a manager or HR partner is part of the process and is committed to supporting the development of the individual (the coachee). This representative from the organization often sees where the coachee's effort is breaking down. They can play a very useful role, providing feedback to both coach and coachee on what is or is not working for the client in the organization. These sponsors are typically quite savvy about the process of coaching and do not expect to be privy to the confidential conversations between coach and coachee. However, it is important to be clear about this upfront when contracting. Using a framework helps you to explain when and how the sponsor can be a part of the process.

The Basics of Coaching with an Analytical Framework

In this section, I will review my model of "Coaching with an Analytical Framework" along with the Jungian model for analytical consultation (psychotherapy). You will see both overlap and where deliberate differences make this approach viable and necessary in our very challenging contemporary organizations. In this and subsequent chapters you will note where other theorists, their constructs, and ideology have played into the development of this model, and yet, how subsumed many of these concepts are in Jung's ideas and theories.

Step One – Confession / Aspiration

In the Jungian Psychoanalytic Model, the analyst begins with "Confession." Akin to the Catholic in the confessional, this is the time when we open up to someone we trust and put voice to what is troubling us – our concerns and disappointments, fears, and overwhelment. A psychoanalytic term for this is *abreaction*. This is the act of reliving, purging, and grounding emotional experiences in a safe environment. Perhaps you would call it *catharsis*. Sometimes, this is when repressed trauma comes to the surface. Unlike the confessional, however, this is when a person might share the aspirations and hopes that have been difficult for them to express in their lives. It is a time to bring thoughts and feelings to consciousness, to work toward individuation, and to increase awareness of and connection to the Self.

In the "Coaching with an Analytical Framework Model (CAF)," this first step is that of "Aspiration." Like in Jungian analysis, it is the beginning of a conscious effort toward the client's individuation, self-awareness, and the clarifying or voicing of their reality—the realities your clients are happy with, the hopes and dreams they have, as well as those aspects that are disappointing, frustrating, or confusing. As a coach, you consider the goals of the organization and what the manager might want from the coachee, as well as what the individual wants for him/herself—especially where there is a rub or lack of alignment. We first ask questions like: Why do you want to engage a coach? What are your personal goals? What are your professional goals? At what do you want to become more effective? Why does your manager want you to have a coach? What does your HR partner think? Have you ever completed a 360° assessment or other assessments? What did you learn from that? What do you aspire to? How have your aspirations led you to where you are today?

While these are some guiding questions, the coach must be agile—adjusting the line of questioning based on what is heard from the client. If you hear anxiety, concern, or apprehension, you might ask: What concerns do you have about coaching? What makes you uncomfortable about this process?

If you hear enthusiasm, excitement, and the energy to proceed, continue on. This is a time to confirm that coaching is the right developmental process and that the individual is committed to the time and effort required. It is a time to discuss the "rules of engagement."

One night, my husband and I were at dinner with Dr. Jim Hollis when he relayed a story about Marian Woodman (famed author, analyst and workshop leader) and her expectations of new analysands (patients/clients). She would tell them right up front that if they weren't willing to spend an hour a day working with their dreams, they weren't ready for analysis. We laughed at her moxy, but we agreed that it is good to have some expectations. I give clients a journal when we start and let them know I expect them to write something in it regularly. At the beginning and/or end of each day might be ideal, but at the beginning and end of the week is a good start for those who have never been reflective. They can use it to make session notes during or after our sessions or to jot down issues as they arise relative to goals. One physician challenged me, saying he keeps all his notes on his mobile device and won't use the journal. If that's the best you can do, okay, but it is not the same as putting pen to paper and allowing yourself to get carried away with a thought that explodes into multiple tributaries, opening up consciousness on some issue.

"The daily journal is like a mirror. When we first look into it, the blank pages stare back with ominous emptiness. But if we keep looking and trusting in what Rilke calls "the possibility of being", gradually we begin to see the face that is looking back at us." (Woodman, 1982)

Sometimes, a client's more challenging issues come to the surface early on, e.g., alcoholism, abuse, difficult memories from youth that get in the way of their effectiveness, anger, etc. This is a good time to mention the employee assistance program (this is part of most organizations' benefits programs) and inquire about experience with therapy. In some cases, you'll feel comfortable to refer someone to therapy, but this usually comes later once the relationship is developed. Coaching and therapy together can work wonders for an individual who is in a stuck place or when you get the sense that a person is quite fragile or hasn't developed the coping skills necessary to function with consistency.

But again, as a coach, we don't try to be therapists. We are not trying to work with and make sense of the traumas of the past. The conversation simply informs us and provides a bigger picture of the individual. Some caution is necessary (a) not to become too empathetic, moving into co-dependence; (b) not to support a victim nature; and (c) to be aware of any bias the information has given you. Sometimes, you will feel a collision with your own values, and it is very helpful to note this and manage that discomfort without reacting to it. At other times, you will feel a merging of values, which makes it easy to over-identify with the client.

In the book, *Psychotherapy: The Purchase of Friendship*, the point author William Schofield makes is that psychotherapy is not *just* a friendship, I think this is also important to consider in coaching. Some people do need a friend of a sort, a confidant. I am reminded of Gallup's idea of a best friend at work[1], which moved them to study this further. That research led to a book called *Vital Friends*, in which author Tom Rath outlines the eight important friends to have in the workplace. In many ways, a coach can play these roles, too. But the essential learning a coach can instill in the client is the wisdom of developing relationships with people at work who can play those roles – mind-opener, collaborator, champion, etc. And, at times more paramount, is the ability to call on these characters within.

In contracting conversations, we inevitably get around to the topic of meaningful work. Of course, this is a great fit with the aspiration and inspiration conversation. After discussing work aspirations with a new coachee, I will ask about personal aspirations. We develop this idea together as we move through the coaching engagement. This work is often followed by a deeper intake of the individual's past experiences by drawing up and analyzing a career and life line. Looking at the client's

---

1   Best friend at work debuted with an employee engagement 12 question survey you can learn more about at q12.gallup.com.

aspirations, disappointments, and accomplishments over a lifetime produces patterns and further understanding of meaningful work of and for the client.

This is primarily the work of the ego, the aspect of the psyche that is responsible for consciousness. However, the life line work can bring up subconscious material (just below the surface, but accessible to our conscious memory), and in some instances, even unconscious material. While we might start this process in step one, it is an important discussion throughout the coaching engagement.

In the aspiration phase, clients are usually excited about change and the opportunity to make adjustments that will serve them well in their jobs, with their managers, and in their lives. They rarely realize what that truly means until they complete the coaching process, however.

As you are probably aware, it is important not to create a plan for the client in isolation, but to get their involvement with the development plan and process early on. Some will resist setting goals, or at least goals that are very meaningful. That is okay; just keep asking and reminding them that goals are important. Find out if this is an issue for the client in other parts of life and how it impacts them. If it is a problem it might be an opportunity to dig in and get to work on it from a more holistic perspective. Ironically, there are times when goals aren't clearly identified until the end of the engagement, but you discover that you were working on them all the time, allowing them to deepen and evolve. We might say that they eventually become *speech ripe*.[2] Forcing the issue can result in a false commitment and an inability on the part of the client to get to work on their real "stuff." Understanding systems thinking and believing in emergent properties allows for this loose-tight flow.

---

2   Speech ripe is a term used by Jeremy Taylor, dream worker extraordinaire, referring to information from our night dreams. While there might be ideas we know a bit about, it isn't "speech ripe" means that it is still a bit hazy (perhaps not entirely conscious), and we can't express it clearly yet.

Step Two – Elucidation / Assessment

The second step in the Jungian Psychoanalytic Model is "Elucidation." This is the process of months, and often years, of conversations and transferences[3] that arise in analysis. This work requires great skill and is a constant balance of toughness and tenderness, of questioning and empathy. The analyst works with dreams and uses active imagination[4] techniques. Some clients draw or paint, and that becomes an important part of the work.

The work of elucidation can take a very long time, and it might never elicit the more wounded aspects of the inner Self. The "ego-Self axis" is a common phrase in Jungian circles that describes this communication between the ego (conscious self) and the Self (unconscious self) at the center of the psyche. The ego needs to stay in contact with the Self as it originates from and is regulated by the Self. It can be a bit confusing to grasp the Jungan idea of Self, as it is both the entire psyche and the center of the psyche.

"While the cathartic method restores to the ego such contents as are capable of becoming conscious and should normally be components of the conscious mind, the process of clearing up the transference brings to light contents which are hardly ever capable of becoming conscious in that form. This is the cardinal distinction between the stage of confession and the stage of elucidation." (Jung 1954)

Complexes are a part of the psyche and often at the root of our despair. Jungian analyst, author, and speaker, John Beebe[5], noted in an October 2013 workshop brochure, "Today's psychotherapy patient holds knowledge of the complexes in a much more canny way than earlier generations in analytical psychotherapy. Yet, psychological sophistication

---

3   Transference, very generally, is the conscious and unconscious idea exchange that might include inferences, personal impressions, and biases that are transferred onto one another in the analytical process.

4   Active Imagination is Jung's phrase for working with associations that come up from a particular idea, word, experience, place, person, etc.

5   John Beebe has been an ardent supporter of the MBTI® tool and type theory, reminding us often of Jung's initial work on Psychological Types and his own contributions to the theory.

in the culture means that therapists and patients have more than ever to do to uncover what the unconscious still intends us to grasp about our complexes" (Beebe, 2013). Too much "knowing" brings a false security. As we think we are self-aware, we lose our interest and belief that we need to become more self-aware.

The second step of the CAF model is "Assessment." This is the work of developing self-awareness. It is not a discrete step because it often merges with step one and especially with step three. Each person has a unique threshold and approach to Self work. Orienting with tools like the MBTI® instrument (re: personality), VAL® (Values Arrangement List, re: personal values), and FIRO-B® (Fundamental Interpersonal Relations Orientation-Behavior, re: needs), and sometimes using a 360° process, we bring more information about the person to the foreground. We look to make sense of what delights our client and what exhausts or frustrates the client, ever mindful of our projections. A hazard of assessments is painting people into a box. We must use them only to the extent that they are useful – not to project characteristics or behaviors onto an individual that do not fit, or only fit to some minor degree. One must be aware of the "scientist" within who is happy to categorize and standardize.

When I pull assessment data together for individuals, they get quite a good look at themselves – what they value, what they need, how that relates to their personality style, and how others might perceive them. It gives us the opportunity to overtly question certain suggestions and note items that might not be a fit. Sometimes, the leader has been through one or two of these assessments somewhere along the way, with some level of debriefing from a cursory glance to a somewhat satisfactory immersion. Often, the person notes how illuminating such an experience is for him/her.

When I think we have struck a resonating chord and developed a closer relationship, it is then that we begin to discuss the value of gaining some deeper self-awareness (maturity) along with developing more tangible leadership skills, e.g., strategic thinking, decision-making, or delegation skills. Among those who have studied both the "harder" side of leadership and the "softer" side of leadership, we often note that the softer side is "harder." This should come as no surprise for two reasons: 1) Most of our clients have not studied the social sciences, emotional intelligence, or relationship management (and if they have it has been in relationship to marketing or sales); they've been focusing on their specific area of expertise; and 2) there is widely used research that shows this – for example, the Lominger research shows us that it is harder or hardest to build most emotional intelligence-oriented skills (e.g., interpersonal savvy, conflict management, dealing with ambiguity, etc.). (Lombardo and Eichinger, 2002)

During this second step, we often return to our career and life line conversation. This is a part of the spiraling that enables the coach to go a bit deeper. This time, we make attribution for successes and failures, joys, and sorrows, and then we discuss these thoughts further. This is also when the development plan, goals, priorities, and action steps tend to get tightened up. Assessment provides an opportunity for further clarification, calibration with the manager/sponsor, and greater insight for the individual. Clients have a more robust language at this point for expressing themselves more fully. While most clients know themselves to some degree, many insights have not been brought to the light of day.

> "People measure their self-knowledge by what the average person in their social environment knows of himself, but not by the real psychic facts which are for the most part hidden from them." (Jung, 1990)

We might say that elucidation is necessary, especially when a fixation or strong bias arises. In many cases, a client is so sure that he/she knows what the problem is that we first need to unearth self-deceptions and information that has been blocked.

From a very early age, we are taught how to rationalize, betray reality, and justify ourselves. At some point, we become aware that we all have blind spots...yes, even the person who looks back at us when we brush our teeth in the morning. Assessment data often neutralizes those aspects that have appeared as "negative" and all of this groundwork aids in trans-formational change.

Some of this work is ego work, and some of it is breaking through to the unconscious realm. Of this unconscious realm, there is the collective unconscious or the objective psyche (Jung says, it is "...universal: it not only binds individuals together into nation or race, but unites them with the men of the past and with their psychology" (Jung 1956) and the personal unconscious (unconscious shadow material – all that we dislike about ourselves and the material we don't want to remember and certainly don't want others to see).

Step Three – Education / Coaching

The third step in the Jungian Psychoanalytic Model is "Education." New habits are developed because we exercise new thinking, but this requires education and insight. Jung asserted that "the patient must be drawn out of himself into other paths, which is the true meaning of education, and this can be achieved by an educative will" (Jung, 1954).

The analyst shares a variety of thoughts and ideas throughout the sessions. In this process, the analyst attempts to challenge and enlargen the patient's world, enabling him/her to stretch at a manageable pace. This does not generally come easily, however, it requires patience and perseverance. Sometimes, the analyst suggests a book to be read, a museum exhibit to visit, and/or further work on (amplification of) dream symbols. The analyst might share information about another culture, about beliefs and norms, or tell a personal story, all in an effort to educate, inform, challenge, and, ultimately, expand the client.

"You can be a wonderful listener and technician of the emotions, but ultimately the force and the flow of change comes from an unknown place that neither you nor your client can name, measure, or claim. What you hope is that the quality of your skill and presence and dedication, and the quality of desperation and readiness in your client will together combine to put you both in the way of change, the way of grace and the way of transformation."

JOHN O'DONOHUE
(O'Donohue, 2006)

For CAF, the third step is the full-blown "Coaching" aspect. The sessions with the client focus on support and challenge, all in service to the personal and professional co-created goals. We endeavor to further insights, enable new perspectives, develop new skills, and/or unleash capabilities in some of the same ways as the analyst goes about educating. Sometimes, I suggest a book or movie as I do at the end of these chapters. We work with the client's real life challenges and try new approaches to personal and work frustrations to strengthen leadership engagement and personal fulfillment. Additionally, we discuss how to maintain and build on successes and strengths.

The intimacy of the relationship grows with attentive listening and observation, and deeper discussions emerge that further illuminate and explicate. We hope to gain some access to the Self at the center of the psyche in this stage, making the most of insights that bring forth trans-formation. There is little backsliding once you have a firm new lens on old behaviors.

Some relationships trigger (bring to the surface) a person's stuff faster than others, and that in itself is important to observe. Even with some self-awareness a triggered complex will put one right back into old behaviors and routines, and this is why coaching takes six to nine months and sometimes longer. A coach helps the client carry the millstone. Of course, we are never finished with our development and gaining insights and consciousness. But each time we come around to an old issue, we have a slightly different lens on it. We see another aspect of it or see it just a little more clearly. Growth and individuation, in particular, are lifelong processes. This is why we educate clients on the benefits of staying curious.

"Growing up sounds easy on paper, but how many of us are really grown up? If I take responsibility for my life, I lift the burden off others, but I then have a whole ton of stuff to carry myself; moreover, I will find myself very much alone when it comes to the critical decisions of life. If I look within, then I have to stop blaming and acknowledge that I am the party responsible for these outcomes that I deplore, and even these symptoms that rise to annoy and trouble consciousness. Growing up is difficult, and one's powerful position in life, whether as a parent, or a CEO of a multinational corporation, has absolutely no correlation with one's emotional maturity." (Hollis, 2005)

> "If you're paying attention each successive year will make you intimately more acquainted with all of your flaws, the blind spots, the recurring habits of thought."
>
> BARACK OBAMA in the *Audacity of Hope*

One client I had been working with over a couple of years (on and off) finally said to me one day after some new insight, "Okay, this is enough for me. I can't take any more; it's time for you to work with some other people in the department." She just couldn't take responsibility for more maturing at that time. This is an admirable declaration, as anything more we would have tried to do would have only created a negative response.

In this stage, rapport is continuously developed through listening, clarification, and a deep interest in the other. We challenge the client to see a situation more clearly and ask questions from our own insights. Updates with the manager or HR are intermittent as requested or appropriate to the work. It is important to create support from within the system so as not to create dependency on the coach; yet, we always want to ensure safety for the person making the transformational change. Plans are modified as we go in order to enable the best outcomes.

> "For two personalities to meet is like mixing two different chemical substances: if there is any combination at all, both are transformed."
>
> JUNG, Collected Works #16

Step Four – Transformation / Transition

The final stage of the Jungian Psychoanalytic Model is "Transformation." In the more difficult analytical situations, the patient just wants to be normal. But those who have led a normal life wish for something more, which may be considered an abnormal or unsocial life. The analyst or "Doctor" must abandon preconceived ideas of how a case will go because there is no telling what course it will take. The doctor-patient (analyst-analysand) relationship greatly influences the outcomes.

The analyst must be open to being influenced in order to have influence in the analytical relationship (and this is the same for the coach in the analytical coaching framework). Due to this mutual opportunity for influencing, insights occur for both parties, and they are both transformed by the experience.

The fourth and final stage of the CAF Model is "Transition." This is a time of closing out the process with the client in order to "transition" them back to the full support of the system – manager, HR, and other stakeholders. This is a time for celebration[6] of change and transformation. New habits have been formed, new perspectives and attitudes adopted, and a more resilient leader is ready to get back to the business of leading in a fully focused and more confident way. However, the ending is not without a plan for some continuation of development and for thoughtfully and deliberately looking for insights. It might be a minimal focus at first and then get more challenging again at some later, undetermined date.

Rarely are these steps pure or discrete; we go back and forth between them. It is a psychosocial dance and an iterative evolution. Psychotherapy is a great deal more than a well-documented technique – just like coaching. There is art and science to the work.

I imagine that most coaches who are using a model believe that they are using the best model for their efforts or at least a comfortable

---

6   When I say celebration, I note it with a bit of caution. When we get "high" on ourselves, we move into narcissism, elation, or ego enlargement. This is fine when it is conscious and we know how to get grounded once again. Life is full of "highs and lows," "depressions and elations." Getting stuck in an elation is just as detrimental as getting stuck in a depression. Some coaching models thrive on "highs" and "fear tactics." I don't see this as a solid developmental approach, as it leads to dependencies and is difficult on fragile personalities. I also don't mean that anyone should throw the "graduate" a party, but a bouquet of flowers or lunch or dinner plans with the sponsor might be nice.

TABLE 3 - AACT NOW

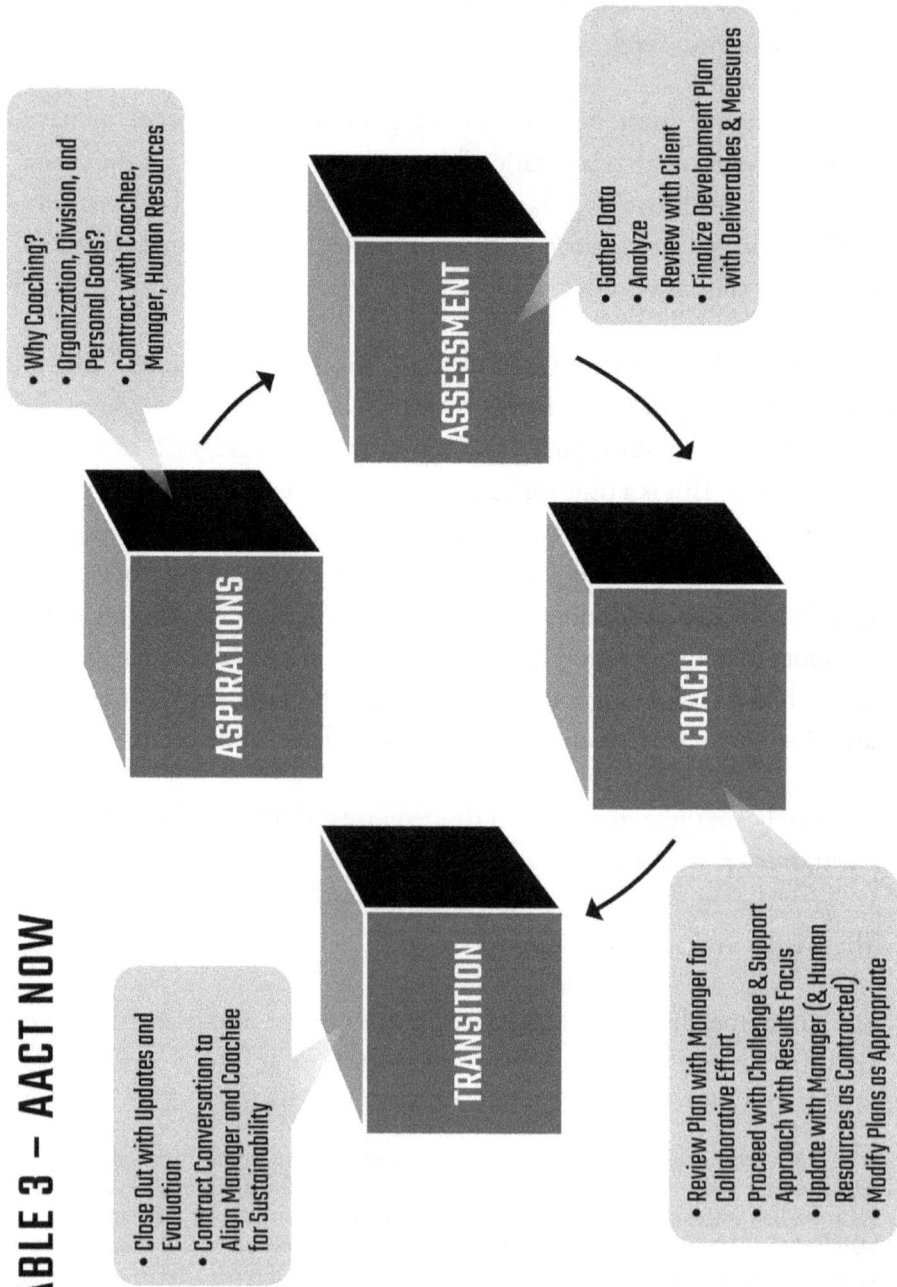

ASPIRATIONS
- Why Coaching?
- Organization, Division, and Personal Goals?
- Contract with Coachee, Manager, Human Resources

ASSESSMENT
- Gather Data
- Analyze
- Review with Client
- Finalize Development Plan with Deliverables & Measures

COACH
- Review Plan with Manager for Collaborative Effort
- Proceed with Challenge & Support Approach with Results Focus
- Update with Manager (& Human Resources as Contracted)
- Modify Plans as Appropriate

TRANSITION
- Close Out with Updates and Evaluation
- Contract Conversation to Align Manager and Coachee for Sustainability

TABLE 4 – FRAMEWORK FOR COACHING

aligned with Jung's framework for analysis

ASPIRATION

Why do you want to engage in coaching? What are you wanting to do better, or be more effective at? What are your personal goals? Professional goals? What's your purpose? What does your manager think? What does HR think? Have you had a 360° assessment and what does it suggest? What do you aspire to? How have your aspirations led you to where you are today? Aspirations vs. inspirations? Rules of engagement (ie: confidentiality).

CONFESSION

Recounting the truth of the moment; getting it out – giving voice to issues, concerns, realities. The act of having some trusted other hear your realities. Abreaction (Wikipedia 1/20/12) is a psychoanalytical term for reliving an experience in order to purge it of its emotional excesses; a type of catharsis. Sometimes it is a method of becoming conscious of repressed traumatic events.

ASSESSMENT

Gather data through assessments; analyze and review with client; finalize development plans and connect with client sponsor. Assessment provides an opportunity for clarification and insight on "you" and a language for expressing yourself more fully. While most clients know themselves to some degree, much of the real insight has not been brought to light; elucidation is necessary where the point of fixation arises.

ELUCIDATION

"While the cathartic method restores to the ego such contents as are capable of becoming conscious and should normally be components of the conscious mind, the process of clearing up the transference brings to light contents which are hardly ever capable of becoming conscious in that form. This is the cardinal distinction between the stage of confession and the stage of elucidation."

COACHING

Sessions with client where support and challenge are utilized to develop new skills and insights. Rapport is continuously developed through listening and clarification. We challenge the client to see the situation more clearly and ask questions from our own insights. Updates with manager or HR are intermittent as requested or appropriate. Plans are modified to enable the best outcomes.

EDUCATION

New habits are won because of exercise and this requires education. "The patient must be drawn out of himself into other paths, which is the true meaning of education, and this can only be achieved by an educative will." The analyst may share a variety of thoughts and ideas allowing the patient to stretch, challenge and enlarge their world.

TRANSITION

Closing out the process with the client in order to transfer them back to the full support of the system – manager, HR, and stakeholders. This is a time for celebration. New habits have been formed, new perspectives and attitudes adopted and a more resilient leader is ready to get back to the business of leading in a fully focused and confident way. However, not without a plan for continuing their development and ongoing insights in some thoughtful way.

TRANSFORMATION

The doctor-patient relationship is very important to the outcomes. "For two personalities to meet is like mixing two different chemical substances: if there is any combination at all, both are transformed." The analyst must be open to influence in order to have influence in the analytic relationship. With this mutuality insights occur for both parties and they are transformed by the experience.

model for their experience and knowledge. I suggest that incorporating a focus on consciousness for both the coach and coachee could make a major step change in the work and create a sense of fulfillment. You'll learn more about why I say this in *The Wounded Healer, An Exploration of the Coach-Client Relationship* Book 2 of *The Red Book Series,* which focuses on what happens in our intimate conversations with another. For now, suffice it to say that greater awareness on the part of both the coach and coachee makes for better work and longer lasting outcomes.

A consciousness approach can be married up with other models. You can incorporate a consciousness thread with performance coaching, strategy coaching, and career coaching, for example. Even business coaching can insert the value of consciousness and behaviors that support it.

When working as an internal practitioner in an organization, I became both aware of and wary of a particular consciousness coaching model in which the coaches were quite selective. They wanted consciousness around some things but not around others. For example, they wanted to hide (perhaps self-deception) that they were creating a dependency between coach and client, and they kept the personal power trip they got from watching a coachee quake with fear in his/her boots for sharing with their colleagues back in the home office. They engaged fear as a mechanism for ensuring the client learned what the coach wanted them to learn. This is a distortion of the word "learn." The client might memorize or exhibit a behavior in order to please, but it isn't getting the fundamental benefit of "seeing with new eyes," of understanding it at a deeper level so as to want to be a new way. This is not sustainable behavior change unless the behavior is getting you something else you want – attention, accolades, money, etc.

Final Thoughts on the Analytical Framework

Early on in the CAF relationship, typically during the *Aspiration* phase, the coach uses some type of intake. Along with getting the basic contact information needed and understanding the aspirations of the client and sponsors, this is a time for the coach to really begin to understand the person they're getting into relationship with. Typically, this carries over into the assessment phase. You'll find that some people are more trusting and comfortable with self-divulging; some people are not conscious of what they have to disclose or may simply have less to reveal.

Along with what the person thinks about all of the questions asked, I want to know how they *feel*. How do they feel about their situation – their role, their boss, their office, the company's values (real and espoused), their purpose, and the organization's purpose? How do they feel about their work and their coworkers? Why do they feel that way? What do they associate these feelings to? I want to learn about the person in five to ten-year life spans – what happened to them, what did they remember learning, who did he/she particularly like and why, and who didn't he/she like and why? What was early life like, and what led to where he/she is today? Hearing about the changes that took place for this individual in terms of their relationships and understanding of themselves tells me about their maturing process. Where did their confidence or lack of confidence come from? Why do they work (other than what might be the obvious financial reasons)?

These questions are no good, however, if you don't know why you're asking them. That is why we'll talk in Part Two about how you develop an authentic framework.

The information I gather helps me to understand where my clients are along the individuation path. How identified are they with others and with various groups? I want to have some understanding of how socially adept they are ("normalcy" versus socially unacceptable behavior). I want to see how their values play out.

While going through his values prioritization, one client kept saying, "I would have put this here; I would have made this higher and this one lower." I thought, "But you made the list (through the VAL® assessment process)." This was a red flag for me and a realization that he was not yet clear about what he values and how his values support his decision-making, what motivates him, and why he gets into conflict. Knowing about this lack of alignment created a shift in my work with him so that we could develop and strengthen his core.

I also want to see if my client has had any experiences with "midlife," as Jung defines it. Are they still in the establishment half of life – the building and protecting mode – or are they beginning to focus on the meaning of their life? Coaching will take a much different route depending on such information. When people don't understand the fuller image of midlife, they want to hide any thoughts that might suggest they have less commitment to their work. That creates lost time because we're working with a false self and not the real person.

All of this impacts our ROI.[7] It does no good to get a super, hyped-up, artificial, highly potentialized, *non*-human being who knows new behaviors that he hopes make him look ready for larger leadership opportunities. Unfortunately, in a situation like this, the ego-Self alliance is very weak. This is not sustainable. This person will fall apart in the first difficult encounter.

To elaborate on the third step of the coaching model, I endeavor first and foremost to bring more focus to consciousness. How self-aware is this person, and where can we build more self-awareness? How can we help this person gain more maturity? Much of what benefits everything else we do is about "growing up." When we are self-aware – conscious – we can self-manage more effectively. Once we can manage ourselves better, we can manage in social situations with greater ease and success.

My knowledge and insights in this arena have come from Schein, Kegan, Goleman, Kofman, Gestalt psychology, Ackerman-Anderson, and of course, Carl Jung. As Jung noted, the biggest problem with the unconscious is that it *really* is *un*conscious. The biggest problem for

---

7   ROI or "Return on Investment" is a business term that gets carelessly bandied about. In the case of coaching it becomes a scientific approach to measuring human behavior. But if you're paying attention at all, you can see that the process is not entirely scientific. It has a strong foundation in science, but it requires intuition and spontaneity as well. We must be able to adapt an approach to ROI that allows for shifts, course corrections and diversions.

coaching relationships is that clients don't know that this is critical to all of the other work they might do.

Organizations have spent billions on teaching emotional intelligence, and with good reason. If we can raise the EQ, most other capabilities ramp up naturally. I don't mean to suggest that if you're not good with budgets and finance that now you will be, but that you will have the confidence to better manage your resources to deal with such a void.

As we've been told repeatedly, the biggest problem in workplaces and in relationships in general, is communication. When we are communicating, we often don't know *what* we're communicating. I've seen reports quoting that 55-75% of communication is body language. This has been taken out of the original context of the work of Albert Mehrabian (UCLA) and his book *Silent Messages*, which I encourage you to review. But for our purposes let's take a look at the analytical communication model highlighted in the box.

TABLE 5 – ANALYTICAL COMMUNICATION MODEL

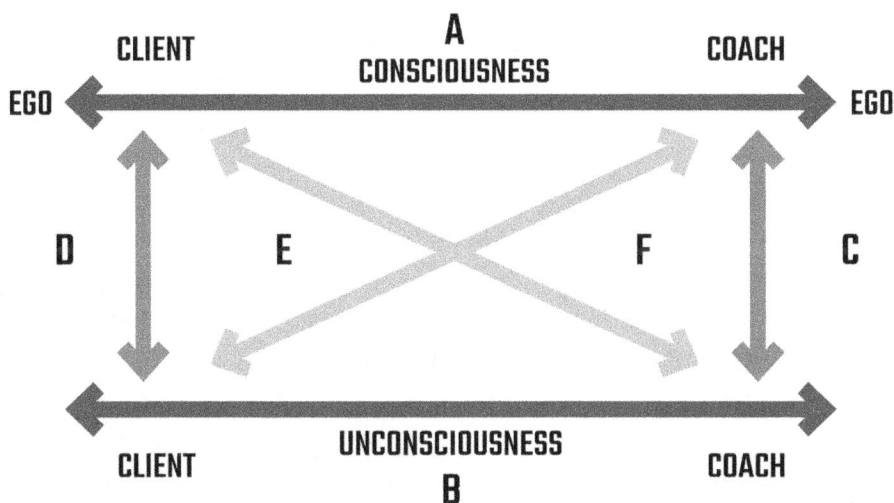

This model[8] shows that at any given time that we are in communication, we not only have the ego-to-ego (a) conversation, but we also have several other, mostly unconscious conversations: My ego to your unconscious, or vice versa (e and f); my ego to my unconscious and/or your ego to your unconscious (c and d); the unconscious (yours or mine) to the ego (c and d in the opposite direction); and the unconscious communication between parties (b).

This is a lot to compute and it is much easier to tow the party line that body language is some disproportionate percentage of our communication. We know communication is certainly about more than what we say. If you can grasp the essence of this model for just a short while and understand some of what it suggests for even a couple of your conversations in the last 24-48 hours, you can begin to understand why and how we get into trouble. Again, it is about making *conscious* what is *unconscious*. Another way of considering this is to make what is subject into object. This work enables us to get closer to and clearer about what we communicate and why we might communicate such a message. It can give us the presence of mind to realize we need to change direction. It also helps us to observe where a group is getting stuck and devise a question that gets communication moving effectively again.

"An inexperienced youth thinks one can let the old people go, because not much more can happen to them anyway: they have their lives behind them and are no better than petrified pillars of the past. But it is a great mistake to suppose that the meaning of life is exhausted with the period of youth and expansion.... The afternoon of life is just as full of meaning as the morning; only, its meaning and purpose are different." (Jung, Collected Works #7, 1953)

In the fourth and final stage, *Transition*, we bring our coaching to a close by reviewing what has transpired. We take some time to consider

---

8   The model was taken from a Jung course at the Philadelphia Jung Seminar. I had been introduced to it previously at a Media Round Table program.

how to sustain learning and insight, as well as how to continue the growth through accessing feedback and contracting with those who can be a resource internally. We connect back with the manager and enlist ongoing support and challenge as appropriate.

On the matter of therapy vs. coaching, I want to highlight a couple of final thoughts. It had been explained to me that in therapy, most of the hours are spent on the past, while in coaching, most of the time is spent on the present and future. Coaching, then, is thought to be much more goal-oriented. Perhaps this was traditionally true, but it is not necessarily the totality of my experience. I do believe the early days of therapy were more past-focused, but today, I think there is a fair mix of past, present, and future. Many therapists are quite goal-focused. It just depends on the individual (and perhaps the insurance plan). I do think the therapist or analyst can go much deeper with a person and take some risks (what would not be so risky for the trained therapist/analyst could be very risky for the coach) based on their qualifications. I feel very strongly about the "first do no harm" rule in the psychologist's code of ethics. Coaches also must keep this front of mind and monitor themselves. Codes of ethics are beginning to pop up for coaches, in particular from the ICF (International Coaches Federation).

Jungian analysts believe that the function of the second half of life is to become psychological – to make sense of the things that cause confusion, disruption, and frustration. These ideas resonate with my experience of working with hundreds of leaders and executives. In order for a leader to lead from a place of strength and authenticity, it is important to reconnect with some of the split-off parts[9] of oneself. If we work with psyche (the aspect of brain functioning that is keeper of conscious and unconscious material), we are naturally becoming *psychological*. Why would we have a psyche if we were not going to use what it has to offer? This is actually an inaccurate question because psyche is functioning whether we call on it or not.

---

9   Split-off aspects of the individual (which will be discussed later in greater detail) are those parts of our personality that have been lost, or are carefully managed to fit into certain compartments of one's life.

You might wonder if I focus too much on the "soft" side – the intrapersonal and interpersonal – but this is the bulk of what the work is about during this stage of life. We are working in relationship all the time. We can all learn skills and behaviors fairly quickly when we decide it is something we want to do and it fits with our personal mission. But sometimes, we need to learn why we have been adverse to learning something or why it has been impossible for us to recognize we either *don't* do "it" (i.e., respect others, have a good attitude, etc.) or we *do* "it" (i.e., have nervous twitches/body language, laugh inappropriately, interrupt people, etc.) And sometimes, we *do* know we do "it" and don't realize it's a problem.

For example, one female executive I worked with had a little magnet on her door that said, "I don't do perky." You might have an *"ouch"* response to that. Some would be intimidated or flustered by such a message, and others might attach negative names or adjectives to its owner. Learning to work with issues like this requires "soft" skills, but skills that are, nonetheless, highly important to leadership success. These issues say a great deal about how someone is feeling below the surface – anxious, nervous, fearful, depressed, or overwhelmed. When we understand these more base issues, we can work on the real stuff of creating fertile lands from which to grow all sorts of capabilities.

Other Theorists of Importance to the Model

There are several contemporary researchers and authors who have had a big influence on me, including Peter Senge, Robert Kegan, and Ken Wilber. Many of their ideas and paradigms resonated with me, influenced my perspective, and enhanced my model.

Peter Senge (Professor at MIT's Sloan School of Management, Founding Partner, Innovation Associates and SoL) has been one of the most compelling and integrative management-leadership thinkers of the 80's and 90's. His *Fifth Discipline: The Art and Practice of the Learning Organization* set many an organization on fire. I, for one, used it to help with the development of a learning organization training program for the company I was working for at the time. Senge's ideas on "Shared Vision," and "Personal Mastery"[10] fit right into the work I was doing on emotional resilience and leader development.

"Systems Learning" and the incorporation of Chris Argyris' work helped me to make sense of organizational development in parallel to my studies in a Master's program. Argyris' left-hand column exercise is about making the unconscious conscious, and it helps clients to "get it." These ideas teed up curiosities that were later fed further by my Jungian studies.

One lucky day (in 2004 or 2005, as I can best recollect) when I was at a professional luncheon at Becco's in New York, Dr. Senge was standing momentarily alone against a wall by the buffet table. Lunch had not started yet, so I took the opportunity to talk with him. I introduced myself and mentioned my various connections with his material and seminars and my work at Fielding Graduate University. He was very familiar with Fielding and favorable about the people he knew there, especially the amazing systems professor, Will McWhinney. We talked about the parts that systems and sustainability played in the work that each of us was doing. I told Peter about my connection to Jung, and he voiced his support of consciousness and individuation. We also talked about his current work with Otto Scharmer, Joe Jaworski, and Betty Sue Flowers on *Presence: Human Purpose and the Field of the Future*. We were very aligned, and the resonance in our work and passions was encouraging. I thought, "If these things – purpose, generativity, consciousness, collective impact, potential, etc. – are important to Peter Senge, I must be heading in the right direction." (Okay, there's a little projection there.)

Of course, I had been aware that most of these things were important to him, which is why I wanted to talk to him again in the first place. But I had forgotten the influence he had on me over the years. I had forgotten how I hung on his every word at conferences. After our discussion, I felt like we were part of the same community.

---

10   Also, the work of Robert Fritz, who Senge drew from relative to ideas such as tension seeking resolution and the importance of knowing both our aspirations and our current reality.

Robert Kegan (professor of adult learning and professional development at the Harvard University Graduate School of Education) developed a theory of maturity describing five developmental stages. These stages and his subject/object work have been very useful in coaching. Kegan likes to encourage us to take the subjective stuff out and look at it – not to be so identified with our concerns, triggers, and issues that we can't find some objectivity and sense-making. For me, his thinking is very much like Jung's here, and he believes we can begin to develop our self-awareness and take responsibility for our behaviors and relationships if we take the time to do this work. He incorporates the ideas of technical vs. adaptive thinking from fellow Harvard Professor, Ronald Heifetz.

Simply put, technical thinking is basic skill development, and adaptive thinking requires an increase in complexity of the mind. It is what I've been referring to as transformational learning. Kegan's five orders of consciousness recognize that the ability to tolerate, hold and develop complexity is necessary for growth to occur enabling higher levels of consciousness. He notes that there are "big assumptions" that keep us from learning. These might be categorized as introjects or complexes. He appears to have been influenced by Gestalt, Freud, and Jung.

When I was working on my doctorate, I first read Kegan's book, *In Over Our Heads: The Mental Demands of Modern Life.* I found his ideas to be spot-on in terms of what I was studying about emotional and leader development, as well as in terms of Jung's ideas on consciousness, complexes, opposites and individuation. He has built on Piaget's theory of child development with three additional levels of adult development. Most adults will be in the third or fourth stage (or between stages), with a few stuck in a more childish, self-oriented perspective (stage two or between two and three), and a very few ordering their worlds at a highly objective, dialectical level, or almost entirely theoretical ("Post Modernism" - stage five). In his work, I find a lot of parallels to the ideas laid out in one of my favorite leadership books, *Leadership and Self-Deception,* by the Arbinger Institute.

In Kegan's third level of development, he notes that we begin to shift and expand our thinking to no longer view others as a means to an end. (The Arbinger Group refers to this as not viewing people as objects: as a vehicle, an obstacle, or as irrelevant (Arbinger 2002).) At this level, (a) we recognize needs and desires of our own and others as valid, even when different, and we have separated from the need to be like our friends and colleagues; (b) we realize that it is a subjective opinion to see one value as better than another, and we find it quite acceptable that others have differing subjective opinions; (c) we can integrate other value systems with our own.

Kegan's third order of consciousness sounds like the Jungian analytical paradigm and the process of looking at our complexes, dissociations, identifications, etc., reflecting on and talking about them until they change shape. This is the two psychic systems at work, enabling us to grow (or referred to earlier as the ego-Self axis). Kegan (1994) asserts, "We cannot be responsible for, in control of, or reflect upon that which is subject." It is only when we make subject object – that is, take it out of the subjective (unconscious) realm and objectively look at it and scrutinize it – that we can take responsibility for our perspective. As it relates to our complexes, Jung says, "We don't have *it, it* has us." This is why we work with the unconscious so that we can take responsibility for our stuff and move into more mature living.

My incorporation of work with the VAL®, is about enabling the client to gain clarity around those values that shape their decision-making and life choices; to bring clarity to how they prioritize their values and why; and to understand that it is not wrong when others prioritize their values differently. Kegan and Associate Professor Lisa Laskow Lahey take values on in their book, *Immunity to Change: How to Overcome It and Unlock the Potential in Yourself and Your Organization.* This process enables us to find the *big assumptions* that hold us back and keep us stuck.

For example, in one client situation, a woman who runs a large department very well and has great technical skills struggles with what senior managers refer to as her image. Her big assumption is if I change my image I will lose my friends. I have great relationships and people listen to me because we have a connection. If I change I will distance myself from them, lose control, and lose my friends. Leadership has to accept me for who I am. I'm very good at my job.

"We don't see things as they are, we see things as we are." — Anaïs Nin

Kegan notes that the third order individual cannot philosophize. They struggle to take the best of several ideas and merge them into a fresh and personal idea. I often ask clients to read certain articles on leadership. Some can have a viable discussion about what they read, noting their perspective on the topic and what they didn't agree with. As we get into the dialogue, there is often new thinking that takes place for both of us. But other clients just dismiss it with "Yeah, it was interesting" and go on with the same thinking they had before reading the article – almost as if it was never seen. Perhaps that is because it was read but not "seen." Ludwig Wittgenstein, an early 20th century philosopher of math, the mind, and of language, said that we cannot enter any world for which we do not have the language. This becomes such a fundamental truth as we grow and develop.

In the fourth stage of Kegan's model, there is another step up in terms of consciousness, abstraction, and meeting a higher self. In fact, at this stage, he speaks of an awareness of self in the terms "self-regulation" and "self-authorship." This is known as "self-formation." Here, we consciously and authentically say what we believe and move away from rhetoric, hubris, and an unconscious, subjective stance. As we move up each stage, what was subject in the previous stage is now object. Kegan writes, "We have object; we are subject" (Kegan 1994).

We hold beliefs from a very young age, and some are harder to make object than others (complexes). Gestalt psychologists refer to these beliefs as "introjects" – we take them in as truths with no consciousness of what we really believe. Jung also used this word and the phrase, "interpretation on the subjective level." The more we can make understandings, choices, values, and positions conscious through examination, the more complexity we deal with, and the wider and deeper our worldview becomes.

For Kegan, transformative learning happens with what I now refer to as a "metanoia" – this is when someone changes "not just the way he behaves, not just the way he feels, but the way he knows – not just what he knows but the way he knows" (Kegan 1994). Each level represents a qualitatively different way in which reality is constructed. It is wonderful to see this dawning, this revelation in conversation with a coaching client. And it is equally exciting when you feel it in yourself. Sometimes, it is fleeting, and a coach can help the client keep it in consciousness by saying something like, "Remember last session when you said X, and it was like a thunderbolt? You went on to tell me how that changed your perspective on the whole idea of leadership. See if you can get back there." We work on our consciousness and that of our clients, as it is consciousness that can make a real sustainable difference in the growth of an individual and can impact the collective. It is our default, however, to go unconscious and move on autopilot much of the time.

The fifth order of consciousness is very rare and certainly never seen before midlife. It is a little more likely to see a small percentage of adults in the transition between the fourth and fifth order. At this level, we have moved on from identification with an inner system and find internal systems limiting. This is a time of seeing more similarities than differences as we look across at the internal systems of others. This might equate somewhat with Jung's fully individuated person (which is just as unlikely). This individual is very balanced, very conscious, and open. There is interconnectedness of subject and object, as well as subject and subject. They see themselves as more whole when in relationship with others. (Or as Jung might say, they recognize the other in themselves.) They understand and deal with paradox well as they are less likely to see polarities and dichotomies

"I absolutely believe that people, unless coached, never reach their maximum capabilities." – Bob Nardelli, former CEO, Home Depot

in the world around them. Nobel Prize winning physicist, Niels Bohr (early 20th century), is known to have said that on the opposite side of a profound truth is another profound truth. So, individuals at this level easily entertain the opinions of other governing bodies, even those that might be quite esoteric, believing that there is something to be gained from all perspectives. This is a self-transforming stage.

In Kegan and Lahey's book, *How the Way We Talk Can Change the Way We Work*, they roll out the system of *Immunity*. The *immunity to change map* helps us see why, even though we may really want to make changes, we have great difficulty doing so. This system is a very respectful and attentive approach to engaging people and their behaviors in a way that shows how we can work against our very own goals.

When I work with clients on their values, we get to some similar conversations on competing values and apparent contradictions. These competing values create a tension, so it is often easier to give up than to face these tensions, which are often at the root of our projections. In other words, it is easier to get angry with someone else – project it outward – than recognize that a competing value within may be the crux of our frustration. Kegan and Lahey's Immunity to Change programs and book are very informative and valuable to those of us who work as coaches.

Ken Wilber is another whose work has been influential for me. He is an insatiable reader and a prolific writer. Like Jung in his day, Wilber is an integral thinker extraordinaire. On the Integral Institute web site, it notes that Wilber is the "internationally acknowledged originator of Integral Theory and founder of the Integral Institute." Integral theory is: an all-inclusive framework that draws on the key insights of the world's greatest knowledge traditions. Wilber has read everything he could get his hands on relative to philosophy, religion, and human development. And believing that everyone has some piece of the truth, he went about putting together a map. The awareness gained from drawing on all truths and perspectives allows Wilber and the Integral thinker to bring new depth, clarity, and compassion to every level of human endeavor – from unlocking individual potential to finding new approaches to global-scale problems.

I like to draw on Wilber's AQAL model of "all quadrants, all levels" (including all lines, states, and types). His quadrants are an integrative representation of everything, of manifest existence. It is complex and, therefore, not easy to use in any perfunctory way, but I refer to him, to his work, or to his ideas when a teachable moment[11] arises and allows for a little extra explanation of theory. He has discussed Jung in podcasts and presentations, and Jung is definitely a part of his integral model. With books like *The Spectrum of Consciousness*, *A Theory of Everything*, and *A Brief History of Everything*, he is impossible to summarize.

On Jung

Jung said, "Learn your theories as well as you can, but put them aside" (Sedgwick, 1994). I think this is extremely important and very sound advice. We must build our foundation on something of strength, but we must be aware that anything can happen. Then, we must be *open* to those possibilities and not try to be prescriptive or shoe-horn someone into a theory. The analyst, like the coach, is continually striving to understand a person (client) from his/her very unique and personal experience. A curious and receptive disposition helps to manage transference.

Jung influenced many and was surely influenced *by* many. He read most of the same works his contemporaries were reading, as well as many other authors and thinkers. And still he says:

And yet each of us can carry the torch of knowledge but a part of the way, until another takes it from him. If only we could understand all this impersonally – could understand that we are

---

11   Noel Tichy was the mastermind behind the development work at General Electric. The teachable moment and teachable point of view comes immediately to mind with the mention of his name. The Leadership Engine is the book in which he introduces the idea of building a leadership pipeline, and in Control Your Own Destiny or Someone Else Will, he addresses the initiative we take on behalf of our own careers. These are two of my all-time favorites.

not the personal creators of our truths, but only their exponents, mere mouthpieces of the day's psychic needs, then much venom and bitterness might be spared and we should be able to perceive the profound and supra-personal continuity of the human mind. (Jung, 1954)

Please re-read this quote, as it is foundational to this book and my work. As you reflect on the various theorists you learned about as a student, it may seem that Jung gets ignored at times. Some of this is due to his writing style and complexity. But part of this is due to his belief that we don't own our ideas. Yet, I want to emphasize that many of his contemporaries and our current developmental specialists have been heavily influenced by his work, as well as Freud's.

It is often difficult to tease out who influenced whom at this fertile time in the life of psychology. Reading Jung's collected works and the writings of many Jungian analysts helps us understand his amazing commitment and the tremendous contribution he made.

The work of analysis is long and arduous. It is a deep, personal commitment, a philosophy, a way of life, and a commitment to the Self. It is a process that can be neglected or short-changed because the cost and number of sessions necessary are not always feasible. Therefore, a coach working from an analytical frame can be a great partner and guide. This work is not meant to be and could not be a replacement for analysis, of course, but the two can work wonders together where appropriate. Clarifying, cleansing, and consciousness-raising go a long way in the cycle of development. For the person not interested in or unable to take the long road of analysis, this provides a depth approach to learning that opens people up to abilities they didn't know they had.

Of course, we should not feel as though we have to analyze ourselves, or work on ourselves, every minute of every day. The goal is not perfection. So, we shouldn't forget to take some time to just "be."

It is my belief that if we, as coaches, are merely ego-focused with our clients – targeting the next achievement, promotion, raise, or award – we do our clients a disservice. If we are only ego-focused in our own lives – targeting our next client, our next article, or some bit of recognition – we also do our clients and ourselves a disservice. Having an understanding of human development and adult learning is critical to how well we support our clients' authentic growth and self-understanding.

Most of our clients are in the second half of life or moving in that direction. Remember that it is not an age that distinguishes this shift, but a mindset – a readiness for something more meaningful. Jung did not spend much time expanding on childhood development theories. If you have curiosities in this arena, read Piaget's four stages of cognitive development or Erikson's eight stages of development. Erikson was known to be a good friend of Jungian analyst Joseph Wheelwright, who started one of the first Jungian Institutes in San Francisco. It has been suggested that Erikson was quite influenced by him.

While Jung did not target the development of children, he was very knowledgeable about how the ego develops in our youth and how important the ego is to our development. Again, ego is not "bad." Being egotistical can be, however. Without ego, we cannot locate Self. The ego is the "I" – that which differentiates "me" from "others." It enables us to know what we like, what we need and how to deal effectively with social issues. That is why it is part of Erikson's stage theory—with each stage the ego is stronger, healthier and ready to support the individual for the next stage of maturity.

While we can choose to go after our work aspirations and achievements with pure ego, doing it with connection to Self (with greater consciousness) will enable a satisfactory transition (transformation) to mid-life and beyond.

Gerard Manley Hopkins is a courageous and insightful poet, and one of his poems illustrates what I've been talking about in this section. In a daring poem that starts with the line, "As Kingfishers catch fire, dragonflies draw flame," he concludes the stanza with "Each mortal thing does one thing and the same: Deals out that being indoors each one dwells; Selves—goes itself; *myself* it speaks and spells, Crying *What I do is me: for this I came."* Ponder that!

Finding out why we came – being *inspired* – provides the impetus for continuing a robust life that, in turn, provides the meaning that stimulates our activities from day to day. Have you met people who always seem exhausted? Maybe they're just bored. We drink so much coffee and Coca-Cola today (and now there are 5-hour energy drinks) that we don't even know when we are exhausted. We just keep moving because we know we have to be at such-and-such place at such-and-such time or complete such-and-such task before the close of the week or day.

Jung posited:

> Wholly unprepared, we embark upon the second half of life. Or are there perhaps colleges for forty-year-olds which prepare them for their coming life and its demands as the ordinary colleges introduce our young people to a knowledge of the world? No, thoroughly unprepared we take the step into the afternoon of life; worse still, we take this step with the false assumption that our truths and ideals will serve us as hitherto. But we cannot live the afternoon of life according to the programme *[sic]* of life's morning; for what was great in the morning will be little at evening, and what in the morning was true will at evening have become a lie. (Jung, 1960)

Perhaps coaches are the answer to the colleges we don't have for forty-year-olds. With that in mind, are you an inspired coach – inspired to do this work? Do you believe it is the work you're meant to do? Are you drawn to do the personal work that is required to do it well?

To get a good look at yourself and what has impacted you, it can be very useful to look at milestones and personal progress in five-year spans. Finding the spirals, rhythms, and patterns of your life tells you a lot. What conferences and workshops did you attend? What certifications or degrees did you gain? What speaking engagements did you take on? What have you been reading? Who has influenced you? What has been compelling in your work and in your life? What feels particularly notable? Are there rhythms of busyness and relaxation; extroverting and introverting?

What in particular inspires you right now? What has been the big, focusing question in your life? How well do you think you know yourself? Do you recognize where you are in your own stage of development? How can you take more time to tune in to your inner voice? Do you need to be more aware of the inner voices of your clients? Sometimes, in order to hear our answers to these questions, we simply need to shut out all of the noise, to rest, and to just have the intention to listen.

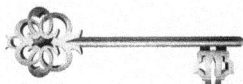

Your Notes

Jot down anything that has come to mind for you personally at this time:

What are you feeling right now? What surprises you from your notes? What insights did you get about yourself? Any other thoughts right now? Anything you want to do, communicate or absorb because of this reflection?

Additional Reading and Resources

Poems

- » *As Kingfishers Catch Fire* by Gerard Manley Hopkins
- » *The Swan* by Rainer Maria Rilke

Books

- » *Balancing Heaven and Earth* by Robert Johnson
- » *Leadership and Self-Deception* by the Arbinger Institute, and the prequel, *The Anatomy of Peace*
- » *Mutant Message Down Under* by Marlo Morgan
- » *Presence* by Peter Senge, Otto Scharmer, Joseph Jaworski, Betty Sue Flowers
- » *Also, see Senge's SoL, (www.solonline.org) that focuses on community learning, organizational learning and development opportunities.
- » *Spectrum of Consciousness* by Ken Wilber (http://www.integralinstitute.org/)
- » *The Path of Least Resistance: Learning to Become the Creative Force in Your Own Life* by Robert Fritz
- » *Ten Poems to Set You Free* by Roger Housden
- » *Writing Down the Bones* by Natalie Goldberg

Movies

- » *As it is in Heaven (2004, Swedish)*
- » *Black Swan (2010)*
- » *The Equalizer (2014)*

PART II

Authenticity is a Gem

Developing a language for expressing who we are and for understanding others' behaviors is a major step in development.

Chapter 1

The Authentic Self

"There would appear to be a sort of conscience in mankind which severely punishes everyone who does not somehow and at some time, at whatever cost to his virtuous pride, cease to defend and assert himself, and instead confess himself fallible and human. Until he can do this, an impenetrable wall shuts him off from the vital feeling that he is a man among other men" [or, a woman among other women].

Jung, *Problems of Modern Psychotherapy* (1929)

In my work with coaches, I have asked the questions of authenticity: Who are you as a coach? And does that align well with how you see yourself? How and when do you manage your ego in order to do your best work? What motivates you? What are your core values? Do you have internal conversations? Can you be compassionate with yourself when things don't go well? How do you know when you're risking your authenticity?

The work of authentic living and emotional development is life-long. We can reflect on our emotional strength in any area of our lives. For example, I played golf twice this week, and neither were particularly proud moments. Golf is one of those games that reveals the level of emotional intelligence you have in just one fairway bunker experience, one shank, or a hook that results in a lost ball. It forces you to get to the point where you either realize or decide that you're out there to have fun. You're not going to be invited to go on tour, and no one's asking for your autograph. I'm sure there are as many people quitting golf as taking it up on any given day. It can wear you out – no doubt about it. When playing golf, it can be very useful to note our emotions, disappointments, and fears of not being accepted by better players. The ego's need to win and be seen as competent in that situation helps us understand ourselves in the workplace, too.

We've been hearing about *emotional intelligence* for some time and especially since Daniel Goleman produced *Working with Emotional Intelligence* in 1998. Goleman discussed ideas of self-awareness, self-management, social skills and relationship management over the years of refining his model. (You might review the model on "Raising Consciousness" on page 56 to recall how the emotional elements fit into a larger developmental framework.)

Authenticity requires emotional clarity. We must develop some *insight* into our emotions, including where they have gone underground and where they are underdeveloped. One *strategy + business* article by David Rock and Jeffrey Schwartz entitled, "The Neuroscience of Leadership," expands on the idea of insight as an imperative to change and to enable learning. The authors explain that the mind's mapping system requires a jolt – some new notion must leap out. They say, "Leaders wanting to change the way people think or behave should learn to recognize, encourage, and deepen their team's insights" (Rock and Schwartz, 2006). They emphasize that the insight must be "generated from within, not given to individuals as conclusions" (Rock and Schwartz, 2006), because of the importance of the rush of adrenaline people experience when they make a connection. An insight brings about a new "mindedness." We begin to see the world through a new lens with a new perspective. This can also be referred to as a metanoia.[1] When we experience a metanoia, we (1) have an insight as to how we have hurt another person, (2) feel remorseful, and (3) gain a new perspective from that sense of contrition. It is true change – transformation. We cannot go back to our former

---

1   Alden Josey introduced me to the word metanoia as he presented this idea in a workshop at Roundtable Associates, Media, PA, in Nov 2006.

way of seeing things. This deeper perspective is particularly important in diversity and cross-cultural development, both of which require a good deal of emotional intelligence and transformational learning.

As I have said, the discipline of EQ has resonated strongly with me and has had a significant impact on my thinking and on the models I've constructed to help me discuss these issues with others. While Goleman, Senge (*Personal Mastery*), Kegan (*Self-expansion*), and Jung have all evolved my thinking in this arena, there are many others we can draw on. You may already have a few of your own favorites.

One way I have found to move into this self-awareness and consciousness frame with my clients is through the MBTI® instrument. I use this assessment in most of the

"The illumination of any lifeworld has something to say about human experience. What I discovered in analyzing these lifeworlds is that the way to human maturity may be arduous, but it is fitting that we undertake the journey. As Hegel emphasized, historically, the knowledge we have accumulated about human development and human communities has moved us in the direction of greater self-awareness."

VALERIE BENZ, *Becoming Mature*

coaching that I do, as it gives the client and me a language for discussing energy, emotions, strengths, and weaknesses. It often brings up challenges to aspirations – that moment of reckoning when the client sees himself or herself anew. "These results are spot on; no wonder I'm so stressed out" is not an unfamiliar response. (For a quick refresher of the Types go to http://www.capt.org/mbti-assessment/type-descriptions.htm). Just the act of learning about our personality type helps us to be clearer and more effective in many of our relationships.

If you are accustomed to the expanded MBTI® assessments, such as *Step II*™, you know that along with four global dichotomies of Extraversion – Intraversion; Sensing – Intuition; Thinking – Feeling; and Judging – Perceiving, you also have five Facet scales for each of the eight preferences. A client may not score all Facets on the side of his or her type preference, which gives us more insight into that client's individualness. For example, he or she might be a "Quiet Extravert," or an "Enthusiastic Introvert." The MBTI® Type profiles provide a very effective way of expressing personality with a focus on strengths. If you are a committed practitioner of the MBTI®, you might try reading Jung's "Psychological Types" (Collected Works #6). If you decide not to use this tool in your work, I still strongly suggest completing the assessment and getting feedback from a Certified Practitioner for your own personal growth.

A very useful companion piece to the basic *Introduction to Type* book, by Isabel Briggs Myers, and extremely valuable in surfacing triggers and stressors, is Naomi Quenk's book called *In The Grip: Understanding Type, Stress and the Inferior Function* (Quenk, 2000). It acknowledges what Jung would refer to as the shadow and helps us to recognize a side of ourselves that we prefer not to expose, or have learned not to expose. My copy of the booklet is in tatters because I find it to be an invaluable resource in working with clients on stress and anxiety. Exhaustion and agitation often go hand-in-hand and allow impatience, impertinence, or criticism to get the better of us. When we know about our triggers, we are more likely to recover before a situation becomes problematic. Also, knowing that everyone is challenged in this way enables us to be less defensive and more compassionate with ourselves and others. Because of the depth of Jung's theories, you can mine these ideas for a lifetime, and many analysts have contributed to the resources available for our continued growth.

> "First, you need a deep self-awareness and the ability to manage your own anxiety."
>
> ROBERT ROSEN,
> *Just Enough Anxiety*

Values Assessment

As I've mentioned previously, the VAL® is an assessment I use along with the MBTI®. While the MBTI® assessment looks at personality and reflects some of the values most relevant to a particular type, the VAL®

is a dedicated tool that forces the ranking of personal values – both short-term focus (Operational Values) and long-term vision (Life Values). Our values form our personal belief systems.[2] Our core values tell us what is important and preferable, and they are at the seat of our motivations and aspirations. They enable us to make good decisions and help us to know why a decision was a bad one; they are also at the root of our conflicts. You might wonder why, with all the power that values hold, we don't take more time on this subject in our educational institutions. Netflix is known to have a simple talent management strategy. They note "7 Aspects of our Culture," with the first one being "Values are What We Value" (McCord, 2014). They want to "hire, reward and tolerate only fully formed adults" (McCord, 2014).

Clients get a lot of insight from these two assessments and are grateful for this foundational work that provides a language to express who they are. An exercise that brings the importance of values closer to home involves journaling about good and bad decisions in relation to a person's reported core values. In this reflective activity they make connections, adjust their priorities as appropriate to their insights (sometimes their lists start out as more ideal than real), and make this a salient tool. Together with the MBTI®, the VAL® is a rich source of affirmation and resonance. Often, clients recognize abilities they haven't attended to, note values that they have neglected, and start to see themselves more authentically. Some feel more confident knowing that there are others like them even though they are, at the same time, quite unique.

During one group session with ten leaders in which we had just completed our review of the MBTI®, a man of about 40 looked startled and asked, "You mean I'm just like those two? I don't see that." After completing the review of values, he said, "Now, I get it." It was interesting to find that several of their highest and lowest values were flipped, making his experience of these other leaders foreign to his own style.

---

2   Much of what I have come to understand about values stems from my work with ORA and Dr. Ed Golden, Dr. John Golden, and Dr. Don Johnson, who developed the VAL® and VALOR® instruments, and others who were part of developing technical guides. Much of their work was based on the work of Milton Rokeach, Abraham Maslow, and Gordon Allport.

Both tools can provide some direction for the framework you are now working on for yourself. Take what you know about your personality and the values that you hold dear, and make some notes. To what can you attribute your interest in coaching? What is it about your personality that is a good fit, and which of your core values drives your interests and ambitions? Summarize what it is about your personality and values that support your work as a coach and any success you have had to date. What is a unique attribute, a potential niche? In what ways can you authentically support client growth and development? If you have prided yourself on the many ways you can assist a client, consider trimming your list of offerings to those that really align with who you are, and see if that lowers your stress levels. On the other hand, if you have found great support for your list of offerings, think about how you could market yourself more deliberately.

Discovering Your Own "Myth"

Working to develop my own self-awareness and become more conscious of my choices, my emotions, and the Self led me to a Jungian challenge to discover my own myth. This is not an easy task, but it is very worthwhile. The work helps us discover more deeply who we are and *why* we do what we do and act as we act. Our myth does not provide us with direction. It does not tell us how to live our lives, but it does help us unfold some of the mysteries and launches us into greater self-awareness, stimulating even greater intention for self-discovery.

As I began this process, I decided to first look at my ancestry. My mother's parents were immigrants to the US from Slovakia, and my father was born in the US (to an Austrian mother and German father) but lived his first 14 years in Germany. It was not a good time to be in Germany and not a carefree childhood. All of this plays into my own sense of *who I am* – my strong sense of responsibility, hard work, and waste-not-want-not mentality, or *my* "immigrant complex."

Jung said, "there is no difference in principle between a fragmentary personality and a complex… complexes are splinter psyches" (Jung, 1960).

Jung believed the complex acts as an independent being within us. He referred to it as an "autonomous splinter psyche." Remember that we are not trying to get rid of complexes, but only to acknowledge them and engage with them so that they don't act out at inconvenient times. The more shadowy, the less success we have with that. For my parents, I would imagine that this complex carried more negative images and ideas with it as they were trying to fit in and assimilate in the great "Melting Pot." For me, on the other hand, it is quite positive. I value the connection to Europe and to cousins who live there today, all of which has inculcated a more global citizenry within me. We took a family trip to six countries in Europe for six weeks when I was ten. I fell in love with the mystery of languages, the tastes of interesting foods, and the character of the architecture. I studied German in junior high and high school since I could speak it with my father. I later also studied French, which I was and still am enamored with. My English was littered with a few Slovak words, and because my mother grew up in New York City, some Yiddish words were "normal" to me. I didn't even know some of these words were atypical for most of my friends and in our community until I was told.

My first year at college, as we were all getting ready for our Christmas break at the end of the first semester, someone asked me if I celebrated Christmas. I didn't know why she would ask such a question. So, I replied, "Of course. Why?"

"Well," she said, "I thought you were Jewish. You used Yiddish words when we played ping pong in the student center at orientation."

As it turned out, I had said that something wasn't *kosher*. And, yes, I do use that word as if it was any other word in the English language, even though I've not had the experience of being Jewish.

That was another point of reflective learning for me. It didn't bother me that someone thought I was Jewish. It bothered me that using one Yiddish word made Jewishness a foregone conclusion. But this was her projection. She might have hoped there was another Jewish person she could relate to.

Others have mistaken me for different nationalities, including Italian, Asian, and Middle Eastern descent. I have enjoyed knowing there was some mystery to me. My work in global organizations has been a perfect fit because it's part of my myth —the fabric of my life.

A way to consider your own myth is to think about your ideologies and fallback routines. For example, if I'm confused, hurt, or angry, I go back to learning. What do I need to understand better or get more information about? Sometimes, that means I have to learn how I've been misinformed or made an incorrect assumption. Curiosity, learning, and the teacher-learner archetype are all part of my myth.

What are the patterns that are revealing themselves to you? Consider the stories and fairytales you enjoyed when growing up. Is there a familiar thread? When you're not reading for work, what are you drawn to read? What institutions and programs get your financial (and other) support? What makes life livable for you? As you dig into these ideas, try to understand some of your story and maybe even some of the challenges (complexes) your myth has created in your psyche. Remember that complexes are neutral until triggered in some way that elicits a negative response. Even then, it is not necessarily "bad" or "wrong." If complexes went away, we'd lose much of our personality. When we struggle with being honest about aspects of ourselves, others see it, we betray ourselves, we miss opportunities for learning, and we make ourselves sick with depressions and other neuroses. Are you making notes relative to the questions and insights that are popping up for you? I hope so, because this is good stuff! It will not only help you with your framework, but with your web site, your promotional materials, and your contracting efforts. You're beginning to reveal the "naked" truth – the authentic self. This is the creative and interesting person you long to be and who the world is waiting for.

The Johari Window

It may seem like a lot of work to develop ourselves, to become conscious, and to find this authentic person within, but it's worth it. A tool I find useful to bringing some simplicity to much of these ideas is the Johari

Window.[3] In working with assessments, a person will experience the obvious and also have blind spots. The Johari Window is a model of four aspects (quadrants) of communication: Open, Secret, Blind, and Closed (see table).

The "Open" windowpane is just that – open, visible to others and to the subject.

The "Secret" pane is there to show that there are things the subject is not comfortable with sharing or having other people know about him/her. This information might feel personal or private. The acronym "TMI" might have been born out of instances of sharing too much from this window. We all have varying tolerances for what we wish to know about others, and there are generally unwritten rules about what is socially acceptable within a community or culture.

The "Blind" window is there to let us know that others are aware of things about us that we are unconscious of. We all conceal certain aspects of ourselves unknowingly. In that same lack of awareness, we leak out emotions, feelings, and thoughts that others pick up on. In the analytical model, this is the "shadow" material I mentioned earlier. I don't know if the authors of the Johari Window had any knowledge of the Analytical Communication model (p. 93), but there are similar messages.

Finally, there is a square called "Closed," which covers the territory of the unknown – unconscious to the subject and unrecognized by observers. These are "deeply repressed feelings and impulses, hidden talents or skills, unconscious potentialities" (Schein, 1988). Schein notes that for his and his readers' purposes, this is irrelevant. Within an Analytical Coaching Framework, however, we know that this exists in everyone, and that everyone can benefit from making some of what is unconscious conscious.

---

3   The Johari Window is very effectively described and discussed by Edgar Schein in his book, Process Consultation, Vol 1. Although I learned and use different descriptors, he credits J. Luft from a 1961 article, so I am sure they have been adjusted for ease of communication over time. Schein's book is one I think all coaches would benefit from reading.

With this awareness, coaches can pay attention to hunches and glimmers of insight that help inform their work with a client. In my experience, these indications sometimes lead to my suggesting a period of analysis or therapy in order for a client to break through a block. If you've never worked with a client who is also in analysis/therapy or has had some analysis/therapy previously, you might not be able to appreciate how enhanced growth can be when coaching and therapy are taking place in parallel.

TABLE 6 – THE JOHARI WINDOW

	KNOWN BY ME	NOT KNOWN BY ME
KNOWN BY OTHER	OPEN	BLIND
NOT KNOWN BY OTHER	SECRET	CLOSED

While the Johari Window is depicted as equal parts (thus the window metaphor), we each have our very own customized proportions depending on our consciousness, personae, and complexes. Surely, the two unconscious quadrants are larger than the two conscious quadrants, which may come as a surprise. This alone is germane to our work as coaches. One important question we can ask is: "What don't *I* see?"

And, of course we need help from others in determining that. The 360° feedback assessment tool is one solution to this challenge. Even with what we do see and know about ourselves, we can ask: "What is there still to understand?"

Shadow is often clarified by noting that there is both light and dark shadow material; it is not all of a negative ilk. Sometimes, we go around with mounting projections on a particular teacher, speaker, or guru, giving away all of our own bright light and keeping ourselves quite small… and perhaps, safe. But this is not growing and developing; this is not the work of individuation. We are not meant to re-live the lives of those who came before us or who are seemingly ahead of us on the path.

It might be interesting and mind-expanding to stay in conversation with these individuals and their ideas, but we must also pull away and determine what is real and true for us individually. What is it that we feel slightly differently about than these teachers? How can we enlarge the thinking in a particular area? I hope you can see this book as my effort to do that with Jung. I don't see myself boxed in, but I use his work to open me up to new ideas.

Consider, for example, where some interest of yours coincides with another interest that will give you a unique yet authentic niche. There is no end to the interesting and attractive careers we can create for ourselves. I listened to a radio show[4] on equine coaching with a woman who had an interest in leadership development and noticed leadership in her horses. She has put the two together for some very interesting developmental opportunities for leaders.

A consultant, Rick Tamlyn, and I met at a Silver Bay leadership program. He named his company, IAMU® – It's All Made Up – a title he chose to press the point that if we don't like our lives, we can change them because they're just *made up*. In other words, our lives can be anything

---

4   Kate Ebner, Internet radio host, "Visionary Leader - Extraordinary Life," on Voice America Business Channel with guests Ariana Strozzi, Linda Kohnanov, and Mel Szarek.

we want them to be. Of course, in my mind, this is true to an extent. If our complexes act on their own (they are autonomous, as Jung says), we might not be fully responsible for where we are and what we're doing. But this is all the more reason to work on consciousness.

Rick's process with former business partner, Laura Whitworth (now deceased) is called, "The Bigger Game," and it is a very useful approach to helping us step up to a *compelling purpose* and a meaningful life.

Often, we have a question that helps direct our path in life. Some people have small, fundamental questions that work well in ordinary situations and well-managed lives, while people who have big questions tend to enlarge their lives. They look to continuously challenge themselves and their thinking. Of course, perhaps we all have big questions yet to be discovered beyond the difficulties and entanglements of the day-to-day. Small questions, however, usually equate to fewer aspirations. For some, fear of greater responsibility or of stepping out of a comfortable place can keep their questions and their lives small.[5]

When the psyche (keeper of all our psychic processes) has been dominated by the events and experiences of a person's childhood, it's easy to get stuck. Sometimes, the support of a skilled and thoughtful coach is all that is needed to get unstuck through exercises that help us disidentify with old stories and experiences. Often, however, this work needs to be done over time in the safety of the analytic space.

One coach I worked with was very proud of her ability to go deeply with her clients very quickly. Before doing this kind of work, we must know that we have the appropriate skills to go into that space and that the individual has the necessary safety for that depth. Even as I write this, I feel the need to caution you to leave much of the deep work to the analysts. Yet, I also realize that there is little transformational change

---

5   My thinking on little and big questions started when reading the Birth of the Chaordic Age by Dee Hock, but it was greatly enhanced through conversations and workshops with James Hollis.

without going to *some* depth. Knowing generally where your client falls on the fragile-to-agile continuum will help guide your steps. Staying attuned to fragility and working with an analyst yourself can also help guide you to effective outcomes.

Certification in and use of the 16PF (Cattell's 16 personality factors) or LSI (Life Styles Inventory) assessments can be very useful in understanding a client's level of anxiety. And reaching down to the deeper places within yourself first will further strengthen your intuitions as a guide.

> "Socrates said that the unexamined life is not worth living. Now that I am old enough to amend Socrates instead of merely quote him, I want to add one thing, for the record: if you decide to live an unexamined life, please do not take a job that involves other people."
>
> PARKER PALMER in
> *Leading from Within)*
> (Intrator and Scribner, 2007)

What are some of the questions that have guided you in your decision-making about the nature of your work with clients, as well as your personal career choices over time? Does authenticity play a role? Is it inspiration that fuels your questions? And where do aspirations come into the equation? Is there alignment? What might you want to do differently as a result of this discussion?

The Role of Persona

Is there a *masked man or woman that* tags along with your aspirations? Think of Batman, Zorro, and the Phantom of the Opera. We all have *personas.* The word comes from the Latin word for "mask" and brings to mind those worn by actors.

Why is a mask necessary? The ego uses a mask or persona to help make a connection to the outer world when it is not ready or confident enough to make that connection head on. There are times in our lives when more masks seem necessary and other times when we feel completely comfortable being "just plain me." We need our personas, but if we identify with them too much, we become more fragile.

Can we truly be "authentic" if we have a persona? I think it is a good question for considering how others see us and how we see ourselves. Is there a gap? As human beings, we can be mighty self-delusional. One way of pressure-testing your hopes for authenticity is to look for a persona. Is there some mask hiding your true face and feelings? How big or complicated is the mask? Do you ever feel like one or several of the dancers at a masquerade ball? Do you change your attitude or develop some swagger or elitist style to your speech when talking about an aspiration? What does this tell you? Do you have any insights from those questions – any at all…even that little one you just tried to ignore? Ask someone close to you when they experience you as your most authentic self, or – if you are ready to hear the answer—ask them about when you aren't). You might learn something about yourself. And don't forget to write down any and all insights…even if your backup thought is, "Well, I already knew that." Look for the slightest bit of new information, a nuance, or a minute revelation. It is this continuous work of discernment that enables us to live meaningful lives and to support others in their life journeys.

The Formative Years, Differentiation and Becoming

Research psychologists have found that the formative years – the first six years – are the most influential to our lives. This is an acknowledgement of the impact of our early relationships – mother, father, grandparent, sibling, babysitter, teacher, etc. (Also consider how the personas they used to manage their lives impacted us during those formative years.) We enter this world with/from wholeness or oneness, and during the formative years, we move out of that wholeness toward seeing and experiencing dichotomies—girl/boy, mother/father, top/bottom, black/white, rich/poor, good/bad. It is a time of separations—first from mother, then from siblings and father. Many of us have to manage through the rebellion of teen years. We must learn to separate in thoughts, needs, desires, reactions, and beliefs. We need to be different and to be *differentiated* in order to individuate.

Sometimes, parents don't think we should separate and don't want us to be different. You might find yourself not wanting your children to pull away and find themselves. But life must take its course. This developmental process is a natural ebb and flow throughout life. We do what we need to do in order to fit in, and we take some risks in order to express individuality.

Take the interview process for a job. It is a great microcosm in which to observe the behaviors of differentiation. The interviewee wants to make a connection to the interviewer and to the company, to show how he might fit into the culture and their current projects. At the same time, he wants to show what he brings that is above and beyond or at least *different* from what they have. What makes him a unique and sought-after talent? Then, when he gets hired because he has something new to offer, he again falls into the conundrum of wanting to fit in—to be liked—as well as to be novel and special. Some people take the risk of being too authentic too quickly. In this situation, others may experience the individual as abrupt, confrontational, or intimidating. Others move too slowly to risk and are not recognized for bringing anything new or for having much to offer. They stay small and insignificant. They won't be on anyone's high potential list and rarely find their way to the "emerging talent" list. Of course, it isn't everyone's path to be on such lists.

The coach has to leave space for clients' unique myths, paths, and evolutions, while encouraging them to keep growing and finding their way. Since coaches are often goal-oriented, this can be challenging. But our goals must be for the individual, and we must meet them where they are. We must watch for points of access and utilize those for the development of the individual's goals. We are there to be catalysts to our clients' insights and maturation.

We can often find points of access in our formative experiences. Early in our lives, certain experiences shape the questions we ask and the degree to which we are comfortable with risk-taking. We can usually point to some of those experiences quite clearly, while others surface over time. For example, I was in the Brownies and Girl Scouts as a child. It must have been in the Brownies, as we were playing "Whisper Down the Lane," when I had just such an experience. I was seven or eight years old, and it finally came around to me to start the message to send "round the lane." I couldn't think of what to say, so I quickly grabbed a familiar phrase and sent it on its way. The girl next to me passed it on to the next girl, and she looked stunned and whispered something to the troop leader. The troop leader paused, and said, "We're going to pick a new phrase." The leader then asked that girl to get a message started. I was *stunned*, embarrassed, and a little angry, as I wanted my turn completed. As I reviewed the phrase in my mind, however, I wanted to die, to just disappear into thin air. "School is for retards" was my phrase. It's one of the few things I still remember from that time period today, and it still embarrasses me. The worst part of this situation is that we had a handicapped girl in our group, but I had never thought of her as *retarded*. It was just a word everyone used, like its opposite, "groovy." But there was nothing groovy, cool, or keen about it. I was so thankful that this other girl was sharp enough to catch it. Yet, I was mortified that I was so *careless* (unconscious?) to have missed something so potentially hurtful. I vowed to never be so negligent again, as I hung my head in shame. This sobering experience is one that gave me the opportunity to see with new eyes and to grow up in a meaningful way. I could no longer look through a person with a handicap I had to *see* them. I learned to choose my words more carefully and consider my responses in many situations before speaking. It slowed me down but kept me from making thoughtless remarks. I think it was a mix of my birth inheritance, my parents' expectations, and experiences like this one that shaped my communication style. Integrity and ethical behavior have been key values throughout my life, and they impact the questions I ask, the comments I make, and the way I try to live.

"One way or another, we all have to find what best fosters the flowering of our humanity in this contemporary life, and dedicate ourselves to that."

JOSEPH CAMPBELL

Another personal shaping experience occurred for me in the third grade when our teacher had us take part in a reading contest. Our studies were focused on the American Indian, so for every book we read and summarized for the class, we received a feather for an Indian headdress. The one with the biggest headdress in the end would receive a prize. I was at my girlfriend's house one day, just playing and doing the things kids do. At some point she disappeared into the bathroom, and after ten minutes, I was beginning to worry about her. I was getting bored and finally called to her. She said, "Just a minute," and came out about five minutes later. She was reading a book! I couldn't believe she was using our time together to read a book and advance her own place in the reading standings, while I sat daydreaming in her kitchen. I got smart very quickly and learned something about *how to read a book*, long before I read a book by the same name by Mortimer Adler. I discovered that I didn't need to read every word. I learned how to skim and pay attention to summaries at the end of the chapters. I wound up doing quite well in the contest and feeling better about myself, rather than being some naïve *chump*.

When I look back on this, however, I wonder about the integrity of the actions – hers *and* mine. Who's to say I had more integrity? Understanding how competition plays into our ethics and observing our behaviors in such situations is important to our acting consciously and in alignment with our values.

What do you remember from your early years? What is hard for you to remember, and what do you delight in reliving? How have those lessons shaped you?

A Gallup poll queried individuals in their 30s, 40s, 50s, 60s, and 70s with the same challenge – "Name your one most serious concern."[6] They were shocked to find that for each group, the same number one concern was, "What am I supposed to do with the rest of my life?" There are few if any of us who will not at some point/s become caught up with examining, probing, challenging, and studying our reason for living: Is it a good life, a worthwhile life, a life to be proud of? What should I do today for tomorrow's benefit? Am I being too selfish? How am I impacting my community, my industry, my country, the world? What is the legacy I will leave?

---

6   Noted in a sermon given by Gregory Knox Jones on January 23, 2011.

The Hero's Journey

What we've been talking about is the "hero's journey," also called a "monomyth" by Joseph Campbell.[7] The hero's journey (and, of course, this includes the heroine's journey) is a pattern that not only shows up in myth all around the world, but in all of our lives, decade after decade, century after century. We are *all* living the hero or heroine's journey.

A myth is typically thought of as a timeless story full of symbols that helps to explain something – an idea, a feeling, an experience, a person, or a tribe. In fact, myth is often thought to be a false or made-up story, but that is not really so. Some myths are a mix of real life with some embellishments or "the story as I remember it." One such heroine's journey or myth would be that of Joan of Arc. You or I might feel like we're living the "Joan of Arc" myth because we are passionately carrying some ideology forward because we must, because we envision a better future for our kind if we do. Some contemporary, high profile heroines' journeys include that of Amelia Earhart, Margaret Thatcher, Grace Kelly, and Katherine Graham. Some high profile heroes' journeys are easily seen in the Kennedy's, the Wright Brothers, Sir Edmund Hillary, and Bruce Springsteen. But, of course, we all have our own.

This idea will be a familiar thread throughout the series because it is our journey and our myth that leads us onward, that draws us to individuation, which is never fully realized – we can only work toward it. My work on "coaching with an analytical framework" (CAF) is part of the process of uncovering my own one-of-a-kind journey and discovering more about my personal myth – realizing what kind of a childhood led to what hopes and dreams in adulthood. It is just as important for the coach to reflect on his/her journey as it is for us to work with our clients on this effort. If we don't, we risk losing ourselves in the process – living

---

7   Wikipedia, Spring 2010 posits this about Joseph Campbell's term monomyth, "also referred to as the hero's journey, refers to a basic pattern found in many narratives from around the world. This widely distributed pattern was described by Campbell in The Hero with a Thousand Faces (1949). An enthusiast of novelist, James Joyce, Campbell borrowed the term monomyth from Joyce's Finnegan's Wake."

the hopes and dreams and lives of others. This often happens in the case of people who live out the lives of one or both of their parents who didn't get to accomplish their dreams in their own lifetimes. Parents have a way of unconsciously projecting on to children their unmet needs and desires – often making children feel guilty when they don't follow a path that has been laid out for them.

What about your journey, your family's myth? Is there an existing myth that speaks to your experience of life? One woman I worked with identified with the Ugly Duckling. She didn't feel that she was wanted as a child, and she never felt that she fit in with the rest of her family. This flowed over into her work family. She was always the different, one-of-a-kind member of the group. (I say "group" because she had a hard time being a part of a team.) Once we see the myth for what it is, we can objectively challenge the reality of it, or change the direction we're going because of it, by consciously choosing a myth that is energizing and has integrity for us. We don't have to live out the Ugly Duckling story or any other … or maybe we do, but we can do it as consciously as possible. Again, I say, "maybe we do," because of those autonomous parts of the psyche that don't consult the ego and just push forward.

In his book on masculine psychology, *He: Understanding Masculine Psychology*, explaining the road a male travels from boy to man, Robert A. Johnson wrote,

> But certain psychologists and anthropologists are now helping us see myth in another light, to understand that mythology reflects underlying psychological and spiritual processes taking place in the human psyche. C. G. Jung in particular, with his theory of the collective unconscious, had pointed out that myths are spontaneous presentations from the unconscious of psychological and spiritual truths. For Jung, myths have meaning for everyone because they represent in story fashion "archetypes," that is, patterns of life that are universally valid. (Johnson, 1974)

You might be curious why "Star Wars" was such an overnight and lasting sensation. It resonated for most males as a part of their myth. It also resonated for women because it has strong, heroic female characters and connects women to that part of themselves. Of course, "Dorothy and the Wizard of Oz" is a powerful monomyth for women. Both of these stories have what Joseph Campbell referred to as the "Call to Adventure," "Initiation" and "Return" aspects that make them so relatable. Luke Skywalker and Dorothy were called to take a journey. They matured through difficult situations and initiations. They risked everything due to their curiosity and need to be fulfilled. Without a call to venture forth what would their lives have been? What calls you to venture forth?

How Curious Are You?

What calls you away from your comfort zones? Why do you get out of bed in the morning? What is the journey you are on? What challenges and initiations have you endured? What is the carrot that calls you forth to the work of coaching? Are you curious about learning and adult development?

As a consummate learner, I was always adding new ideas and developmental technologies to my portfolio for my work internally in organizations. Then came that fateful day when I decided to exit life inside the organization and go out on my own. I had every opportunity to be a "mediocre-at-best" coach when I got started. I thought I *knew* how to coach. I knew I was a good problem-solver and that I could be fairly influential and inspiring (*oh, no!*), I had a background in human and organizational systems, and I had worked in several large organizations from differing industries. I had studied Leadership and Coaching for quite some time, and I had my array of certificates and degrees. But, all of that is inconsequential if you lose your learner disposition. Fortunately, I also understood that being a *knower*[8] could take a lot away from being a *learner*. I knew that coaching could go very badly. I'd seen it, and I had experienced it personally. To my great fortune, I have always been curious and interested in understanding better and more deeply. I wanted to do the personal growth work.

---

8   Learner and Knower were ideas I learned from Fred Kofman in a train-the-trainer program in New York City in 2005 and since have come across the idea in a variety of other places.

You have to want to be fully mindful of what it means to get involved with another person's life and psyche, and you have to take time to be introspective and to continue to do your own hard, personal growth work.

What does that mean for a coach using an Analytical Framework? It doesn't mean that you attend a conference or seminar once a year or get a few CE's. Coaching others is a commitment to personal growth that starts with your own continuous, courageous exploration of Self. The last thing you want is for your own "undigested emotions and feelings"[9] to pollute the work you do with others. Lack of deep self-understanding often leads to feeling as though we know what is going on with our clients, but the reality is that if we leave the space for the real understanding to emerge, it will likely be a new, third thing – not what the coach thinks and not what the client thinks. Jung referred to this as the transcendent third thing. We don't need two parties to come to the transcendent third. We can and do use our various selves to get there when we have competing values, needs or ideas. While this competition or friction is quite unconscious it is still very alive within us, often leaving us feeling stuck. You might wonder why you're "dragging your feet" on a particular decision. Given time the psyche will create a solution that exceeds where we can consciously arrive. "The tendencies of the conscious and unconscious are the two factors that together make up the transcendent function. It is called 'transcendent' because it makes the transition from one attitude to another organically possible, without loss of the unconscious" (Jung 1960). It is a self-regulating process within the psyche in which, at some point, the unconscious does a handoff to the ego.

Hill, et al., speak of this handoff in their book, *Collective Genius*, when discussing decision-making and the value of *creative abrasion*: "The third way, integrating ideas—combining option A and option B to create something new, option C, that's better than A or B—tends to produce the most innovative solutions"(Hill, 2014).

---

9   The perfect expression for what I am trying to convey from Michael Fordham as noted in the journal article, "Vision, Interpretation and the Interactive Field," by Schwartz-Salant.

I was once working with a client and had just "learned" a concept the week prior in a seminar. So, I *knew* where he was going. Except, I actually was not quite right, and he had to tell me twice before I let go of my "answer/interpretation." Even if I was partially right, I was being a knower and reductionistic, and I ruined the opportunity for the moment to evolve in just the right way for this individual. I also ruined the opportunity for me to learn something new. "…[T]he interpretation must stem from what Winnicott would call "unknowing" (Schwartz-Salant, 1991) – back to the idea of an "insight." Also, reminiscent of Jung's transcendent third, which includes conscious and unconscious – he reminds us we must take into account the "one-sidedness of consciousness" (Jung, 1960).

Now, fortunately, there is still the opportunity to repair the situation if we're conscious of it and curious enough to work through it. Repairing the rupture[10] between coach and client, like that of analyst and patient, is done through apologizing and then listening and summarizing what you have heard until the individual feels that he/she has been heard correctly. This is a new opportunity to connect with the client, and it is sometimes a stronger connection because of the acknowledged imperfection of the coach/analyst and the co-creation of the outcome.

Donald Winnicott[11] (1896-1971), a contemporary of Jung's, is famous for his idea of the "good enough mother" (or good enough parent). I suggest that in the same way, there is also the "good enough coach." I see this coach as someone who safely holds what the client puts out into the room so that through patience, the client is allowed time to come to his/her own answers through his/her own curiosity and reflection. The client alone will have the right answers. Perhaps that is all we can hope to be – a container – and often, that is enough. Too much knowledge entices us to provide too many *answers* – to think we *know*.

---

10   Kohut – "Empathic stance": empathic failure can ruin the bond between analyst and patient and empathic attunement can repair the rupture. Can read more on Kohut's construct of "selfobject."

11   Donald Winnicott did psychoanalysis with Melanie Klein, a Freudian, and he was most interested in object relations theory – a theory which speaks to the importance of early relationships formed with others – especially the mother, in order to have success in relationships later on. Object relations theory comes from the work of Melanie Klein.

I am reminded of a poem by Jalaluddin Rumi in which he says, "Out beyond the ideas of wrongdoing and rightdoing, there is a field, I will meet you there." That is the field where we do the best with our clients.

The Analytical Coaching Framework and the Corporate Environment

Now, I do realize that we are coaching in corporations and organizations that have a bottom line to protect. My clients are all under a lot of pressure and to put that burden aside for a short while and just listen and think and be is a great gift. It truly enables better, stronger, more authentic actions and outcomes. I have been fortunate to have very astute client sponsors who understand that what is best for an individual is best for them (sponsor is typically the manager) and the organization. You can fool some of the people some of the time, but you can't fool all of the people all of the time. And you can't fool them forever. That goes for both the client you're coaching and the organization you're serving.

There are a lot of programs available today for the development of coaches, and I'm often asked my opinion of the best ones. It depends, of course, on the individual, what their curiosities are, and what they hope to become. Some programs are big, some small, some full of hubris or fancy processes, some loose and uncontrived, and some falling somewhere in the middle. That's where I find myself – somewhere in the middle, in a loose-tight paradigm. I'm an integral thinker and want transformational outcomes. I want to work in partnership with my clients – learning *from* them and offering something *to* them. I absolutely want a "return on investment." However, I see that as bigger than a number you can put on it.[12]

---

12   Relative to ROI, there are leading and lagging indicators in the determination process. We do not have enough interest in longitudinal studies to capture the value over the long haul. When coaching with an Analytical Framework we're coaching for a person's overall growth and maturity. If a coach-client effort ends with greater maturity you have elevated your coachee's ability in all categories, not just two or three skills or behaviors.

I've had very good conversations with executive leadership about coaching. I'm happy to share my approach as a scholar-practitioner.[13] This means that the practical is every bit as important as the scholarship. It does not mean I force the scholarship on others; it means I have the scholarship to back up my decisions and my approach in a results-oriented, practical environment. Like Noel Tichy, I will find the "teachable moment" and use it to the extent that there is an appetite on the part of my client. Additionally, I'm steeped in systems thinking and don't just look at my client in a vacuum, but my client within a system, within a system. I encourage regular environmental scans of the external environment as well as the internal environment. With all the projects, meetings and presentations it is easy to become myopic and insular, but it is not an effective way to lead.

Phenomenologically, I gain a great deal from hearing someone's story of living their lives, of their experiences, of high points and low points. In a difficult situation, a disappointing outcome, a conflict, I want to get specific and know exactly what has happened, how a situation was created. But without knowledge of the people involved, it is nothing more than an activity of teaching some conflict management skills that may, or may not apply and may, but probably won't, be remembered in the future. If the individuals learn something about themselves in the process, have an insight, make connection to a complex or trigger or pattern, then we've really learned something. Then, we have change and new vision, and we elevate ourselves in terms of our emotional intelligence, our capabilities, and our authenticity.

Sometimes, it may seem that coaches are coming out of the woodwork. But, organizations and their leaders are expected to downsize, right-size, merge, acquire, or become an acquisition, go global, go viral, meet the customer, converse with Wall Street, value every employee, and set a tone for the culture along with their daily work. Whew! Coaches become a

---

13   My PhD is in Human and Organizational Systems from Fielding Graduate University, Santa Barbara, CA. My focus was on leader development, integral and transformational learning, and organizational systems.

god-send. And coaches that understand the environment, stress and the human experience are a truly essential resource.

For the internal coach, HR, or talent development partner, you may be providing some coaching in your organizations and ensuring there is a pool of qualified external coaches for leaders to draw from. It is important that the pool have a diversity of backgrounds and experiences. Taking time to consider where your organization is in its life cycle and what you're trying to accomplish in the culture will help you make stronger choices.

In my work interviewing coaches I use a thorough protocol to really understand what a coach is about and what priorities and values shape their approach. I have met coaches with an understanding of family systems who work with family businesses; those who target small (under 100 employees) or larger (10,000+ employees) organizations; those who work with middle management, or just the C-suite; a particular industry; non-profits; performance coaching; those who do improvisational coaching; business coaching; and the list goes on. So, if you're a coach, you see the importance of clarifying who you are and what you do. And if you're an internal HR leader, you see the importance of your strength of purpose in this process. Finally, if you're a leader in an organization, you see the importance of making a good choice for yourself (and the *Self*).

If you're reading this book because you are serious about becoming a good, authentic coach, find the right training, whether that is in university or at a training institute. If it feels to you like coaches are being mass produced in a program, beware. If there is concern about too many rules, too much precision, and rigidity, causing the work to lose some value or potency, keep looking. If you feel like you're part of a coaching mill, perhaps you need to find something smaller or more intimate. If you feel like you're becoming an automaton, look for something that focuses on you as an individual. Don't become a perfectly molded product looking for a client to work your magic on. If it's too much science and feeling reductive and confining, find a program that is more holistic, more integral.

Coaches, do you have a perfectly predictable approach? Or are you comfortable with your ability to adapt and adjust from one client to another? Do you challenge yourself to think? To feel? Do you have the agility to meet whatever comes your way? Are you losing your individuality or gaining it? I think we all have to come to our own truths. What I am encouraging is reflection and consciousness in your efforts. I hope I am providing a platform that can inform your personal knowing of what is right for you. What are your emotional sensibilities telling you?

> Adaptability requires flexibility to take into account multiple perspectives on a given situation. This flexibility depends, in turn, on an emotional strength: the ability to stay comfortable with ambiguity and remain calm in the face of the unexpected. Another competence that supports adaptability is self-confidence, particularly the sureness that allows someone to quickly adjust their responses, even dropping everything without reservation as realities shift. (Goleman, 1998)

We all experience days when we're emotionally challenged. We all have blind spots, and that fact doesn't go away. It especially does not go away with success. The likelihood is that it gets worse with success. As soon as we feel our successes, there is a tendency to become inflated and to believe "we've got it now." *"I'm on a roll; I get it; I've got the formula down."* Remember *The Gong Show*? (I suppose I'm dating myself.) But, this is the moment when the big gong sounds. In analytical psychology, we look for the archetype that constellates with these types of feelings. It could be many, but I want to consider the charlatan, who has some overlap with the magician and savior archetypes.

The Charlatan Knocking at the Door of Our Own Authenticity

We typically think of a charlatan as someone who is bad, is shifty, and uses trickery. We can start from a neutral ground, however – not good or bad, but depending on the intention and the consciousness with which we as coaches engage our internal charlatans. To our clients, we seem to have magical powers, and that, of course, is a projection. Sometimes, we readily accept that projection. It certainly is nice to feel our value and know that others appreciate what we do. Some of what appears as magical power, however, is the ability to see a situation without the client's emotional trappings.

Some coaches have a model or a formula for everything, and that can appear to be magical. During my experience of interviewing coaches for various organizational coaching pools,[14] I sat with an HR employee who was partnering with me on an interview of an external coach. The HR rep paid a big compliment to her former coach, whom she obviously admired, saying that the coach indeed had a model for *every* situation. The coach beamed in an "awe shucks" fashion (as I can now see myself having done on various occasions), appreciating the compliment with no sense of the power over this individual that she had helped create. Coaching is not a dependency model, and it is not a "better than" model. To guide you in more clearly understanding my pronouncement let me share some examples of some experiences I had as an internal consultant/employee with leaders who were coached by coaches who appeared to me to have clear moments of working out of the charlatan archetype.

In one instance two coaches co-leading a meeting came down hard on a leader, saying, "you're not showing up, what do you want?" The individual was embarrassed in front of his peers and only gave them what *they* wanted for fear of a reprisal. He learned to mimic this in order to make it look like he "learned" something. He learned something alright, but not something that was of deep value.

Another senior leader this pair had been coaching for some time and had a lot of influence over was given to bouts of rage…clearly saying what he wanted, but I doubt really influencing the hearts of people. On one occasion he shocked me by pulling me aside and reading me the riot act. He finished by giving me an ultimatum and sending me on my way. As the receiver of his message I was

---

14   Starting with my work at AstraZeneca, where I developed a global coaching initiative consisting of developing our HR Business Partners as internal coaches; developing our leaders to utilize coaching skills; and working with external leadership coaches.

very confused and lost my respect for the individual. While he may have been clear about what he wanted, he wasn't able to engage me in a way that enrolled my support and conviction.

I was left to wonder the value of his coaching. Was this the result of the charlatan archetype at play? What authority was this leader speaking from? What was creating this false self?

In another experience, a coach brought the charlatan into play in order to move the energy in the room. At the time I referred to it as "stirring the pot." But the intervention was successful. In this instance he didn't belittle or diminish anyone, he simply put a charged question to the group about their thoughts on gender bias, shifting the stuckness into new movement on the issue at hand. Could this be an example of the positive charlatan? It seemed so.

We must be aware of paying homage to false gods. They rule any coaching we do to satisfy pride, greed, gluttony, and other vices. If instead we are working with a value for virtues like humility, charity, and temperance we have greater, long-term impact. I'm learning to be alert to whenever the charlatan archetype is at work in my psyche so that I can weigh the real value I'm bringing for both my client and me. I'm taking opportunities (i.e., being conscious) to effectively manifest the positive charlatan.

"So why do I say we should lose this idea that we hold special magic?" You may still be questioning my thinking. You might be under the assumption that we sell ourselves on our special abilities. That is quite understandable until you think it through further. What happens when the client can't make the necessary changes, can't effectively commit, or gets fired? Where's the magic then? If you're struggling with this idea, it might be a good time to do some journaling. Step away from the text, and write down what you're thinking. Keep writing every thought without editing. Just keep writing until there are no more thoughts. Then, reengage with the text.

But actually it [the psychoanalyst's work] is a tricky and not undangerous calling. Just as all doctors are exposed to infections and other occupational hazards, so the psychotherapist runs the risk of psychic infections which are no less menacing. On the one hand he is often in danger of getting entangled in the neuroses of his patients; on the other hand if he tries too hard to guard against their influence, he robs himself of his therapeutic efficacy. Between this Scylla and Charybdis lies the peril, but also the healing power. (Jung, 1954)

Coaching is not "undangerous" work. We get our training from somewhere – but is that the whole answer – is that "truth"? We have clients that feed our egos, telling great stories about us. That always feels good, but another challenge to be wary of is the need for admiration. The coach who chooses a route of flattery and affirmation will at some point have his/her come-uppance, just as a coach who keeps a sterile and objective point of view. It can appear preferable to some coaches, for example, to focus on the positives or to create positives in order to develop what they think is "relationship." This can be a rather problematic start and can create more issues than it resolves. (Does it have integrity?) The person who tries, on the other hand, to keep everything very objective does not allow for the intimacy that is necessary for transformational change. In speaking on the values of depth psychology, Lionel Corbett says that healing comes from "the complexities of the relationships and from the appreciation of the depth of the soul." (Corbett, 2013)

So, let us first consider what a relationship is: It is based on closeness and suggests care for one another – a connection, a bond, a relatedness. I have taken on the idea of a *thinking partnership*[15] with my coaching practice as I believe the work is collaborative, and I believe the relationship requires an equality or parity – both bring something to the table. A thinking partnership brings a focus to what the relationship

---

15   Saj-nicole A. Joni is a senior leadership coach who introduced me to this term at a leadership development presentation.

is about – what our intention is. We are coming together to think and to work together on resolutions. We will bring some ideas and tools, and the client will do the same. Together, we will find a way forward. We can be a mirror to our client, reflecting what we see, hear, and experience in the relationship. This is known as "use of self" or the "self as instrument" in the field of organizational development. We have a responsibility to work with information that we're getting and assist the client in making sense of it. This can be very hard, as sometimes we get directives from management about our client like, "Joe is a bully, and he has to change." Yet, the person saying this is not willing to have that conversation with Joe. And the 360° data is not clearly showing that others in the organization feel that way about Joe. So, what do we do with these conflicting inputs? We could ignore the opinion of management, assume it's just an outlier perspective, and go on as if it doesn't exist. Or we could say, "Hey, I've got some information that's going to be hard to tell you, but I think it's important that you hear it." And, "no, I can't tell you who said it."

Another way that the charlatan shows itself is when we develop a great relationship, we really like the other person, and they are equally complimentary. Yet, there is little truth in it. If we create this kind of enmeshment, we both suffer. There is likely no opportunity for psychic development or personal growth if we merely affirm the client. Yet, depending on the fragility of him/her, it can be difficult and potentially even a mistake to move on. That's why we are continuously assessing and discerning our way forward and balancing our own thinking and feeling functions.

The charlatan may also show up when we attempt to create a relationship with the client's boss. Our ability to get along with this individual has no bearing on the client's ability to get along with him/her or other stakeholders. I like the ideas of positive psychology and appreciative inquiry. These should not be confused with fanatical idealism and a singular focus on strengths as some anticipate by the names alone. We don't want to purely focus on adulation of what one does well – building their one-sidedness. We must also deal with areas of difficulty. Not to be glib, but we all, of course, have strengths and weaknesses. There's a line from a popular song in the late 1970s that I'm reminded of: "It will sure do me good to do you good, I can help." On the positive side of the charlatan, we have a diplomatic and influential individual playing a role to make a point. On the negative side, we have a cunning, devious liar.

We must, therefore, be aware continuously of why we're in this profession. How does it make me feel – popular, superior, competent, powerful? What is my need to "help" about? How do we understand these feelings and needs and put them in

> "I should not talk so much about myself if there were anybody else whom I knew so well."
>
> HENRY THOREAU

their proper place? Are we just feeding our own complexes? "Helping" is probably not the best paradigm. If I'm helping you, I'm putting you in a one-down position, and I'm under the assumption that I have knowledge or capability that you don't and that you *need* my help.

On the flip side of this coin, of course, is the bully coach. This coach thinks that his tough, brash feedback is a good fit for working with the leaders of the organization. Break them down, and let them know who's in charge. But fear and intimidation are not effective motivators over the long haul. They do not build the authentic character of a person. Often, when coached this way, a client will go on to "coach" his/her direct reports in the same manner.

When coach and client meet each other with authenticity and as equals, they can work through and tease out the real issues and come to better answers together. In that process, if I, as coach, project onto the client's situation, I stay in a conscious space of *"This may have some value to your conundrum, and it may not."* This allows me to continue to listen to the client rather than push my own agenda, my own "brilliance," which may, in fact, not be the right direction for my client.

Taking on a coach is a little scary (even for coaches who decide *they* need further development) because coaching asks us to take the risk of being who we really are or *finding out* who we really are. When one has spent a lifetime carefully constructing a persona that seems to be holding up quite well, this can be a shocking suggestion. As mentioned, we generally have several "personae." In our clients we might recognize a persona for the boss, one for peers, and yet another for the direct reports. Then, there may be a home persona and an in-law persona, and all the other "me's" that help me "fit in," "get along," or manage the many situations we find ourselves in. Persona is not necessarily a negative, however – quite the contrary according to Jung.

> Jung saw that the persona functions as mediator between the outer world and the ego, a mediator comparable in importance to the anima/animus, which serves as mediator between the ego and the unconscious....Far from shattering the persona, Jung saw the persona as a vital sector of the personality which provides the individual with a container, a protective covering for his or her inner self.

> In the best case, the persona is appropriate and tasteful, a true reflection of our inner individuality and our outward sense of self. (Hopcke, 1990)

> In this best case scenario, then, we are authentic.

The coach works with his/her own personae and defenses while working with the same in his/her clients. No wonder this is tricky work and why some sort of supervision is necessary. If a client is not ready to see personae and defenses, the coach provides the container (a holding unit) until they are. But as time goes on, the goal is for the individual to strengthen his/her ability to take this work on personally so as to realize more of the potential of the Self.

As coach or client, at times, a false self can get the better of us, and we have to stop and reflect: Who am *I* really? How do I want to show up? What do I want to stand for?

These are the questions of midlife and of developing greater self-awareness – the doorway to emotional and social intelligence, to authenticity, and to individuation. In order to position ourselves in the marketplace in a unique way, we need to have some answers to these questions. We need to reflect on our experiences and do our own work.

So, I recommend that you find your voice, find your authentic self, and be your own coach first. What do you need to do in order to bring more consciousness to your work?

On Jung

Persona is an archetype. Something that is archetypal is imaged and understood everywhere and always was from the beginning of time. We need our personae, and Jung is quick to confirm that we don't want to get rid of these "masks" we wear, but that we can help ourselves if we are more conscious of them. He worked very hard at recognizing and confronting his personae, which is clearly depicted in his *Red Book, Liber Novus*. "The persona is thus a functional complex that comes into existence for reasons of adaptation or personal convenience, but is by no means identical with the individuality." (Jung, 1971).

Recognizing how we adapt and what we do to make situations tenable or effective enables us greater control. These insights provide us a window into what aspects we may need to grow, where we may need to challenge ourselves, and where authenticity may be lacking and resulting in stress or frustration.

In his early 80s, Jung was persuaded to tell the story of his life to his trusted, long-time colleague Aniela Jaffé for the development of his biography, "Memories, Dreams and Reflections." He died in 1961 at 86. He begins the Prologue with, "My life is a story of the self-realization of the unconscious. Everything in the unconscious seeks outward manifestation, and the personality too desires to evolve out of its unconscious conditions and to experience itself as a whole." He continues in the next paragraph: "What we are to our inward vision, and what man appears to be sub specie aeternitatis, can only be expressed by way of myth. Myth is more individual and expresses life more precisely than does science." (Jaffé, 1989) And so he shares his personal myth – stories that make up his personal truth.

Jung worked through a lot of what was unconscious in the work of *The Red Book,* which contains his reflections on his visions and dreams. In it, Jung shares the difficult conversations he has with various aspects of himself and provides us a look into his inner journey over a 16-year period of maturation and movement toward individuation. Not everyone can, or should, go to the lengths he did, but Jung's brave, shared experience gives us a chance to see what it might be like for us to take on such an epic effort. It gives us an idea as to what we might do in lesser degrees. He encouraged others to take up this challenge to work toward "re-membering" their inherent wholeness.

Early in my work in Training and Organizational Development, my driving question was: "How can we shorten the cycle time to a person's development?" What kinds of exercises and experiences could I provide to individuals seeking to grow and advance themselves as leaders in an organization? That led to my curiosity and work with emotional intelligence, positive psychology, and, eventually, to my PhD work, Jung, and analytical or depth psychology. Jung wrote, "Often this work is wearisome and difficult, because it cannot be accomplished by intellectual shortcuts or moral recipes, but only by careful observation of the inner and outer conditions" (Jung, 1989).

While I'd have to agree that there are no shortcuts to the personal work we each have to do, half of the work is realizing it needs to be done. My work is enabling coaches to see that there are many benefits to facing their personal growth work and many ways to go about it.

If your interest lies here as well, I hope you will venture into some of the suggested readings. You might find some of them useful to your clients, too. One client said, "I never read an HBR article; these are great!" We all gain value from reading outside of our typical resources. If books seem too long and too much like work, watch a good movie or read a poem and ponder its message for you. Keep a journal even if you only write a sentence or two a week about how you're feeling; what's exciting, disappointing, or new. Like the highway signs say, "Stay awake, stay alert, stay alive!"

Your Notes

Jot down anything that has come to mind for you personally at this time:

What are you feeling right now? What surprises you from your notes? What insights did you get about yourself? Any other thoughts right now? Anything you want to do, communicate or absorb because of this reflection?

Additional Reading and Resources

Poems

- » *If I Had My Life to Live Over* by Nadine Stair
- » *The Art of Disappearing* by Naomi Shihab Nye

Books

- » *The Bigger Game* by Laura Whitworth, Rick Tamlyn, and Caroline MacNeill Hall
- » *Care of the Soul in Medicine: Healing Guidance for Patients, Families, and the People Who Care For Them* by Thomas Moore
- » *The Change Leader's Roadmap* by Anderson and Anderson
- » *The Dark Side of the Light Chasers* by Debbie Ford
- » *The Hero Within: Six Archetypes We Live By* by Carol S. Pearson
- » *Inner Work* by Robert Johnson
- » *Intelligence Reframed* by Howard Gardner
- » *Just Who Will You Be?* by Maria Shriver
- » *Memories, Dreams, and Reflections* by C.G. Jung
- » *The Path of the Everyday Hero* by Lorna Catford and Michael Ray
- » *Running with the Wolves* by Clarrissa Pinkola Estes
- » *Searching for Wisdom in America* by Tony Schwartz
- » *Where Have I Been All My Life* by Cheryl Rice

Songs

- » *Man In the Mirror* by Michael Jackson
- » *Is That All There Is?* by Peggy Lee
- » *Puff, the Magic Dragon* by Peter, Paul and Mary

Movies

- » *Good Night Mr. Tom* (1998)
- » *Hitchcock* (2012)
- » *Precious* (2009)
- » *Sweet November* (2001)

TED Talks

- » *How to Overcome Our Biases* by Vernā Myers
- » *Where is Home?* by Pico Iyer

Chapter 2

Designing a Framework that Fits You

Leadership over the long term requires self-knowledge.
You can learn managerial functions and develop managerial
skills, but, sustained leadership requires self-knowledge,
self-realization, self-discipline, and self-development.

Barr and Bar, *The Leadership Equation*

Self-knowledge is critical to our ability to be authentic in the world and to form an authentic framing for our work. We might even say that it is "key" to our effectiveness and our leadership. After all, we are all leaders and have a responsibility to take that seriously. That does not mean that we have to be out front and center asserting ourselves. It does mean, however, that we have to know how to get things done and how to talk about what it is we do. We have to know how and when to use our voices, as well as how and when to act. It requires doing our own work first and forever.

We lead in so many ways and often don't realize that what we are doing is leadership and that it expresses our values. For example, I interviewed coaches for an organization's coaching pool, asking each about their leadership. Here are some of their responses:

» I am a leader in the community with children's sports leagues.

» I am on the board for the local hospital.

» I serve on my church leadership as an elder.

» I lead groups at Habitat for Humanity.

» I mentor at the Catholic church and help children with their homework in the evenings.

» I organize breakfasts for the homeless.

» I support crisis response through our synagogue.

» I run for breast cancer.

Another question I have asked coaches is what they've done in the last year for their own development. This is some of what I've heard:

» I read the *Wall Street Journal* and *The New York Times* every morning.

» I take yoga classes.

» I meditate.

» I attended an industry conference.

» I went to a workshop on decision-making.

» I am in a mindfulness program.

» I read books – some on leadership and change management and some on ideas that are new to me, like beekeeping.

» I was certified in the MBTI® assessment.

» I'm getting certified in the Enneagram.

So, how do you communicate your style of leadership to a new client? The first way that you might do it is by sharing your framework for how the work gets done. You can express what is important to you, how you initiate developmental work with a client and some possibilities for how it might evolve.

When I ask people about their frameworks and on what they base their ideas, they usually provide a nice diagram and a brief explanation. Sometimes, I get a host of handouts, including an intake, checklists, charts, and graphs. One woman handed me a packet that was nearly an inch thick. I'm sure it was every process she'd ever come upon. Some people are dogmatic and rigid, while others overflow with ideas and possibilities. Some are knowledgeable about business and financial markets, some marketing, communications or PR, and others are more knowledgeable about particular theories, philosophies, or assessments.

I have mentioned some of the researchers, authors, psychologists, development theorists, and poets who have impacted me in my development and in my understanding of leadership. Hopefully, you've been thinking about the ones who have impacted you. If you haven't already, take some time now to write them down. Next to each entry, put a little note about what is most interesting to you about this person or theory and what in particular resonates with you, your myth, and your work.

As your myth continues to unfold in this process, take note of what models you return to again and again to explain the human condition and adult development. Maslow's hierarchy of needs and the Johari Window are a couple of good basics that everyone seems to know about. But what do you personally know about their strengths and weaknesses? Do you know the work of Kurt Lewin or Fritz and Laura Perls? Who is doing work today that attracts you, and what forms their theoretical underpinning? Who are the founding fathers and mothers of the various theories of human development? What leaders do you admire and why? What are the strengths and weaknesses of your own leadership? As you respond in your head to these questions, continue to add to your notes. This is the beginning of creating your own framework.

An Introduction to Human Development and Motivation

For those who are unfamiliar with the fields of human development and motivation, you will find below a brief introduction to assist you in getting started with your own research and discovery. You might be reminded of Psychology 101 class and *Behaviorism, Humanistic Psychology,* and perhaps even *Gestalt Psychology.* Maybe Piaget, Erikson, Rogers, Satir, Herzberg, Loevinger, McClelland, and McGregor ring a bell, but you can't quite identify their ideas. You've likely heard of Peter Drucker, Ram Charan, and Gary Hamel. All have contributed to the fields of personal and organizational or management development, leadership, and strategy, and most lived at the same time as Carl Jung.

The intermingling of ideas and the evolution of psychological constructs was at an all-time high in the mid-20th century. I imagine it was a very exciting time to be in the field. And, of course, it still is.

This is by no means meant to be complete or conclusive, but to encourage your understanding of the importance of knowing the fundamentals. Psychology is integral to coaching.

Behaviorism – Pavlov and Skinner

The behaviorist school of thought began in the 19th century, from which you might remember names like Ivan Pavlov and B. F. Skinner. You'll likely recollect the experiments with bells, whistles, and the use of pain in order to manage or curb behavior. You might think of the conditioning of the Von Trapp children, popularized in the "Sound of Music." Ideas of reinforcement and punishment are popular themes. The idea here is that through certain conditioning in interaction with the environment, new behaviors or habits could be developed. Once developed, a habit is very hard to break, of course, even when that habit is not in our best interests. The addition of Albert Bandura's work offers us useful, less mechanical approaches in terms of social learning through observation, modeling and rehearsal. Recognition, praise, affirmation is all very important; and withholding such also impacts the individual. Behaviorism is happening whether we plan for it or not. It is important to recognize that we are always being reinforced in a variety of ways, some stimulated by our environments and some by those we interact with or admire.

Unfortunately, behaviorism leaves much of the individual out of the equation. It is one-dimensional and doesn't incorporate deep learning. While it makes collection of data and ROI more observable, it is quite limited in how it can help leaders develop integrally and morally. Many times, behavioral efforts become a "check-the-box activity." But will it stick? Operant conditioning may work on our youth and in the military, but it does not fit the adult learning model. After all, authentic leader development and individuation is not Pavlovian.

I think most of us prefer to see people make deeper, more meaningful change that is sustainable over time. Leadership coaching shouldn't just be about satisfying a manager or a goal in the moment. I know there are coaches who work from a narrow, behaviorist theoretical base, which does not fit the holistic paradigm that I am advocating. I'm not saying that there aren't any behavioral efforts worth employing, or that when the organization is footing the bill, every client should get to choose what they want to learn in order to fit their authentic view of themselves. I realize that there are and will be expectations from a boss, but I think most of those can be more effectively dealt with from a thoughtfully negotiated, mature adult-adult interaction. And, of course it follows, that it is mature, centered adults that would make the most of behavioral learning methods.

Humanism

Maslow

Humanistic psychology offers another option in the development of the individual. A founder, American psychologist Abraham Maslow (April 1, 1908 – June 8, 1970), may be the most recognizable human development figure to the greatest number of people due to his pyramid diagram of the five levels of motivation (see table on page 54). Maslow felt that in order for any one of us to make it to effective levels of management, we had to have some basic needs met. This is where Maslow's theory starts. He targets physiological and safety needs in the first and second levels of his pyramid.

Maslow believed that when each need is met, we are compelled to try and meet the next level need. The third and fourth levels are what often bring us to organizations – belonging and self-esteem needs. We join all sorts of organizations over a lifetime, starting with the Brownies, Cub Scouts, Little League, 4-H, and such. Are you on Facebook or other online communities? We often join spiritual organizations and ethnic networks, as well as other community and national organizations. Some of these are aligned to our personal lives, and some are aligned to our professional lives. But they are all for the sake of belonging and connection.

At the belonging level, we seek love and affection. This may be seen as admiration, appreciation, inclusion, and affiliation. Once fulfilled in this way, we feel drawn to meet our self-esteem needs. We have a certain need for a high level of self-respect and respect from others, Maslow posited. We often get this from awards, certifications, promotions, and titles. It targets what affects our self-worth.

When Maslow wrote his 1943 article, "A Theory of Human Motivation," the top of the pyramid was Self-Actualization. He believed that this level begins to call us when all other needs are met. Self-actualization is not as much an aspirational calling as an inspirational one. The focus is on what a person was "born to do." Until we can become conscious enough to access this space, Maslow theorized that we have some restlessness within.

As he aged, Maslow saw that there was more to self-actualization – the even higher reaches of wisdom and consciousness, the more spiritual domains or self-transcendence. He referred to the "peak experience" as a euphoric one and felt that these should be cultivated for the sake of personal growth. For me, these are the higher level insights I find so important to mature development. My perception is that as Maslow continued to develop his thinking on self-actualization, it came to look more and more like "individuation."

Jung and Maslow were contemporaries, and Maslow is said to have been influenced by a Jungian analyst friend. In The Farther Reaches of Human Nature, Maslow clearly states commonalities and connections with Jung, and he specifically noted the influence of Jung and Rogers (discussed next) in at least two of his books, Motivation and Personality and Toward a Psychology of Being (Schott, 1992). Maslow was also influenced by Alfred Adler, Erich Fromm, Karen Horney, and Gestalt psychologists Kurt Goldstein and Max Wertheimer (Ibid).

While Maslow has received a fair amount of criticism from scholars for only studying high functioning people in the United States, his work is continuously used in schools and training programs. We know he did not study the mentally ill or clinically neurotic individuals, and it's said that he had a relatively limited scope of the human psyche. However, his nicely packaged hierarchy of the important fundamentals of needs always seems to resonate with people, and it has the benefit of being easy to remember. This is one of the challenges for Jungian psychology – you can't pack it up nice and neatly in a table or chart.

Rogers

Carl Rogers (1902-1987), also a Humanistic psychologist, is well known for his ideas of unconditional positive regard and a client-centered approach. This stance requires listening empathically, seeing the value in each person, and being genuine. His work and research showed the value of empathy over the long haul. Empathy, from Roger's perspective, is one of the most powerful tools of the therapist.

He also believed that the only worldview we can understand is the reality we face in each moment of our experience. Rogers felt that these beliefs and this humanistic approach enable individuals to open up and express themselves more clearly and move toward personal congruence (personal authority). He saw people as trustworthy, resourceful, capable of self-understanding, and as having the ability to resolve their own problems in order to live productive lives. His work is at the heart of what we refer to as "Emotional Intelligence" today.

In terms of typology, the Feeling (F) type would likely have more inclination to this approach, possibly becoming too one-sided, and the Thinking (T) type might need more of this empathic listening skill. Jung's attention to such opposites and the reconciliation of such forces is foundational to his work and germane to our unique functioning.

It has been my experience that people in the coaching relationship respond to empathy and positive regard when it is genuine, and it must be genuine for the integrity of the relationship and the work. However, with only the tool of empathy, we will not get very far in accomplishing our goals.

Rogers also had a sense for the "search for self" in what he termed "Becoming." He noted that a person "is increasingly listening to the deepest recesses of his psychological and emotional being, and finds himself increasingly willing to be, with greater accuracy and depth, that self which he most truly is" (Rogers, 1961). He published his writing on this the same year that Jung died at 86 years old. It certainly resonates with Jung's individuation theory.

Cognitive School of Thought

Cognition is about perception, thought and knowing. Cognitive therapy deals with the negative emotions that come from what is considered "bad" thinking. Albert Ellis and Aaron Beck are key contributors to the work of cognitive development. The cognitive therapist belieives we should tell people when their thinking is flawed. But in many ways for me that is like playing god. We need to be careful of making judgments about other people's thinking. What makes my thinking right? How do I know if someone's thinking is bad or if there are deeper issues that their thinking is helping to elevate? More pragmatically, I believe there is a more profound place for cognitive development with middle managers than with senior leaders. As managers try to get comfortable with the basic skills of getting work done through others they can benefit from learning how to organize, delegate, present materials and strategy the right way by getting direction from those more skilled. If one tends to be a naysayer he or she may benefit from cognitive therapy to adjust these thinking patterns. But remember, there are times when such thinking is important and necessary for healthy decision-making. If our emphasis is on guiding people to be more self-authoring we support them in thinking (and feeling) about their thinking.

The adult learning model directs us to assist others in being more self-authoring:

Adults with a self-authoring way of knowing have the developmental capacity to generate their own internal value system, and they take responsibility for and ownership of their own internal authority. They can identify abstract values, principles, and longer-term purposes and are able to prioritize and integrate competing values. (Drago-Severson, 2008)

Cognitive therapy seems to assume that the therapist knows and the client/patient does not. In coaching we have a fundamental belief that the client knows most of what they need to know, the coach is there to help the individual access that knowledge. It is not a model of fixing others but of unleashing the inner knowing we each hold. That being said, perhaps cognitive therapy lends itself best to performance coaching.

Herzberg

Frederick Herzberg (1923 – 2000) was one of the early thinkers on business management. His two-factor theory included the consideration of motivation and hygiene factors. You'll probably remember his studies of what brings satisfaction and dissatisfaction to people's work lives. He aligned the factors that bring satisfaction to employees with "motivation" and differentiated those factors from others that are "maintenance" oriented and might even be aligned with dissatisfaction.

The motivation factors – such as achievement, recognition, the work itself, responsibility, advancement, and growth – were said to be necessary to avoid dissatisfaction. On Maslow's hierarchy, these might align with belonging, self-esteem, and self-actualization in some cases. And the hygiene factors might align well with Maslow's first two needs. (If you're interested in this theory, you might also find Victor Vroom's Expectancy theory of interest.)

McGregor and Ouchi

In 1960 Douglas McGregor unveiled Theory X and Theory Y to help business people understand motivation. Theory X people inherently dislike work and will avoid it if possible. Theory Y people see work as natural as play and rest, and they put the same amount of effort into work as they do into their personal lives. In the 1980's, William Ouchi posited a theory Z, which was based on the effectiveness of Japanese productivity and perspective. The theory Z organization is people-centric. Trust is very important and is built from modeling trustworthy behavior. For example, Ouchi said, "As long as the vice-president regards the president as a fair and well-informed person who will arrive at a fair appraisal of his performance, the contented employee will let the hierarchy operate unobstructed" (Ouchi, 1981).

These organizations are described more as "clans" than hierarchies due to the intimate nature of their associations. The decision-making process is a more participative one, as people are drawn into the shaping of important issues. The espoused values and beliefs must be carried out and expressed in concrete ways in order to overcome skepticism and enroll new employees into the culture. The orientation is a holistic one among all employees. It was the dawning of ideas on participative management, incorporating trust and transparency.

McClelland

In many organizations where I have worked, the management or leader development programs have had some connection to David McClelland's (1917-1998) "Human Motivation Theory" (sometimes referred to as achievement motivation theory or acquired-needs theory). Human Motivation Theory targets three needs: The need for achievement, affiliation, and power. These needs are typically abbreviated as: nAch (the need for achievement); nAffil (the need for affiliation); and nPow (the need for power). McClelland believed these needs were acquired over time and that our life experiences played into the strength of our needs in each of these areas.

Achievement

People with a high need for achievement (nAch) seek to excel and, thus, tend to avoid both low-risk and high-risk situations. Achievers avoid low-risk situations because the easily attained success is not a genuine achievement. In high-risk projects, achievers see the outcome as one of chance rather than their own effort. High nAch individuals, therefore, prefer work that has a moderate probability of success, ideally a 50% chance. Achievers need regular feedback in order to monitor the progress of their achievements. They prefer either to work alone or with other high achievers.

Affiliation

Those with a high need for affiliation (nAffil or nAff) need harmonious relationships with other people and need to feel accepted by other people. They tend to conform to the norms of their work group. High nAff individuals prefer work that provides significant personal interaction. For this reason, they perform particularly well in customer service and client interaction situations.

Power

A person's need for power (nPow) can be one of two types – personal or institutional. Those who need personal power want to direct others, and often, this need is perceived as undesirable. Persons who need institutional power (also known as social power) want to organize the efforts of others to further the goals of the organization. Managers with a high need for institutional power tend to be more effective than those with a high need for personal power. (NetMBA.com 2002-2010)

Schutz

William Schutz was another needs-oriented theorist whose theory of interpersonal relations surfaced in 1958 in a book called Joy. His more technical book of the same year was entitled, FIRO: A Three-Dimensional Theory of Interpersonal Behavior. We know this work best in our organizations today from an assessment called the FIRO-B®. The three fundamental needs are the need for Inclusion, the need for Control, and the need for Affection. For each need, we gain insight into how much we want it met by others and the level to which we express it to others.

In 2011, the FIRO-B® was updated to FIRO-Business®, and the three needs were adjusted to link more effectively with business-speak. Inclusion became Involvement; Control became Influence; and Affiliation became Connection.

The assessment outcomes enable us to understand our approach to interacting with others, and they are very useful in team effectiveness work. Our needs change based on whether or not certain needs are being met at a given time. They also change based on our current life situation or work context and our need for relationships or control in that context. I've found that some people experience changes in their MBTI® assessment results – their innate type doesn't actually change, but their assessment results can change each time they complete the Inventory due to life pressures and adaptations. This is why self-validation prior to looking at report results is important.

Kohlberg, Gilligan, and Levinson

Other theorists that have been influential to me are Lawrence Kohlberg on moral development, Carol Gilligan on women's development, and Daniel Levinson on adult development, especially as relayed in his books Seasons of a Man's Life and Seasons of a Woman's Life. All of these theorists and their works provide us with context and opportunity to understand the possibilities of a person's experience. They also help us to see how multifaceted human development is and how impossible it is to land on one explanation for any surfacing issue.

Gestalt and Perls

Gestalt psychology, founded by Fritz Perls and his wife, Laura, has offered a plethora of ideas to organizations and continues to do so through organizations like the Gestalt Institute in Cleveland. As noted in the online Gestalt Cleveland approach to learning, "Gestalt theory is rooted in perceptual psychology, holism, and field and systems theory" (Gestalt Institute of Cleveland, 2011). You will find Gestalt psychology firmly embedded in a good deal of OD (organizational development) work in many organizations. The AU/NTL (National Training Labs) program at the American University in Washington, D.C. had its beginnings in Gestalt psychology, but it now has more of an integral approach and has added quite robustly to its initial platform, thanks to the curiosity of founder Edie Seashore.

There is a lot of overlap between Gestalt psychology and Jungian psychology. Perls was a contemporary of Jung's. It is my understanding that through Otto Rank (psychoanalyst and colleague of Frued and Jung), they corroborated on a lot of Jung's ideas. How their ideas may have been expanded through Jung's work, however, I don't know. He and Laura both studied first as psychoanalysts (Freudian school). The Perls adopted bodywork into their platform from an understanding of dance (from Laura's training), and they studied dream work from Asclepios to Freud to Jung. In the end, Fritz developed his own style of dream-working and the open chair (often referred to as second chair) method of therapeutic work.

Drucker

I cannot not mention Peter Drucker, the father of modern management. Today, he might be considered an integral thinker (see Wilber, Part 1, Chapter 3) as he drew on ideas from psychology, philosophy, sociology, history, culture, and religion to invent management theory. He developed one of the first Executive MBA programs in America. Wikipedia notes that he thought of himself as a "social ecologist."

He was surely one of the most widely influential thinkers on management in the 20th century. He highly valued the idea and activity of lifelong learning and introduced the idea of the "knowledge worker" before anyone else saw it coming. He worked with many organizational leaders, and his writing appeared often in Harvard Business Review. You might start by looking at his 2001 book, The Essential Drucker.

In these last several pages, I have attempted to include a thumbnail sketch of several of the key thinkers who have explored, excavated, and built strong foundations for the work of organizational and leader development. It is clear that this is work that is necessary and meaningful. If we want to make the most of our psyches and our abilities, we must continue to do the investigating, sowing, and harvesting. We must be hermeneuts – digging, discovering, spiraling through psyche, interpreting, and reevaluating, and then looking again after a time to once again experience aspects of ourselves we thought we knew.

We must distinguish between what is *knowledge* and what is *understanding*. These theorists provide us with direction for understanding where our clients are in their development when we meet them. They help us to consider people from many angles. They ensure that we have sound models, information, and research to support our observations. But to be sure, when we sit with an individual we must set aside our knowledge and see the client as unique so that we can *understand*. In explaining these ideas – knowledge and understanding – that are "diametrically opposed" and "mutually exclusive attitudes," Jung says, "This conflict cannot be solved by an either/or but only by a kind of two-way thinking: doing one thing while not losing sight of the other" (Jung, 1990).

In the bigger scheme, developmental work tends to fall under the umbrella of humanistic or social sciences and is sometimes referred to as "moral sciences." No doubt you're hearing that from my perspective, it is an imperative that leadership coaches study this field as well as business.

A coach once called me when I was still working internally in a corporate environment, and she insisted that she be included in our coaching pool because there were two individuals in our organization who wanted to enlist her as their coach. She felt that based on her line successes in another organization within the industry, she was totally qualified. However, she had completed no studies in human development. I made some suggestions as to what she might do to prepare that side of herself and her ability to be a more effective coach. To say the least, she was not happy with me. She called me back six months later to ask again to be included in our pool of coaches. If she had been personally tutored for those six months, it still would not have been a likely possibility as she would have missed the most important part – her own deep learning. That would have required practice, perhaps some mistakes that shed light on new perspective, and more practice and insight. An experienced and skilled mentor (teacher, supervisor, guide) might have increased her ability appreciatively. She tried to "check the box" on a couple of things, noting that she was scheduled to be certified in the MBTI® tool in a few months. Of course, this hardly seemed sufficient and only reaffirmed my initial belief that she was not ready to coach individuals on their development. There is a moral obligation within coaching to do the right thing, but you wouldn't know what the right thing was if you had no knowledge and experience of this extensive field.

This information is accessible through a myriad of books, the Internet, and courses you can take at your local community college or university. My notes are meant to be a reminder of this broad discipline and of the various territories you can research. Clearly, there is a threshold of knowledge in human relations, personal growth, and leadership that is necessary for a coach to explore, just as there is a threshold of knowledge for our clients and the work that they do.

Additionally, I wanted to make some connections to Jung and to begin to demonstrate the vastness of Jung's work in comparison to many of his contemporaries.

Looking at Your Leadership History from Another Angle

In another effort to learn how to learn from a place of consciousness and prepare for how you will position yourself in the marketplace, take a moment to reflect on the transformations in your life. On paper or on your computer, create a continuum of these transformations, with the jobs you've held written along the top (including stay-at-home Mom or Dad, barrista, a *less than* genius at the Apple store, or nanny). Note under each job title the aspects of the job that brought you the most happiness—whatever was most interesting, exciting, and meaningful. Then, list your successes during that time. What experiences were transformative? How did you change or grow? Where did you refuse the invitation to grow?

> "Since it's a journey you can become what you need to be. Good managers are made, not born."
>
> Linda Hill & Kent Lineback,
> *Being the Boss*

It can be discouraging to see that you have refused the opportunity to grow at times, but if it is an important learning for you, you can be sure that you will come around to it again.

One of my favorite words in Jungian psychology is "circumambulation." Not only is it a five dollar word, but it is rich in meaning and resonates with my experience of learning. We often revisit themes and ideas that we need to learn in order to get on with our individuation work. Upon revisiting an idea, we might entertain a reflective thinking stream like, "I've been here before. I thought I learned this lesson, but now I see that even though I did learn x and y, there is more to learn here. Wow, this is interesting. I'll deliberate about being more conscious of this now." Then, years pass, you have more experiences and insights, and you come across the idea again. Low and behold, you have yet another insight! It's a "whoops, I could have had a V-8" experience. You recollect former perceptions and iterations of the same connection, and on and on it goes.

> "People become leaders by internalizing a leadership identity and developing a sense of purpose. Internalizing a sense of oneself as a leader is an iterative process." (HBR, 9/13, Vol 91, #9, Ibarra, Hermina, Ely Robin, Deborah Kolb)

Become an Observer

Ron Heifetz and Marty Linsky use a terrific metaphor of "getting on the balcony" in their book, *Leadership on the Line*. The authors make the case for stepping away mentally from a situation for just seconds and *getting on the balcony* to oversee *the dance floor* – to get a bigger picture. The idea is that we can get a better sense of what is actually going on if we step away from it. As you read this book, I recommend that you put this idea into practice. Step away from it, and think about what you find annoying in the book and what aligns with your perspective. This is another way of making the subject the object.

You can also use this concept with client groups. In other words, who is "dancing" with whom? Who has been in the conversation, and who has been sitting it out? What non-verbal communication do you notice? Have your own interactions gone well? Is there someone who hasn't spoken who could shed light on an issue? This is a terrific in-the-moment exercise for making a situation more conscious and clarifying your next best move. (If you're interested in this idea, see Edgar Schein's process consultation work.)

Of course, developing the ability to observe is a very important leadership and coaching skill, as well as an important general life skill, whether observing groups, teams, or individuals. When you begin to intentionally observe your clients, you start to notice all sorts of things that you missed before. When we believe we know a person very well or that a situation is clear, it is a good time to build in some deliberate observation again.

We start by holding our judgments. Just try to get the facts and specifics down. Then, consider potential meanings, and check in with others as appropriate. You might say something like, "I noticed you seemed unusually quiet today. Was I talking too much? or "Did I get off on a tangent that didn't make sense to you?" or "What was your experience?"

You can do this if you're trying to become a better observer of yourself, too. Be sure to begin by restraining any judgments. This is not about good or bad; it's just about "what is". When you objectively have "what is" out on the table, you can talk about what you want more of, less of, and what is working just as it is. So, as an example of working with myself following a coaching session, I might ask some of these questions and lay out my responses in front of me on a tablet. I might, for example, notice that I was particularly quiet, overly judgmental, opinionated, or that I kept talking over the other person. I might want to consider what I've come up with using all four functions of the MBTI®: Sensing and Intuition as well as Thinking and Feeling, just as we do in problem-solving. In that review, without being hard on myself, I can begin to decide what to do with the information. Does it require a conversation with my client sooner rather than later, or is it just a note for the next session? I might decide a simple email will do, in which I write something like, "In reflecting on our meeting today, I realize that I had quite a bit to say about your current situation. I just want you to know that those were my reactions and thoughts, and they might not fit your sense of things. It would be useful if you made some notes about that – what worked for you, what resonated with you, and anything that was particularly off base or that caused you concern. This will help us both as we reconnect next week. I'll be eager to hear where you are on the issue." With reflection and consciousness, I made a useful intervention out of my unconscious behaviors in the meeting.

> "If you want to make the world a better place, take a look at yourself then make the change, got to get it right while you've got the time....
>
> MICHAEL JACKSON,
> *Man in the Mirror*

Much of this work reflects the learning cycle: We're naturals at the first half of the cycle – making decisions about what I or we have to do, carrying out those decisions, and looking for the next task. The second half of the learning cycle—reflection and connection comes only with greater intention. If we reflect but don't make the connections, reflection becomes just another activity that bears no fruit. Spending the additional few moments to consider what the reflections mean, what actions you can take, and/or what plans you can try in the future is the key to success.

Too often, we jump to connections without reflecting, which is equally meaningless, and can bring us extra work in the long run. The journey of self-development is complex and often intimidating. To be useful guides, we must persevere. *We cannot lead where we have not been.*

Earlier in the book, I briefly mentioned Chris Argyris and his exercise called the "left-hand column." He is another theorist who has showed us how to have more conscious conversations in organizations as was popularized in Peter Senge's *The Fifth Discipline*. In the left-hand column exercise, you write down what you can remember of a difficult conversation in the right-hand column of a piece of paper. This includes the dialogue between you and the other person. Then, fill in the left-hand column with what you thought during each part of the conversation but did not say. What thoughts were just below the surface? What might you be able to grasp of that which was quite unconscious at the time you were in the actual conversation?

In this exercise, you begin to make object that which was subject and make conscious that which was unconscious, allowing you to see the situation anew. It sounds fairly simple, but it often has great impact. I encourage you to try it using some conversations you have had in the last few days.

Your Framework

By now you've uncovered a lot about yourself. You've made a lot of notes as to what is important to you and why you do this work. To begin to design your framework, ask yourself these questions: What is it that you want others to know? What stands out to you as the most important ways you interact with others? How do you learn about another person? How do you help them learn about themselves? How are you framing your perspective? What paradigm are you starting from – business, change management, talent development, career planning, family business, marketing, communications, public relations? What does this mean for your coaching framework and your authentic connection with your future clients?

If you can't quite come up with a diagram of your framework yet, try explaining it to someone else, and ask what he or she heard. Note what makes you feel enthusiastic and passionate. Whether you have a stronger way of expressing yourself or you actually created your framework at this point, congratulations. This is a big step.

Now jot down some action steps for yourself. What else do you want to research or get more clarity about? What next steps will strengthen your position? Does your web site or your personal mission statement need some tweaking?

Relax, breathe, and reflect. Make an entry in your journal.

On Jung

While making his own effort at *getting on the balcony*, Jung liked to inhabit his library for some personal analytic discussions:

> There he had his alchemical books on hand, added to which, as he (Jung) put it, the size of the room gave him the mental space for what he termed an out-of-body experience. On these occasions he would "go up and sit on the window, and look down and watch myself, how I am acting, until I see what from the unconscious has caught up with me and I can deal with it." (Miller, 2009)

Jung was meant to be Freud's protégé, and it was upsetting for both men when Jung decided to go his own way in 1913. But this was the beginning of his asserting his authenticity and finding his own framework. Staying with Freud was becoming a personal betrayal. He had become quite clear about what he believed and why, and he began to write and present his own views. Many of his ideas were not immediately accepted by the psychological community, particularly the psychoanalytic community.

In *Memories, Dreams and Reflections*, Jung noted, "...I have been launched upon a single enterprise which is my 'main business.' My life has been permeated and held together by one idea and one goal: namely to penetrate into the secret of the personality. Everything can be explained from this central point, and all my works relate to this one theme. (Jaffé, 1989)

In his preoccupation with his own unconscious images, he determined that he needed to start with the question, "What does one do with the unconscious" (Jaffé, 1989)? In answer, he realized it was about the relation between the ego and the unconscious, and he began to experiment and expand on this.

While Jung was working on this question and his response to it, he was also working on his book, *Psychological Types*. He declared, "This work sprang originally from my need to define the ways in which my outlook differed from Freud's and Adler's. In attempting to answer this question, I came across the problem of types; for it is one's psychological type which from the outset determines and limits a person's judgment. My book, was therefore, an effort to deal with the relationship of the individual to the world, to people and things" (Jaffé, 1989).

Your Notes

Jot down anything that has come to mind for you personally at this time:

_____

_____

_____

_____

_____

_____

_____

_____

_____

_____

_____

_____

_____

_____

_____

_____

_____

_____

_____

_____

_____

_____

_____

_____

What are you feeling right now? What surprises you from your notes? What insights did you get about yourself? Any other thoughts right now? Anything you want to do, communicate or absorb because of this reflection?

Additional Reading and Resources

Poems

- » *As Once the Winged Energy of Delight* by Rainer Maria Rilke
- » *Keep Walking* by Jalal ad-Din Muhammad Rumi
- » *Songs of Innocence (Introduction)* byWilliam Blake

Read

- » *Being the Boss* by Linda A. Hill, Kent Linebck
- » *The Farther Reaches of Human Nature* by Abraham H. Maslow
- » *Human Motivation* by David McClelland
- » *Maslow on Management* by Abraham H. Maslow
- » *On Becoming a Person* by Carl Rogers
- » *Peak: How Great Companies Get Their Mojo from Maslow* by Chip Conley
- » *Personality Types: Jung's Model of Typology* by Daryl Sharp
- » *Points of Influence: A Guide to Using Personality Theory at Work* by Morley Segal
- » *Religions, Values, and Peak-Experiences* by Abraham H. Maslow
- » *A Whole New Mind: Why Right-Brainers Will Rule the Future* by Dan Pink

Songs

- » *Playing God* by Paramore
- » *The Times They Are A-Changin'* by Bob Dylan

Movies & Television

- » *Equus* (1977)
- » *Gentleman's Agreement* (1947)
- » *Jimmy P.* (2013)
- » *Orphan Black* (2013)
- » *Schindler's List* (1993)

Chapter 3

Supporting the Development of Authentic Leaders

We know that our demons are not easily dismissed, that we yearn for more than simply the ability to get through the day. We would like to make a life and not just a living, which—as we know from our own experience and that of others—takes courage.

Paul Tillich

On the very first page of his book, *Why Not the Best*, Jimmy Carter relays a story of authenticity from when he was applying for the nuclear submarine program. He was interviewed by Admiral Hyman G. Rickover for more than two hours about many subjects he knew well – seamanship, gunnery, naval tactics, music, literature, etc.

Carter depicts Rickover as quite an intimidating figure. The Admiral asked increasingly difficult questions, keeping the former president humble and on his toes. At some point, Carter realized that he was sweating from the anxiety of the experience. Then, the Admiral asked what seemed to be his last question, "Did you always do your best?" Carter started to say, "Yes, sir," but then, he quickly reflected on times at the Academy when he "could have learned more about our allies, our enemies, weapons, strategy, and so forth" (Carter, 1975). So, he stopped. Swallowing hard, Carter said, "No, sir, I didn't always do my best."

He remembers that Rickover looked at him for a long time and then turned his chair to end the interview asking a final question, "Why not?" Carter said he was never able to forget this question or to answer it. He sat for a while sweaty and shaken and then left the room. (Ibid.)

Carter certainly portrays himself as authentic in this exchange. But what about Rickover? Did he show up as his genuine self? Was he authentic, or was he acting out of a complex? It sounds like he fit the persona for what you might expect from an Admiral. But, similar kinds of meetings with similar types of characters are taking place throughout organizations around the world. David Whyte refers to the "Shakespearean plays writ large" in our workplaces – "with the nobles telling their truths from the podium while the gravediggers are telling it like it really is in the bathroom. And every epoch ends with a lot of blood on the floor" (Honigmann, 2009). So, organizational life, like the meeting between Carter and Rickover, is filled with blood and tragedy. No wonder we shrug off authenticity.

Political challenges and a desire for self-preservation often cause us to create our next move unconsciously. We've learned how to stay "safe" in many situations. For some, that means "staying just under the radar." For others, it is a matter of "giving people what they want." In either case, staying safe doesn't allow for much authenticity.

> "What locks itself in sameness has congealed. Is it safer to be gray and numb? What turns hard becomes rigid and is easily shattered."
>
> RILKE,
> *Sonnets to Orpheus*

Some personality types are inclined to play it safe, while others are given to risk-taking. Your values in a given situation will force your hand in a particular direction, creating defining moments in which you learn something about yourself and your tolerances.

Coaches are in a unique position to get to know leaders in their fuller authenticity and to support them in bringing that authenticity out in their leadership efforts. We're there to mediate the crude angst and raw desires into carefully considered options.

In Chapter One (Part 2), we discussed how we, as coaches, can connect with our own authentic selves as a precursor to assisting others. Determining your rightful path by considering your values, personality, interests, expertise, and experience enables you to develop a sensibility for what this undertaking is about. You've no doubt lived through taking a stand when something resonates as "right" for you but isn't popular. You've challenged yourself to find meaning in your efforts and to be clear about your capabilities and purpose. You have ascertained what makes you resilient and effective over the long haul and how to sustain your best self. And when things aren't going well, you have learned how to step back, gain some insight, and get back in the ring, stronger for having opened yourself to reflection, to your humanity, and to your truth.

> "I never cease to be amazed at the power of the coaching process to draw out the skills or talent that was previously hidden within an individual, and which invariable finds a way to solve a problem previously thought unsolvable."
> JOHN RUSSELL, Managing Director, Harley-Davidson Europe Ltd.

"I know the truth," Russian poet, Marina Tsvetaeva who lived through the Russian Revolution of 1917 and the Moscow famine that followed, says, in a poem of the same name. "I know the truth, give up all other truths," she asserts. Her confident declaration assures you she's come far to share the truth she knows. This is the journeying we all must do if we wish to understand our own authenticity, our instinctual truths.

Can People Be "Fixed"?

Some coaches are quick to take the position that they are not in the business of "fixing" others. I sometimes wonder if this is more a platitude than a statement made in true consciousness because often, after the statement is made and the coach has shared work examples, what I hear is how he or she has indeed *fixed* a lot of people. I think this issue is a challenge for our discipline, and one we need to clarify for ourselves.

Some of my clients' behavior patterns are explosive and obvious, while other behavior patterns show up in discreet ways that still appear to hamper the clients' abilities to develop or maintain meaningful relationships. I see it as my job to hold up the mirror and help them see what others might see, or to discuss these behaviors and why they think they are as they are. What I believe I do is collaborate with my clients to release the *fixes* from within. Together we seek relief for the challenges they face.

As coaches or HR leaders, we regularly hear of someone needing, say, "anger management" to deal with impatience and outbursts. Is this a fix? If it is meant to be, it's certainly not that easy. A person may be well aware of their anger, envy, need to be the expert, or some other attitude or behavioral issue. But these behaviors are often triggered by a complex. So, even if we, as coaches, provide some skills for managing the problem, it would be trite to think we can "fix" it. (I've made the mistake of trying – quite unconsciously, but trying all the same.)

The coach who works from an analytical frame knows that the tentacles from these problem behaviors reach into deep places within. While Fritz Perls, the father of Gestalt therapy, is known for saying, "awareness in and of itself is curative," the behavior is likely to rise up again when the client is least able to manage and recover – despite awareness. This is the work, however – hypothesizing first on the complex (a split-off personality that surfaces and resurfaces as problem or irritant), followed by assisting the client to verify or clarify the complex through effective inquiry. When the client can recognize and name the problem behavior when it presents itself, he or she can develop strategies for managing this splinter personality and enjoy greater success in his/her relationships. This process is different from actually getting rid of the complex, which is not the goal.

> "There is nothing with which every man is so afraid as getting to know how enormously much he is capable of doing and becoming."
>
> SØREN KIERKEGAARD

The "Quick Fix"

One contemporary thinker, Genpo Roshi, an American Buddhist, came up with the idea of "Big Mind." In an effort to work with the damaged self, wake up to his authentic, essential self (or "Self"), and help others, he has designed a teaching process. In one technique in his approach, he calls on his complexes and thanks them for their availability to him, relieves them of the need to be on guard, and assures them that he will let them know when they are needed. This dialoging with damaged (split off) aspects can enable more consciousness in the individual. It reminds us of Perls' empty chair (or two-chair) technique and Jung's active imagination.

Recently, Genpo's work has come under attack, partly due to his sexual indiscretions, but even more so as a result of a dumbing down of a process that takes time and support. He tries to make enlightenment a quick and easy prepackaged process when it is actually a slow progression toward insight and truth. One critic said,

> There's a very good reason why Zen teachers for thousands of years have cautioned their students to go very slowly and cautiously along the path. These sudden breakthroughs can seem very thrilling when they happen. People might even pay good money for them. But they can also mess your mind up in a very big way if you go into them unprepared. (Warner, 2011)

Warner goes on to say that having what I might refer to as a quick and dirty enlightenment experience, is like "giving random people massive doses of LSD and saying, 'Here, it's fun! Now you're going to see God and love everyone in the world'" (Ibid). We all want the quick fix, the amazing insight that opens up "truth" for us. But it doesn't work that way. Gaining insights, learning and transformation are ways of life.

Kegan's five orders of consciousness and Jung's individuation theory help us to see that these processes are life-long and most people never get "transform*ed*," or become "individuat*ed*." We are all on the path, although some may appear more on a path than others. And we all fall off of the path because that's just part of being on the path. This should not be equated with hopelessness. We do progress. Whyte reminds us (paraphrasing poet, Antonio Muchado), that anyone who moves on in the slightest manner, walks like Jesus on the water. It is hard work, but it is work that we are made for.

Reflective Listening

Reflective listening is one of the safe tools that the coach can teach clients who are working on their authenticity. This is a process that came out of Roger's Client-Centered Therapy and involves empathic listening and repeating back so that the individual who is speaking feels heard. It also gives clients the chance to hear another version of their thoughts and have a second chance to reflect on whether or not they have clearly communicated their true feelings and ideas.

The coach often guides the client by offering thoughts about what has been said, inviting reflection and clarification, and then encouraging actions in alignment with the client's purpose and values. In this process, the client stops, breathes, and reflects on meaning. The client might make attribution for his/her feelings or ideas. When we make attribution, we claim some understanding of a connection. For example, a client might say that she knows she gets her *temper* from her father, her *impatience* from her mother, or some other trait from some other childhood relationship or experience. This may sound like blaming, but when skillfully managed, it is an important unraveling of a thread to truth. It is typically easier for people to start with a connection to the external environment and then to be led inside to the inner landscape.

A person might say ("confess") for example, "When someone catches me off guard with a criticism, I'm quick to come back defensively, maybe because I grew up in a highly critical environment." Here, at least, this individual is owning his or her own defensiveness, and this small amount of awareness can be a helpful step toward altering the behavior.

Robert Johnson, noted it this way: "It is a general principle that anything rejected from the psyche becomes hostile. If one understands this, one is well on the way to knowing what to do about it" (Johnson, 1974). But, many of our leaders have not taken these first steps to reflect on why they are who they are, and why they behave as they do. And if you ask them these questions, the response typically comes from the ego.

James Hollis provides a useful metaphor, noting that "our egos are fragile wafers on a vast sea" (Hollis 2013). He goes on to explain, "the ego inflates its importance and proclaims, mostly to itself: *I know who I am; I am in charge here; I know what I know; and what I know is sufficient to make proper decisions for myself*" (Hollis 2013). Surely, we can all recognize this conversation. It is an automatic response that protects us from being in that uncomfortable place of *not* knowing. It is that ambiguity and uncertainty that rocks our world, making us feel out of control. How can authenticity live there? It is a flame that is snuffed out before it has a chance to shed light on anything real and of value to the Self.

The Saboteur

When focusing on authenticity, the coach can look for opportunities to alert the client to the saboteur archetype. We all have the energy of the saboteur within us, so why not normalize it? It is when we are caught off-guard and unable to be objective that we have a tendency to constellate the *saboteur*. How doubly frustrating it is when we find we just created our own demise. One young physician I worked with couldn't help but tell his managing physician that he didn't think he made a sound decision on an important issue. A month later, he found that his job responsibilities had changed and that his future opportunities looked dismal. It isn't that he shouldn't have voiced his concerns, but it would have been useful to stop and think about what he wanted to accomplish first. If this were easy, of course, we would all immediately employ some age-old technique like counting to ten first or writing a letter and throwing it away. But those techniques are not organic, and the emotions only build up as anger and frustration, which one day will find their release. That is not likely to be a happy day.

From a personal experience I can tell you the saboteur works like this:

One morning, I was preparing to leave for a full day with an important client organization. Due to the amount of snow that had fallen a few days before, I wanted to leave 10-15 minutes earlier than the already padded hour I usually gave myself. Somehow, those 15 minutes got away from me, and I actually left with just under the one hour I had made my norm. Within a mile of my home, I realized that I had left my phone at home with my schedule for the day and all of the phone numbers I needed. I decided I had no choice but to go on without the phone. I would simply experience the minor embarrassment of having to ask for help because of my personal failings (disorganized, lack of planning, forgetfulness...whatever this person might think of me). If I stayed on course, I would likely still make it just in time for that first meeting.

But just then, for some reason I'll never be able to understand, I took the wrong road. Deep in my other thoughts, I unconsciously took a road that I use less often and had to take the long way around to get back on route. By that time, I was furious with myself. This was unforgiveable. I went into a tirade and had a moment of near hysteria before I was able to come to terms with the fact that I would surely be 10-15 minutes late ... *and* didn't even have a phone to let them know.

So who is the saboteur? This is the archetypal energy that holds us back from reaching our goals by tripping us up and impeding our effectiveness. When we bring it into awareness, it serves as one of the important checks and balances in the human psyche. Some refer to it as "one of the four archetypes of survival,"[1] as it forces you to reconsider, to reflect. This might sound like madness or justification, but here are some of the useful questions that might make such a frustrating experience valuable:

---

1   Caroline Myss of Sacred Contracts, has popularized the ideas of archetypes, making them easier to understand.

» Are you sure this activity or effort is going to help you get what you really want?

» Should you reach the success you're hoping for what will that mean? Try thinking it through to the end.

» What challenges will that success bring?

» Is this the right time for X? Will there ever be a right time?

» Why and why not?

» How might you be afraid of success?

» Are you fed up with being perfect?

This last one was a trigger for me, forcing me to consider whether I had an unconscious aspect trying to get my ego's attention about keeping up a perfect rate of pleasing everyone else at the risk of never fully pleasing myself. How conscious was I of my efforts that morning when the saboteur was so apparent? What was at the root of my distraction?

Of course, self-sabotage is just one form of overcompensation that attempts to move us toward more conscious living in the second half of life. If we become more aware of these reflexive patterns, we can adjust, moderate, and live more effectively and authentically. My experience of the saboteur caused me to reflect later that day on how I could begin to lighten my load. At first, I was able to adjust through stealing time from my personal life, but only by promising myself that it was very short term. I knew myself well enough to know that it wouldn't work for the long haul because that kind of arrangement was not congruent with the life I want to live. So, with each successive week, I made adjustments to give myself the thinking and down time I needed.

This is not to say that I manage my life perfectly now, but I'm working at living more consciously in terms of the decisions I make. For example, if I say "yes" to X, what am I saying "no" to? Or I ask myself, "Does it fit with my life and my purpose right now to say 'yes' to X? How will it curb other activities? How will it make me less effective at other commitments?"

So, what complex may have been activated in my experience of the saboteur? Was it that old notion of perfection? Was it my father complex, which, for me, is so wrapped up in responsibility?

For one of my clients, the saboteur archetype came up in our first meeting in a self-description of "selfish." He gave me a few small examples of his selfishness and said, "Plus, my mother always told me I was selfish." I immediately thought of Carol Gilligan's three-step model of development that begins with "selfish." In her model, "selfish" is a level of immaturity like Maslow's first and second levels on his pyramid or Kegan's first two to three levels of consciousness using subject-object relations.

The second level of Gilligan's model is "care," and the third is "universal care." Each level is increasingly more inclusive. At the second level, we care for those like us – our families, our communities, people that fall into our race, creed, or national origin. At the third level, we are quite mature, caring for universal rights, freedom, and protection for all.

With a limiting belief like selfishness, we find the saboteur at work – that inner voice that is quick to challenge us, saying, "You'll never meet anyone to marry because you're too selfish" or "You'll never get that job; you don't know how to do that" or "You're not smart enough to get in that advanced degree program."

Likely, in childhood, my client *was* selfish. But more likely, his mother wasn't getting something from him that she needed, or she was jealous or angry to have someone dependent upon her. Perhaps, she couldn't be as attentive to her interests as she might have liked and, therefore, resented her child's freedom, thus instilling in him the belief that he is a selfish person.

The Imposter

An imposter masquerades as someone they are not. This archetype shows up when people are fraudulent and make up the information on their resumes or tell grandiose stories. They don't have the experiences, skills, schooling, degrees, or abilities that they claim to have. They parade around under false pretenses – the quintessential *trickster*. This could be a pathological liar or someone with a narcissistic disorder or some other mental illness. In the work of coaching, we are more likely to run into the leader with an imposter *syndrome* rather than disorder.

The imposter syndrome refers to people in organizations who are concerned that others might find out they aren't who they profess to be. Often, people suffering with this syndrome say things like, "When they figure out that I have no idea what I'm doing, they'll surely fire me." Despite this belief, these individuals are usually very capable and have proven themselves time and time again. Nevertheless, these leaders are likely to attribute their success to external factors – great teammates, the fact that everything worked in their favor (*this* time), or that the data just landed in their laps from some other resource. They downplay their own efforts and abilities, giving away their power. Their angst and despair can lead to getting work in late, appearing scattered or unprepared, or not taking the initiative to volunteer for projects.

And this brings us right back to the saboteur archetype because this kind of imposter syndrome is a form of self-sabotage. For example, some highly intuitive people feel like imposters because they cannot explain how they've performed well. In a sense, it came too naturally for their minds to comprehend it. Very concrete, rather than intuitive, individuals often focus on what they *don't* know rather than give themselves credit for what they *do* know.

Jung notes,

> ...when the thinking depends primarily not on objective data but on some second-hand idea, the very poverty of this thinking is compensated by an all the more impressive accumulation of facts congregating round a narrow and sterile point of view, with the result that many valuable and meaningful aspects are completely lost sight of. Many of the allegedly scientific outpourings of our own day owe their existence to this wrong orientation. (Jung, 1956)

One way to work with a client and their imposter syndrome is to have him/her consider the ideas of overwhelment and fear. These are at the root of most of our issues in life, if not all of them, warns Dr. Hollis. In this exercise I ask my client to turn to a clean journal page and put the idea at the top, in this case, "Imposter Syndrome." Then, I ask her to spend the first few minutes of our session defining or expressing what this idea means to her until she runs out of things to say. This is never an exercise in effective writing skills, penmanship, or grammar, of course; the individual should just write freely. Once these ideas are expressed, I then instruct the client to write how the idea of being overwhelmed might be impacting her feeling that she is an imposter. She then writes as much as possible without bringing the critical brain into the activity. Next, she considers "fear" and writes about how it might be feeding the imposter. Images and interesting insights often emerge, shedding some light on why the imposter archetype emerged at this time.

The Power of "No"

Another way that the coach can work with a client on authenticity and overwhelm is to be supportive of how and when to say, "No." (This can, of course, mean "perhaps just not right now" rather than "never.") Deciding when to say "no" is an opportunity for reflection and greater connection to what is important – i.e., values, purpose, and truth, to the individual.

David Whyte says,

> By saying no, when we can, to many of the activities and things that come our way, we are continually thrown back on ourselves. By learning who is at the center of this activity, we find inside ourselves someone who can say *yes* and at the same time be truly wholehearted. (Whyte, 1994)

Once we assist the client in connecting to the Self, he or she can say "yes" in much more truthful and aligned ways. Because executives are moving so quickly in the organizations of today, their yesses often become automatic, without boundaries or clarity. Whyte goes on to say,

Disapproval from the wrong quarter can be deadly for prospects and advancement. Our intuitive reaction may be *no*, but without a full-bodied reply to back it up, we dislike simply sounding negative. Yes or no, the voice throws us back on what we want for our life. It forces us to ask ourselves: Who is speaking? Who came to work today? Who is working for what? What do I really care about? (Ibid.)

The Coach's Own Authenticity

As coaches, we are there to be a mirror for our clients who may be showing too much reactivity or too much negativity. Listening, sharing our own reactions, summarizing, reconstructing what we heard, and asking good questions are all tools of our trade. When well-placed and thoughtfully chosen, these tools allow us to provide great value.

Reflecting on "leaders" from the past who have fallen provides a lot of lessons for us, as well as our clients. Who could forget some of these personalities: Chainsaw Al (Al Dunlap) noted for his slash-and-burn leadership style; Lee Iaccocca, said to be a flashy executive and one of the greatest salesmen in U.S. history; Jeffrey Skilling and his subversive activity as head of Enron; and Carly Fiorina of Hewlett Packard:

> Some say she was promoted to the top position due to her decisiveness and forceful leadership. Eventually this action orientation led to her downfall and she became portrayed as a leader too focused on action and not enough on evaluation. (Barton and Sutcliffe, 2010)

Andrea Jung, President and COO of Avon, was named to *Forbes* Most Powerful Women's list more than once – the Top 100 list in 2004 and the Top 25 list in 2009. Then, in 2012, she was named to Bloomberg *Business Week's* Worse 5 CEOs list (Wikipedia, 2013). How does this happen? It would require a lot of analysis, of course, and even then, it would be hard to decipher exactly how this occurred.

For the coach, in this situation and, indeed, in all coaching situations, humility remains a key to our effectiveness. If you were Andrea Jung's coach in 2004 or 2009, you would probably have become inflated with her success and identified with the reasons for it. In 2012, however, what would you have done? Changed your identity? Claimed that she stopped working with you? This is the tough part, especially if you tie your success to your client's success.

One coach I supervised related a client experience she found particularly upsetting:

> I was asked by senior management if a particular leader was a potential candidate for succession in a specific role. I was hesitant at first, as was the inquiring leader, but over time, the client made some significant changes. I felt it was only right to make it known that I was putting myself firmly in his camp. I did believe he made the necessary progress to enable his success, albeit differently from the current leader, but successful in his own authentic way. However, over the next two years, he made a couple of obvious mistakes in the broad realm of emotional intelligence, and I began to feel uncomfortable about his potential in the system-wide role he was now considered a successor for. It literally kept me up at night when he aborted his leadership in a high profile situation, and I decided I had to do something. He wasn't willing to meet and discuss it with me, so I was forced (in my mind) to let the senior leader know that I was pulling my support and why.

> I realized that my ego had led me into the problem. I liked being asked my opinion, and I liked being able to say that with the coaching I'd provided him, he showed improvement so that I believed in his ability. Then, I had to eat crow in the end, which I didn't like so much. I didn't like looking wishy-washy or reactive or, worse yet, resentful and potentially revengeful. I thought long and hard before I went back with my change in support, but I felt it was a matter of integrity. What if they put him in that role? How many people might suffer? How might the organization

suffer? How might *he* suffer? I wasn't saying he couldn't do it, but I was disappointed in several choices he made that indicated he might have difficulty in positions of greater responsibility. I left feeling I'd been forced to eat humble pie, and the whole thing still doesn't feel right with me. Where did I go wrong?

Her experience reminded me of how easy it is to take part of the credit or bask in the positive outcomes of our clients, but the truth is that change is very hard. No one knows how long these changes in behavior will stick with any individual. And when people do make changes for the good, for no matter how long, they are the ones who deserve all the credit. When there is a slip back into comfort zones or complexes, it is our job as coaches to once again provide a mirror and a sounding board – when they're ready – to enable insight and growth to the next level. What is subject at one level is object at the next. And so it goes. At each level, we become a little more authentic as we're able to hold on to that which is important to the Self.

In debriefing this issue with the coach, I asked her what bothered her most. She said she was struggling with the integrity of the situation. "How did it become a matter of integrity?" I asked. She felt caught between two senior leaders and wished she hadn't provided her opinion about her client in the first place. She realized that her ego had taken over, and she felt a need to look strong, as well as to please the corporate executive who asked for her opinion.

We talked about what she might have done instead. She decided that in future similar situations, she would stay in her role as a coach and state her commitment to each individual, offering two options: 1) to come together as a threesome for a discussion on succession, how the individual fits in, and what he/she would need to do to become a solid candidate; or 2) as a consultant, offer ways to determine strong candidates for succession plans, including questions to ask, assessments to use, and experiences to provide.

This was a great learning for this coach and good preparation for the future. She actually didn't do a bad job managing her integrity. She was careful not to throw her client under the bus, and she suggested it might be time to do a 360° in-person assessment with the client, naming specific corporate stakeholders that would be germane to the process. She had first offered the client some debriefing opportunities, but he didn't take her up on them. It seemed to her that he was in strong defense mode and unwilling to discuss his recent decisions. Several months later, she learned that he was continuing down a path of self-destruction. Was his saboteur at work? Why? She wanted to get together with him and provide more coaching to help him gain some insight and perspective once again, but she realized it was up to him to reach out. She struggled with being an outside observer.

In an effort to "help," she reemphasized his potential and her admiration for his past work. Having developed a relationship with him and having a stake in the situation, she said she hated not to be able to assist him further. She agreed to do some journaling on the insights and questions that persisted for her.

Is Humility a "Beautiful Thing"?

There is a host of available information about executives who lost sight of themselves (the Self) in their high profile positions. It is an interesting exercise to read how their futures looked early in their careers and see where they got off track … or perhaps never truly got on track. Maybe it was losing touch with the characteristic of humility that made many of the seemingly great leaders lose their way.

Hollis often reminds us that, "What we become will be our chief obstacle at any given time in our lives." When we reach a goal and become something new, there is a tendency to be enthralled with our achievement and to become inflated as a result. That inflation will get us in trouble, and it often takes a humiliation to ground us once again. Of course, I'm not suggesting that we don't take some delight in achieving and reaching new pinnacles, but if we let ego carry us away, we lose our balance and, ultimately, lose our ability to be effective.

Analyst, Adolf Guggenbuhl-Craig challenges our thinking with this assertion:

> A good way to relate to power is to try to get some and then use it ethically. Often we are envious of people who have power, but that envy is an indirect means of damaging the self. So I suggest that we all try to relate to power by not shying away from it. (Henderson and Henderson, 2006)

In an online LinkedIn group called "Jungian Analytical Psychology," I had a conversation with John Brusseau, the originator of a particular thread, in which I commented, "Humility is a beautiful thing."

He responded, "Janet, that's an interesting idea, isn't it – 'humility is a beautiful thing.' Why is that? Is it that humility is a grand revelation of our real context?"

After I stopped to think about it, I concluded that he was right, and I would add that it is a grand revelation of our real context *for "wholeness."* When we are faced with a humiliating experience, time seems to stop for an instant, and a flood of reality rushes in. When we gloat, on the other hand, we tend to leave pieces of reality out. There always seems to be a leveling agent, however, that eventually makes the fuller truth less grandiose than our gloating made it out to be. Some leaders are masters at keeping leveling agents at a distance – we call them the "Teflon Dons," as nothing seems to stick to them. Still, it's usually just a matter of time before the humiliation catches up with them and the truth demands to be seen.

Humor is from the same root as humiliation and humble. The Latin, *humilis* means low, and *humus* means earth or ground. In researching the etymology of humor, I was reminded of the old, physiological aspect and of the fact that good mental and physical health was seen as requiring a balance of the four basic humors: bile, black bile, phlegm, and blood. To be out of balance in the humors is to be of ill temper.

"Rod Blagojevich—governor of Illinois—Impeached in 2009 (charged on 16 criminal counts including racketeering conspiracy and wire fraud) at 52, saw himself a victim of a rush to judgment. Was seen as arrogant and untrustworthy by lawmakers." (Jan 30, 2009, Chicago Tribune)

RAY LONG, RICK PEARSON, Staff Reporters

As coaches, we can play a very useful role in modeling how we keep a sense of humor about ourselves and how we challenge an inflated client. One way of doing this is to work with a compensation like the idea of gratefulness. When *what I'm grateful for today* becomes part of the journaling process, we ground ourselves in appreciation and recognition of all that comes together to make for our successes and the goodness of life. When any of the vices (seven deadly sins) – lust, gluttony, greed, sloth, anger, envy, and pride – show up, we gain value from steeping ourselves in its opposite.

In her book, *Female Leadership,* Karin Jironet does a beautiful job of depicting these vices and virtues in accordance with Dante's *Divine Comedy.* She guides the leader toward balance in managing the difficult terrain of motivations, desires, depressions, and expectations.

The Necessity of Psychologizing

In the introduction, I said that we must become psychological…

Now what is the activity of psychologizing? How may it be more narrowly characterized? We have considered it necessary, hence legitimate; we have pointed out that it occurs unprompted; and we have concluded that it seems to be an attempt of the psyche to realize itself wherever it can. Thus it takes place in many ways and at many levels, from the simplest "figuring out," questioning curiosity, and paranoid afterthoughts about "What do they mean?" and "What else is going on here?" to reflection in tranquility, the most sophisticated scrutiny of signification, and scientific doubting. *Psychologizing goes on whenever reflection takes place in terms other than those presented.* It suspects an interior, not evident intention; it searches for a hidden clockwork, a ghost in the machine, an etymological root, something more than meets the eye; or it sees with another eye. It goes on whenever we move to a deeper level. (Hillman 1975)

We spoke about your authenticity as coach in Chapter One of this section and how insight into your personal myth can be very useful for building confidence and connection to the Self. Similarly, working with and coming back again and again to a *client's* myth – to refine and further define it – enables insight, growth, and resilience. What is the story the client is telling you today? How is it different from the story told when you first came together? How is it different after a "defining moment" (a tough situation/decision that defines what we're about, what we're made of, and what we value).

"But don't be satisfied with stories, how things have gone with others. Unfold your own myth, so everyone will understand the passage, we have opened you."

RUMI,
Unfold Your Own Myth

The authors of an HBR article, *Discovering Your Authentic Leadership*, say: "It is your personal narrative that matters, not the mere facts of your life. Your life narrative is like a permanent recording playing in your head. Over and over you play the events and personal interactions that are important to your life, attempting to make sense of them to find your rightful place in the world" (George et al. 2007).

As a coach working with the MBTI® insturment, I have enjoyed watching someone's eyes light up when reading about their Type, after which they usually announce, "That's me!" There is a joy in being recognized. Maybe it makes us feel acceptable to fit into one of the 16 categories. If they felt different, odd, or even lacking, they now realize that there are many others just like them. Of course, we get clearer as we work with type and individuation that no two people are alike, but they may have many similar patterns of behavior.

Some clients tell me that they are one way at home and another way at work. For some, this is true, and for others, it is just their perception of themselves. When they ask their spouses to read their Type summaries, the spouse says, "No, that's you."

Those who are truly different at home and at work have split off parts of themselves, and this is a cause of great discomfort. For example, someone might have spent a lot of time building a skill, interest, or expertise only to recognize a nagging in the body that says, "This is not your path." It can be very hard to face that reality.

When we help a client through these kinds of "humbling" experiences, we help them to develop resilience and evolve their coping skills. They develop the ability to bounce back from humiliations and other mini-deaths that are typical in organizational life, as well as other social experiences. Something must die off in order for something else to gain life. Equipping leaders with perspective is one of the gifts we bring to the relationship. We do this when we see someone through midlife challenges, empowering them to come out the other side stronger, more confident, and more purposeful.

While we are most fulfilled when we find our authentic self, it doesn't mean we're not adaptable or that we don't stretch beyond Type and natural gifts. For example, when a person thinks their Type is the best Type, you know there is still work to be done. So, how do you challenge clients to develop beyond Type? How can you assist them in becoming less identified with their Type?

This happens over time, certainly. First, the client gains the confidence of their Type – their strengths, capabilities, and contributions. Then, the client begins the work of seeing the value in other Types. You can guide the client to factor in values, needs, and interests in order to find his or her own unique sweet spot.

In one client organization, a leader took on the role of *Type czar*. He often explained things he had begun to recognize within Type. He was very smart, quite intuitive, and often quite right. Of course, he made some mistakes, but he really wanted to learn and use the information effectively. In the process, some of his colleagues made fun of him. If he hadn't taken it so seriously, though, he wouldn't have come so far in his understanding of others. He made the effort to see patterns of behavior in his coworkers, and he was quick to note where the same Types might look different because of values, needs, or experiences. Since he is one of several INTJ's on his executive team, he has become aware that there are possibilities for a lot of differences within a Type group.

I seem to work with a lot of INTJ's. (My analyst says we attract what we need.) Leaders, in fact, do dominate the four corners of the Type table: ISTJ, INTJ, ENTJ and ESTJ. INTJ's are nothing if not curious. They're seekers who want to know. "Knowing is everything" in their eyes. One INTJ executive kept a Curious George monkey in his office as a reminder to his team that they need to stay curious. Because of his own curiosity, he was very engaging to work with. He appeared compelled to understand human nature, and he developed his self-awareness.

One year, after some deliberation, I decided to gift him a copy of *King, Warrior, Magician, Lover*, a book by Robert Moore. I held my breath while I waited for him to read it and hoped my desire for him to have the patience to get through it with an open perspective wasn't asking too much. On the contrary, he caught me in the hall one day and said, "Not fair with that book; you know me too well." I imagine it was his curiosity, his ability to abstract, and his desire for knowledge that drew him into the reading. We had an interesting discussion, and I left him that day with the idea of working on evolving his "lover" – the Feeling side of himself.

Some months later, I saw his understanding depicted in a holiday letter that he sent to his staff in which he demonstrated humor, intelligence, and pragmatism. He provided statistics and an appreciation for a good year. He showed warmth for a colleague who was retiring, and he expressed hopes for the future. It conveyed Extraversion and Feeling, but he spent a lot of time Introverting and Thinking to create it. The capacity for integration was beautifully achieved. I read it several times in admiration for what he had accomplished.

I am often asked about the goal of the MBTI®. Should we all aim to be right down the middle of E and I, S and N, T and F, J and P? No, that is not the answer. The goal is for us to be the best we can be *within Type* – understanding our Facets and Out-of-Preference scores (Step II™); the nuances of how values, interests, and needs impact and shift a Type; and – in the end – to be less identified with *a* Type.

Once in a while, someone will challenge the theory by saying, "Well, aren't you just putting us in a box?" I reply, "Perhaps momentarily." But the thing I like about the Facets and noting where we are out of preference is that we are quickly taken *out* of the box. And certainly we need to look at Type dynamics, but that's for another day.

I don't know if there are two exact MBTI® Assessment profiles in existence, but even if there are, Type is only one aspect of who we are. When we turn to our stories, our experiences and our myth, we bust any box we may have found ourselves in for any amount of time.

We help our clients tremendously when we help them move away from "either/or" and "black/white" thinking. If we can increase the "both/and" possibilities and the "never before and not yet…but maybe someday" options, we do clients a great service. This tends to be the antithesis of how people were taught in school, but for leadership (and especially global leadership), this kind of thinking becomes essential. It opens up relationships and possibilities and makes for smarter outcomes.

There are people who don't like to psychologize, and it even annoys them to have to discuss Type. They don't have the appetite for such "time-consuming" activities, and they struggle with minimum amounts of personal exposure. If such a person has the good fortune to have coworkers who find value in the process and consider the psychology work interesting and useful, however, that individual might be more willing to participate. I'm glad to say that I've seen more than a couple of people shift from their original feelings of doubt or disinterest.

In one executive team I worked with, I was very aware of a leader with little patience for personal insights. His HR VP introduced us and encouraged him to bring me on to develop the executive team. Just before our second team meeting, the leader said to the HR leader that he hoped the work wouldn't entail a lot of "psychobabble." Of course, this provided me with valuable insight about him. He was obviously uncomfortable going inside. The very word he chose, "psychobabble," might suggest a dumbing down ("infantilizing") and an inability to even see it as professional, respectable work. This executive was bright and quick, and he enjoyed thinking up new ideas. But he was also intolerant, divergent, and quickly bored. With an undeveloped and immature personality he had a tendency to be unaware of moods or emotional swings. Spontaneous reactions got him into trouble with others as they didn't know where they stood.

This executive had a long-time corporate background, during which he learned the politically correct way to behave and how to endure some of the "painful" teamwork stuff. When we finished our third team meeting together, I asked him what processes he wanted to see more of and what he wanted less of. He was careful with his words and noted that he wasn't much for theory. "I like the practical," he said. He felt that the exercise using a real work experience "reenergized everyone" and was "time well-spent." (I didn't miss the implication that we wasted a lot of time before that exercise and that everyone was bored, in his opinion.) He would have "liked to spend more time on the practical."

While I tried to withhold any defensiveness I felt and just listen to his comments, I weighed and considered what he was really trying to say and what it meant for our work together. For example, I felt that I wanted to do more practical work, too, but the group had a substantial number of questions on Type theory that ate up a lot of time. Their questions either showed their interest in the theoretical aspects of the work or, perhaps, their desire to put off the practical. We also had a new member to integrate with the team, and it was important to work that individual into the mix so that he could establish rapport and relationship with everyone else. While the leader might not have regarded that activity as *practical*, I thought it was essential for the individual's comfort and connection to the team and for the team's willingness to go beyond courteous conversation with the new member.

The role of the coach is to create a safe place for the individual client or the group. But what happens when there are strong sentiments in the group that impact the coach at the individual level?

One such event occurred when I was working with a small group of senior executives at a leadership development program offered by a business school. Just as I had explained the deeper work we were going to do as a group following their individual 360° feedback, one of the participants mentioned that he thought that might be an interesting idea for other people, but he did not believe this was useful to him ... "I don't really do this". One of the other participants responded immediately and said: " I am glad you mention that because I don't really do that either". We were five minutes into an intensive nine-hour day and it was not going very well ....

I created an intervention which helped us to move on, we navigated the resistance and had a reasonably good day. However, that evening, after the program, I was struck by an unusual and totally irrational fear of flying. The fact that the skies over Europe were particularly turbulent that evening, did not help.

It was instantly clear to me that I had internalized the fear of the group. They may have been safe, but how about me? And was my intervention the best thing to do for the group or would it have been better to leave the fear in the group and support the group to work through their own resistance? How about the role the first participant played? Was this a one-off or part of his pattern to escape unpleasant situations? Could we have broken the pattern in different ways so that the participant experienced he had overcome something, rather than for me to create a safe place and for him to play within those boundaries?

These are the kind of questions coaches learn from in supervision sessions ...a coach-for-the-coach is essential to do solid inner work.

HANNEKE C. FRESE
Executive Coach,
Consultant (EMCCC-Insead)

Finally, when we asked for a real example, the group had a tough time coming up with anything. This does not mean that there weren't plenty of possibilities, but they were not yet ready to be so vulnerable as to venture into such discussions. It was interesting to me, too, that while the leader purportedly wanted everyone else to stay open and hear one another, he only seemed interested in hearing and listening to those who agreed with him. He judged quickly, set the team straight definitively, and closed down conversation regularly. He appeared to be totally unaware of this.

Upon further reflection, I realized that he would have benefited from more one-to-one work. He had a coach he was comfortable with (maybe too much so) because they had years of history together. The situation made me want to reconnect with her, but that was a touchy proposition. I had met her before, and she made it clear that she was in charge and I had a temporary assignment. My sense was that she would have preferred to be responsible for all aspects of the work. I even had some concern that she might be quick to tell the leader my "judgments" or assessments, thereby putting the work in jeopardy. I thought if I could work with some dyads and individuals on personal and professional development in between our full team sessions, we could have more of an impact on decisions with regard to how we spent time in the bigger sessions.

While I was working with his team members much of the time, I realized that I needed to stay in touch with that leader, provide my feedback and thoughts, and continue to listen and integrate his suggestions. Knowing that he would always be critical, as that was the unconscious behavior of his Typology, I took it in stride. After all, it was important for me to know what he didn't like.

What I learned about myself in this relationship was how hard it is for me to not feel appreciated. I didn't feel any reward for all of the time and effort I put into the planning and execution of my work there. It was just an expectation for me to regularly adjust my schedule to meet their ever-changing plans. Of course, I didn't have to do the work. I could have politely said, "I think I've done what I can for you, and I don't sense that I'm aligned with you at this point." But I did think I was having an impact on some members, and I thought I could have further impact. I get drawn into problem-solving, and I like to have a hand in facilitating breakthroughs. So, I wanted to keep pushing forward for that.

Considering that, I had to come to terms with the fact that work with this individual would be tiring, taking energy out of me, so I had to prepare myself for how I would reenergize and find benefit in the work. I was sure there would be learning in the experience for me, and, indeed, there was. I either scheduled a visit with a good friend in the evening after the work or made an appointment for a massage the next day. And I also journaled about my insights and aspirations. All of that certainly helped. I also had to remember to recognize the likeable things about the leader in question and realize that just because he didn't like self-development (especially on the level of psyche), it didn't make him a bad person.

> "We shall not cease from exploration; and the end of all our exploring will be to arrive where we started and know the place for the first time."
>
> T. S. ELIOT,
> *Little Gidding*

When you reflect on my story, how do you propose you will begin to work with clients to make more of the unconscious conscious? How will you help them stay more closely connected to their values? How will your coaching guide them to the adjustments that enable them to defend less and observe more? And, how will you learn from your client experiences?

Dreams

The coach working from an analytical frame has another very important, very powerful tool. Early on, we spoke of aspirations – what might be referred to as daydreams. But perhaps even more important is the night dream. Freud noted a century ago that *dreams are the royal road to the unconscious*, but we still have not yet given the unconscious or dreams the respect they are due. Why is it that we shun our night dreams and the unconscious material they bring up? Time spent reflecting on those odd movies that run in our sleep each night is lost on contemporary society.[2]

Our ancestors did pay close attention to their dreams. Now, centuries later, even though we are so much more highly evolved and living lives of great complexity, few of us take time to draw from this well within. For our own personal insights, it wouldn't hurt us to reflect on the patterns and symbols that our non-egoic minds surface each night. Even without understanding their full meaning, making them more conscious is known to have a positive impact on self-awareness.

> "We are a species, addicted to story. Even when the body goes to sleep, the mind stays up all night, telling itself stories."
>
> JONATHAN GOTTSCHALL,
> *The Storytelling Animal*

To work with a client and their dreams is similar to other coaching. We are not trying to *analyze* or *interpret* the dream. We are merely guiding a process of reflection around the dream material.

Active imagination is a term Jung used for the process of amplifying an idea – an image or a feeling. It works by taking any aspect of the dream and focusing on what comes to mind. For example, let's say an overstuffed file cabinet appears in your dream. You might first consider where you've seen such a file cabinet and what it reminds you of. Then, you can choose to have a dialogue with it. Yes, you would actually converse with the file cabinet in your mind: "So, FC, what is it that you want me to know?" It sounds strange until you've tried it and get a revelatory answer like, "If you put one more piece of information into me, I will explode." Perhaps you've been studying a great deal, doing a lot of research, reading, and cramming, and you need to step away for a bit of time.

> ...if we work with active imagination we soon confirm that we dialogue with genuine interior parts of our own selves. We confront

---

2   Our Dreaming Mind, Van de Castle, is a great place to start reviewing the epistemology of dreams and dreaming.

the powerful personalities who live inside us at the unconscious level and who are so often in conflict with our conscious ideas and behavior. We actually enter into the dynamics of the unconscious: We travel into a region where the conscious mind had not known how to go" (Johnson, *Inner Work*, 1986).

If you think you want to incorporate dream work into your practice, you must first do it yourself, of course, preferably with an analyst. You can use active imagination to understand dreams and inspirations, and, in time, you'll find it to be quite edifying. When reflecting on dreams, note metaphors and plays on words to help you get the message the unconscious Self is trying to relay to you. You might initially be very literal with the characters and experiences that show up in your dreams, but when you take the time to amplify aspects that have some energy for you or pay attention to the emotions in the dream (or even the emotions when you awoke), you can often gain much more insight.

Dreams bring the psyche back in balance just like sleep brings the body back in balance.

I have a consultant colleague who reported that she frequently awakened herself with laughter in her dreams. We tossed the idea around a bit. Then, I mentioned that dreams are often compensatory in nature – meaning that they compensate for something we are currently missing in our waking lives. She quickly said, "That's it! I have been much too serious lately. I need to laugh again." It was a simple idea, but without thinking about it, an important message would have gone unheard.

Often, the very nature of dreams leaves you with an object – something that you look at as separate from yourself (detached) because you have no idea what it could possibly be or mean. This is why the work is so powerful. Time after time, the answers sneak up on you before you've asked the question. The phrases below are taken from real dreams some of my executive clients have shared with me and they provided insights as soon as they were said out loud:

"I'm at a crossroads."

"I'm a turkey."

"I'm not having fun."

"I'm at a transition point."

"I didn't need to wait on her to take me to work – I had other choices." (Steinwedel, 2005)

Metaphor is not as foreign to us as we sometimes believe. It comes up in our work language all the time – "I'm going to do battle on this one;" "Let's tee it up with the boss;" "That was another grenade over the transom."

One such metaphor came up when I was working with a very accomplished woman who mentioned that she had "rose-colored glasses" that she chose to keep at all cost. (In some countries, the term "rose-colored glasses" is positive, noting the ability to be optimistic, and I think this is how she meant it. While that is part of the suggestion in America, it is most often said as a slight, suggesting a person is naïve or can't see what is "real.") There are several ways to work with such information, and while this was not a dream, one way to tease out more understanding would be to amplify rose-colored and glasses, i.e., What are glasses for? When do you use glasses? What other kinds of glasses do you wear? Can you envision yourself wearing glasses in any other color? When? What for? What is/are rose/s? How have roses shown up in your life?

While the client had claimed her own positive conviction about rose-colored glasses quite clearly, it was useful for her to gain some tolerance for the "other" point of view. When are rose-colored glasses not very useful? How can they get in the way?

> "The real voyage of discovery consists not in seeking new landscapes, but in having new eyes."
>
> MARCEL PROUST

This delightful NF (Intuitive-Feeling type) client was living happily with her God-given enthusiasm and idealism until she rubbed up against an NT (Intuitive-Thinking Type) and an ST (Sensing-Thinking Type) in her workplace one too many times. She needed to work well with these individuals, and they didn't share her effusive joy and rose-colored view of the world. Suddenly, she found herself stymied and said, "Being *me* has always worked well for me. I've never come across a situation that I couldn't work through."

In one meeting, she defiantly noted that she *loved* a particular colleague and never wished anything bad for him. But he wasn't feeling the love; he was feeling a false self – something unreal. He wasn't the least bit entertained or attracted by her expression. Whatever relationship they had been able to have had grown thin and thinner...until it erupted.

In a meeting where we began to work through issues between the two individuals, my client noted again that her rose-colored glasses had always worked. But she agreed that maybe the current situation required at least a clear-colored lens. Paying attention, allowing for insights, and making adjustments are all important to enabling the authentic self. When we can't find them elsewhere, our dreams often hold important clues.

Just as we tend to assume that the world is as we see it, we naïvely suppose that people are as we imagine them to be. In this latter case, unfortunately, there is no scientific test that would prove the discrepancy between perception and reality. Although the possibility of gross deception is infinitely greater here than in our perception of the physical world, we still go on naïvely projecting our own psychology into our fellow human beings. In this way everyone creates for himself a series of more or less imaginary relationships based essentially on projection....Unless we are possessed of an unusual degree of self-awareness we shall never see through our projections but must always succumb to them, because the mind in its natural state presupposes the existence of such projections. It is the natural and given thing for unconscious contents to be projected. (Jung, 1960)

Remember that the persona is "that general idea of ourselves which we have built up from experiencing our effect upon the world around us and its effect upon us" (Jung, 1971). The persona often gets in the way of our fulfillment and joy, steering us in odd directions that may be opportunistic or seem intriguing or exciting at the time. If a new job title or the new boss suits my persona's ambitions, I may be apt to take the job without thinking how it suits me – the *real* me.

Again, just as we work with clients on authenticity, we must work with ourselves as well. So, start to pay attention to the masks you wear at different times in your life with the various people with whom you spend your time. Or with the ones who show up in dreams – the wild other, the wise elder, the doctor, or the snake oil salesman. Which ones come to mind? How will you take notice of the masks when they come out? Why are these masks useful to you? While much coaching is focused on *what* and *how,* analytical coaching is focused on *why,* and *what do we want to do about it?* It is about making the unconscious behaviors and activities of our lives more conscious. It provides fulfillment for what is intrinsically motivating and meaningful.

The Shadow

When we were one or two years old we had what we might visualize as a 360 degree personality. Energy radiated out from all parts of our body and all parts of our psyche. A child running is a living globe of energy. We had a ball of energy, all right; but one day we noticed that our parents didn't like certain parts of that ball. They said things like: "Can't you be still?" Or "It isn't nice to try and kill your brother." Behind us we have an invisible bag, and the part of us our parents don't like, we, to keep our parents' love, put in the bag. By the time we go to school our bag is quite large. Then our teachers have their say; "Good children don't get angry over such little things." So we take our anger and put it in the bag. By the time my brother and I were twelve in Madison, Minnesota we were known as "the nice Bly boys." Our bags were already a mile long. (Bly, 1990)

The aspects of our personalities that go into our invisible bags create our shadow side. We don't even know it exists, but we rub up against it repeatedly in our day-to-day experiences, knowing it from our mood shifts and irritability. There is light shadow as well as dark shadow. Light shadow can be harder for us to see as we sometimes have difficulty identifying all that is wonderful about us. One women demonstrated this in noting that she wasn't at all creative but went on to tell me about birding with her niece and playing ninjas with her nephew.

Evidently we spend the first twenty or twenty-five years of life deciding what should be pushed down into the shadow self, and the next forty years trying to get in touch with that material again. (Ibid.)

"We live in the midst of currents and pressures that are immense in guiding our expectations toward certain norms that may be good for humankind in general but deadly for us as specific individuals."

DAVID WHYTE,
The Three Marriages

Coaches get to work in these most intimate affairs of the heart, teasing out with the leader what he/she really loves and where his/her passions lie. A client might tell you that their life is not their own. It is an interesting expression – one we typically dare not delve too far into. You might remember being eager to grow up and be an adult so that you could take control of your life and run it in a way you saw fit. But we all have that experience 10-20 years later of turning around and finding we've lost hold of our lives, and in fact, we often find our lives are running us. We've lost a conscious connection to what we've been doing.

Bringing new awareness to what you do and to the decisions you make is critical to the individuation journey and to a life well-lived. The coach must continuously work on this in order to keep the "instrument" (themselves) clean and effective. My dissertation work confirmed the importance of this idea of purification. It requires a lot of self-reflection, observation, insight, purging, and care. The dream story is very important to this Self-work and "other" support. Each insight brings transformation, a larger perspective, and a more versatile way of being. This is certainly more than transitioning; it's about growing up. It's something we are all called to do, and it enables us to deal with the harder things we are called to handle along the journey of life.

So, reflect on *your* own transformations. Then, help your clients consider their transformations. Making these growth patterns conscious is illuminating and transforming. Try using this exercise, adjusting the questions to suit your client's life journey:

> Just take a moment and think about all of the transitions you thought you were making that were really little transformations (and maybe some big ones). Who would you have been if you hadn't taken that job across the country; in another country; or on another continent? What have you become because of it? Who would you have been if you didn't get fired from that job and land a new and exciting opportunity, even if at first you thought it was humdrum, or even beneath you? What emerged in/from you because of it? What would have become of you if you stayed in that tired relationship…or if you hadn't brought some new intention to an old relationship? What changes occurred in you because of it? Now, what is becoming clear to you?

My girlfriend had a note pad with a quote at the top that read: "I'm becoming the man I always thought I'd marry." Many transformations enabled this sentiment. This is individuation – growing up, taking back the projection and owning it.

For your client's greater depth and insight, I encourage you to have the client sketch out their life's journey to-date in decades, noting the following (and adding in other thoughts that arise in the process):

> What do you remember most about the first 10 years of life? What did you like to do best of all? What was most oppressive?

What did you tell others you wanted to be when you grew up? Where did you get this notion? When, if ever did that change? What did you like to do most in your spare time? What is the first trip you remember taking? How would you individually characterize the people you grew up with? How do you remember feeling, in general, at this time (one feeling word that sums it up)?

How did the next 10 years change some of these memories and ideas? How did you change? What do you remember most? How did you best enjoy spending your time? What did you most like about school? Who was your best friend, and why? Who was your favorite teacher, and why? What else stands out about your teenage years and transitioning from high school to college? What feelings stand out overall?

What about that time period from 20-30? Did you fall in love – once or many times? Who most influenced you during this time? What was your first real job? How did you feel about this job, your coworkers, and your boss? What did you think about your position, your motives, and your being in the world? Did you have children, and how did that change your perspectives and your behaviors? What were your biggest disappointments? What were the best things that happened to you (or that you made happen) and why?

Keep going till you reach your current age. When you finish, consider what stands out for you as you review your comments and lists?

Make attribution where you can for what you see. (e.g., "I'm rather cautious for my otherwise outgoing personality, and I attribute that to my father who was very conservative and hyper-responsible." Or, the person feeling really courageous might say, "I attribute it to never feeling smart enough.")

If you could change any one thing you've noted, what would it be? Even if you can't change it physically, can you change it mentally in terms of how it takes up space in your psyche?

What were the most defining moments? What are some of the lessons for you?

What are you newly inspired to do? Are you any clearer about your aspirations, your inspirations, your authentic Self?

When you work with this exercise with your client, give them some time to complete it. Get them started by asking a couple of questions and having them jot down some notes along a continuum of their years on earth. But then, allow them perhaps two weeks to ponder the questions and make their notes. Suggest that they work on it a little bit at a time. Then, after creating some space for intimacy (i.e., reconnecting and reestablishing rapport), have them tell you what they came up with at a high level. As it feels appropriate to your work with this client, begin to drill down where you hear energy, confusion, angst, joy, vulnerability, etc. You may review bits of this as time goes on. Don't try to work it all in one meeting. Instead, it should be integrated into your work of assessment and coaching. It's the work of elucidation and education, of inspiration and aspiration, of experience and action, of transition and transformation.

Be prepared for what you might hear, too. For example, one man told me about his alcoholism; a woman expressed the deep sorrow of losing a mother at a very young age; another client mentioned early life abuse. You do not need to *deal* with these issues, but you need to hear the feelings behind them, acknowledge those feelings, and allow the client to go on looking for patterns and expressions of who they are. If you feel stuck in a difficult spot, you can encourage the individual to see a therapist (always have the name and contact information of someone available); connect to the appropriate support through the employee assistance program (EAP), which most companies subscribe to; or recommit to AA. In many instances, it's just a matter of allowing a person to purge – shed some tears and regain composure.

Don't shy away from this material, but don't try to fix it or analyze it. Ask how it has impacted the client's life. Ask if there are any actions he or she would like to take in relation to the issue. Encourage clients to journal about the important things that come up. Refer back to the MBTI or other assessment data to make connections and to educate on points of interest.

Some of your clients will be at that point in midlife where they are asking about and exploring the existential questions of life – who am I, and why am I here? Why me? Where is here, and how does it differ from there? What happens when I pass from this world?

Yet, your clients will no doubt stay tethered to the world, aware of a nagging question that supports why they've been attracted to vocational or avocational endeavors. For Jung, this is the natural work of the human psyche – to connect our understanding of Self and existence through our intellectual and emotional pursuits. Insights bring about self-awareness, which brings about the opportunity for integrity. The resonance or internal harmony, known as integrity, helps us to know we're on the right path.

Some people never come to an overt curiosity about the Self and never get around to self-development beyond skills development. Some are one-sided in their intellectual or physical pursuits. We can pretty much be assured that even if we're not working on it, it's working on us.

Masculine and Feminine Authenticity

Although there is enough to say on the subject to fill a whole separate book, I think it is important to at least make a connection to masculine and feminine authenticity. Everyone has both masculine and feminine energy. There are positive and negative characteristics to both. It is worth a coach's consideration for their own work, as well as their work with clients, to evaluate how these energies have shown up in their lives over the years. Has there been more masculine or more feminine energy? Do you see yourself or does your client see himself/herself as more one-sided or more variable? What has that looked like? How do you or how does your client express feminine energy/masculine energy? (Note that everyone will have a different experience, even if only slightly – pay attention to the words used.) One male client for example, told me a of a remarkably satisfying feeling he had when he really took the time to hear about some peronal challenges that a coworker was having. He saw this as his feminine side in play. There is a lot of material on this subject for a coach trained to work from an analytical frame.

Some men, for instance, are harder on other men or can't delegate to a woman unless she's an administrative assistant. Some women can't delegate to men, and they compete with every woman. Some clients compete with everyone, and some aren't aware of their competitive natures. These are important patterns for the coach to observe in order to assist the client in gaining awareness of the patterns in an honest way.

One day when I was working in an organizational job, full of optimism for bringing my creativity and ideas to a leadership program, my masculine ambition got a major closing out, and my feminine naïveté took a direct hit. I was helping the external consultant (who seemed to be threatened by my relationships) and my boss to set up the room for the 20 leaders who would join us for a full day session. "Ms. External" said in a rather coy voice, "So, I hear you had a *good* meeting with 'Mr. CEO' yesterday." (She was his coach.)

"Oh, good; I think it went well," I remarked cautiously.

"Oh, yeah, I don't know what you did (said with raised eyebrows), but boy, he really likes you."

The comment, "I don't know what you did" reverberated in my head. What was she insinuating?

I tried to downplay it and just responded, "Well, I think it was an interesting conversation. I enjoyed it."

I came to assume that Ms. External's comments in her coy and alluring voice were meant for my boss, who had a very good relationship with the CEO and likely wouldn't want someone below her (me) getting his attention – at least not in the way that seemed to be suggested. Ms. External obviously didn't like that I had the CEO's attention either, and she was trying to ensure that I never got to meet alone with him again. And I never did.[3]

Eric Hoffer, a philosopher awarded the Presidential Medal of Freedom said, "In times of change, learners inherit the Earth, while the learned find themselves beautifully equipped to deal with a world that no longer exists." When we do our work and guide our clients in finding their rightful place, we (and the client) can say, like the poet, "Ah dear friends but to the brim my heart was full, I made no vows but vows were then made for me, bond unknown to me was given, that I should be else sinning greatly, a dedicated spirit, and on I walk in blessedness which even yet remains." This is an expression of the integration of Self – the inspiration and the aspiration; the innate ability and the developed skills; the feminine and the masculine. This is William Wordsworth ("The Prelude") speaking with a strong sense of personal authority.

I'm rarely asked to coach executives at this place of fullness for several reasons: 1) they are quite well integrated and confidently on their path; 2) they don't need coaching because they've typically found the resources they need to keep a balanced life; 3) they have left organizational life because they were too encumbered to live their true authenticity there, or they went to jobs that were more humanitarian oriented. This last point is important. If we want balanced organizations that are attuned to people, relationships, collaboration, customers, global working, sustainability, and corporate responsibility, the organizations must find a way to keep these folks engaged because they are key to company success. And they have been key to my success when they show up in teams and groups and bring some synergy to efforts of insight, growth, and maturing.

---

3 We never met again formally and while I was working in the organization, but years later when I was queuing for a flight to London he was just in front of me. I tugged on his jacket and said hello. Only to be met with a curt reply and a look of sheer exhaustion. We only shared a few words. The joy I knew in him had been stripped. This was a dead man walking. Sad, but not to be pitied. He was on his path to individuation with its inflations and deflations.

On Jung

Jung worked at the Burgholzi, a mental hospital and psychiatric clinic from 1900 to 1909, continuing to provide lectures on relevant topics and theory for another five years. He knew the politics and frustration of having ideas that were not valued. He understood meeting the expectations of a boss. And he lived with the challenge of finding the time and support to do what he believed in. He worked with a variety of business people, housewives, and the mentally distressed. He had insight into many different career paths and organizations, cultures and world affairs. He was well-traveled and well-read.

His childhood experiences catapulted his curiosities into much larger spaces than he could have ever imagined when he had this encounter:

> Suddenly I had the overwhelming experience of having just emerged from a dense cloud. I knew all at once: Now I am myself! It was as if a wall of mist were at my back, and behind that wall there was not yet an 'I.' But at this moment I came upon myself. Previously I had existed too, but everything had merely happened to me. Now I happened to myself. Now I knew: I am myself now: now I exist.
>
> Jung, describing an experience at age 12. (Phipps, 2008)

Certainly, this is a human experience, but rarely is it so clearly distinguishable to us and at such a young age. Jung was very self-aware. He was very attentive to life occurrences. When he broke with Freud, he was bereft and went through a period of depression that enabled him to once again find himself. He was initially enamored with Freud because they had many interests and ideas in common. They built on each other's hypotheses and theoretical understandings. But he was pulled in a direction that did not altogether agree with Freud, so Jung needed to sever the tie.

> If you fulfill the pattern that is peculiar to yourself, you have loved yourself, you have accumulated, you have abundance; you bestow virtue then because you have lustre, you radiate; from your

abundance something overflows. But if you hate yourself, if you have not accepted your pattern, then there are hungry animals, prowling cats and other beasts in your constitution which get at your neighbors like flies in order to satisfy the appetites which you have failed to satisfy. C.G. Jung, *The Nietzsche Seminars, Part 6, Lecture 2*

How hard it is to love ourselves. I don't mean to be *satisfied* with who we are or how our lives are developing. I don't mean to be *narcissistic* and self-aggrandizing, but to truly love oneself seems to be most difficult. Many books, lectures and CD series provide guidance toward this end, but it is not a "one and done" activity. We must spend our lives pursuing this intangible.

Unfortunately, people are masters of deception, staving off vulnerability and shame. We justify our behaviors and follow those who will provide justification for us. We're often ignorant to those who call for us to be more of our true self. We find places to fit in and insert ourselves in places that meet with our deceptions. We project onto others what we need them to be in order to keep ourselves comfortable, or better yet, "right."

Marie Louise Von Franz, a close associate of Jung's, defined projection as "a transfer of inner elements to things external" (Von Franz, 1978). In this process we see in others what we don't like in ourselves, and we dislike them for it; or we fall headfirst into a friendship or love relationship because we love in this person what we can't acknowledge in ourselves. If only we could love ourselves, we would be spared a lot of pain and spare others a lot of pain.

This is not only a concern for the individual but for the collective. I recently came across this invitation for a conference entitled, *Civilization in Transition: Jungian Presence in Creative World Change*:

In our world divided, there is a fractious split between old religious concepts and newer, more individual spiritual understandings. Brash greed of giant corporations is juxtaposed against a movement toward greater respect for earth's people and resources. East and

West battle for dominance. Distrust of leaders causes confusion, rage. Vitriolic rhetoric spills over into violent action.

What major forms of individual and collective identity will solidify if human beings continue to split the world with rigid assignments of good and evil, insist on finding the enemy in otherness, and demand simple answers to complex problems?

If it is who we are, not what we say, that effects lasting change, we must consider deeply who we are, who we are becoming, and what our role is in the collective.

Dr. Jung's insistence on the need for introspective awareness does not mean living entirely in isolated contemplation. He himself wrote, lectured, composed long, thoughtful letters, and risked his reputation as a scholar and scientist in exploring unpopular topics and challenging collective assumptions. Our conference will explore what is asked of us as we move into an unprecedented era of rapid travel and instant communication of information and misinformation. Ahead are opportunities for greater accord and understanding, and also dark emotions of fear, despair, suspicion and discord.

> [Excerpt from an invitation to join a conference with the Foundation for International Training (email: Monday, 2/14/11 *Spring Journal*: announcing Nov/2011 conference: *Civilization in Transition: Jungian Presence in Creative World Change*).]

Jungian analyst, Michael Conforti, is Director of the Assisi Institute. The Institute focuses on development of the individual for collective benefit, attempting to help us understand archetypal patterns of behavior. He says,

> This commitment requires more of us than we may have ever realized, and may bring far greater meaning to our lives than we have ever imagined. Recognizing both the riches and abuses that may result from this work, we must adopt a new attitude. Like new parents, we need to embrace the precious opportunity offered

to us, knowing that like tending to a newborn, tremendous care, attention and love is required of us, not for the moment – but for a lifetime. (Conforti, 2010)

The coach's work in guiding others toward an authentic life, never mind staying on the path ourselves, is not an easy task. We're working against negative, ubiquitous patterns of a lifetime. We're working against defenses and socialization and aspirations. We're working against others in our discipline who try to dumb it down to five or ten easy steps. For example, many coaches and leadership development programs suggest paying attention to senior leaders who have been successful and watching what they do. Then, they suggest mirroring that behavior to exhibit leadership. This is not the way to develop strength and confidence in our leaders – never mind their followers. It certainly isn't the way to authenticity.

It isn't enough to say that leaders need to be accountable and results-focused. Leadership is only becoming more complex, spanning time zones, languages, and customs. The economy and the political challenges we face in our world today mean that we all have to be paying much greater attention. We need to be conscious to differences and needs and temptations. We need the diversity of thought and spirit and the ideas that come from that diversity.

Leadership requires more of us than we could ever imagine. It requires conscious decision-making and bringing all of ourselves to the table. We must leave less to chance and to unconscious behavior. We must be aware of our shadows, as well as how and what we deliver from our shadow sides.

The shadow is a moral problem that challenges the whole ego-personality, for no one can become conscious of the shadow without considerable moral effort. To become conscious of it involves recognizing the dark aspects of the personality as present and real. This act is the essential condition for any kind of self-knowledge, and it therefore, as a rule, meets with considerable resistance. Indeed self-knowledge as a psychotherapeutic measure frequently requires much painstaking work extending over a long period of time. (Jung 1969b)

Several years ago, a new book by Kwame Anthony Appiah, called, "The Honor Code," was being discussed on NPR/WHYY radio.[4] One comment caught my attention and caused me to reflect about it later. The person said that we do not have to earn dignity. Every man deserves dignity, but we do have to earn respect. I appreciated this nuance, if it can be called a nuance. And as I was reading in Jung's *Red Book* one day, I came upon a resonant golden nugget from an internal struggle he described:

Believe me: It is no teaching and no instruction that I give you. On what basis should I presume to teach you? I give you news of the way of this man, but not of your own way. My path is not your path, therefore I cannot teach you.... If you live according to an example, you thus live the life of that example, but who should live your own life if not yourself. So live yourselves! ...I will be no savior, no lawgiver, no master teacher unto you. You are no longer little children...Power stands against power, contempt against contempt, love against love. Give human dignity, and trust that life will find the better way. (See also the note[5] of the draft comments accompanying this passage.) (Shamdasani, 2009)

Some coaches may long for "guru" status. This might show an unconscious desire to be esteemed, or it might suggest that they are so much further along the line of personal development than anyone they might "teach." But the reality is that we are all learning all of our lives, and we have much we can learn from one another. The coaching relationship is a partnership of highly capable individuals and equally fallible individuals.

---

4   WHYY radio, late Sept early Oct 2010
5   Footnote #28 in The Red Book, p. 231, adds from the original draft, "One should not turn people into sheep, but sheep into people....Speak and write for those who want to listen and read. But do not run after men, so that you do not soil the dignity of humanity – it is a rare good. A sad demise in dignity is better than an undignified healing. Whoever wants to be a doctor of the soul sees people as being sick. He offends human dignity. It is presumptuous to say that man is sick. Whoever wants to be the soul's shepherd treats people like sheep. He violates human dignity. It is insolent to say that people are like sheep....Give him human dignity so he may find his ascendancy or downfall, his way."

Whether coach or client, we tend to come to our success based on certain strengths. As Lombardo and Eichinger warned us, our strengths become our weaknesses when they are over-used. We earn respect and easily lose it if we're not paying attention. It would seem that our comfort zones only lead us into stagnation and one-sidedness.

> One-sidedness, though it lends momentum, is a mark of barbarism. The reaction that is now beginning in the West against the intellect in favour [sic] of feeling, or in favour [sic] of intuition, seems to me a sign of cultural advance, a widening of consciousness beyond the narrow confines of a tyrannical intellect" (Jung, 1967)

Being aware and conscious, honest and honorable, fresh and yet consistent, is enough for anyone to think about, and that is just the tip of the iceberg. Feeling and Intuition, carefully attended, enable our conscious connection to many relational concerns at one time while keeping us grounded and enabling our authenticity.

> The special role of the dream in revealing the status of a dreamer's integrity is a hallmark of Jungian analysis. I have come to feel that monitoring integrity is one of the chief functions of the dream, and it ought to guide the way we look at dreams and the way we work with them. (Beebe, 1992)

The Warrior

There are two archetypes prevalent in today's organizations that work contrary to authenticity. First, contemporary leaders have been trained to be "warriors" (an archetype that often shows up in our dream landscapes) – travel, time, technology, "do more with less" and "make decisions with 70% or less of the information you need." Leaders meet all times of the day and night in order to collaborate on all continents. And they're expected to be prepared to navigate a calendar that has them double and triple booked at any given hour of the day.

It's no wonder that some leaders get caught up in inflations when riding a wave of delusion and hubris to what is called success. They are gods – Zeus, Apollo, Aphrodite, Artemis, Hermes, Demeter, and Diana – in the flesh. And having been named to all of the top-whatever lists, they can come crashing down – humbled and broken like the statues of Greek mythology I found strewn throughout southern Turkey. They can't sustain the unconscious rise to greatness. What will it take to say, "No, I am not invincible, and no, I can't keep up this pace and this delusion?" What leaders *will* sweat the small stuff so that it doesn't become big stuff?

The Addict

The second archetype of destruction is the "addict." And it is right under our noses – it is you and me. This is not necessarily a "fall down in the gutter drunk or cocaine addict." (I have to say that I was stunned by the movie, *The Wolf of Wall Street*. Are three hours of lewd, crude, and rude behavior what we call *entertainment?* Not only that, but it really happened.) Having worked in the money management field, I have witnessed some small level of this kind of living…or maybe dying.

There are many kinds of addicts who are addicted to one thing or many. We often think of sex, hard drugs, and alcohol when we think of addictions, but in the corporate world, we certainly know work addicts.

A couple of years ago, I became aware of another addiction that is being fed on every corner of the modern world – the addiction to caffeine. It isn't just those fabulous coffee-makers that brew your favorite blend to perfection in several nooks on all floors of the office. It isn't just the chocolate – from Hershey's to Godiva at every street vendor, pharmacy, and Hallmark store. Move over Energizer Bunny! There's a new gig in town. Coke wants to know, "Are you a go, go, go-getter?"

"What's really driving the boom in coaching, is this: as we move from 30 miles an hour to 70 to 120 to 180…as we go from driving straight down the road to making right turns and left turns to abandoning cars and getting motorcycles…the whole game changes, and a lot of people are trying to keep up, learn how not to fall."

JOHN KOTTER,
Professor of Leadership,
Harvard Business Reviews

Yes, that is the suggestion of a little extra "go" than the ordinary person has. And they propose that you be an "Over, Over-Achiever." Are you up for the challenge? How long can you "Stay Extraordinary?" That's *a lot* of energy. We used to talk about burnout, but now, we draw on one of our favorite caffeine addictions and go with the flow. "What do you drink on your way to the top?" asks Coke on yet another billboard.

On my drive on I-95 to visit a client organization, I saw a license plate that read, *RUlate2*. Not five minutes later, I saw another vanity plate that read, *IMbusy*. The year before the Coke ads, Quaker Oats had a billboard that read "Go, Humans, Go!" It's no wonder that there are so many accidents on our highways, and we can't stay off of our cell phones when driving. The messages around us only support continuous action.

You might wonder if you're not doing enough just paying attention to traffic and cruising at a 65-70 mph pace. Are you spinning needlessly out of control? Have you reached a level of velocity that has you *jonesing* for the next can of high octane fizz? Where are you going? What are you trying to achieve? Is there any purpose or focus to the whirling dervish activity you're joining on the highways and byways of your *organization*?

One client called me to say, "Thank you so much for reconnecting me with my values. It's clear that my organization does not value the work that I do. I gave my notice, and my husband and I are moving to Tuscany to ride bikes, cook healthy food, and do what matters to us." What happened to paying attention to employee engagement? She said the company would fill the job, and the new person would take over the Sisyphean task of proving his/her value to the organization. This woman was no slouch. She was bright and energetic. The company lost her.

Last week, we went to dinner with a couple, and the woman asked me if I knew an executive at a company I once worked for. Yes, I did. She said that the woman openly boasted that she worked out so hard that she shut down her menstrual cycle. The woman was also known to be quite a tyrant at work. As a Jungian analytical coach, I might wonder about the nature of the mother complex that drives this addiction to exercise. I would not look to treat this as an analyst would, but understanding the negative mother influence could help me in guiding the woman toward greater balance. It gives me a new set of questions that might bring some insights for this individual in recognizing her addiction and making sense of it.

> The goddess at the center of our wasteland culture is a Lady Macbeth. We don't call her that. We don't know she's there. Like her, we go about sleepwalking with our eyes open and our senses shut. Lady Macbeth personifies the extreme negative mother, one who would dash her baby's brains out and sacrifice love to power. (Woodman, 1982)

In AA, the shorthand is, "Are you a friend of Bill W?" It allows alcoholics to acknowledge one another or to subtly let others know why they're not drinking. You might not know that Jung had his hands in the tenets of AA due to his work with a chronic alcoholic, Roland H. Five months before his death, Jung replied to a letter of appreciation from Bill W (Wilson). In it, Jung expressed his understanding of the craving for alcohol and his experience in working with alcoholics.

Alcoholism is just one road to individuation. Any addiction, difficulty, or passion can get us on the path. What made you conscious of your individuation journey? Do you know what prompted you in that direction?

Many companies talk about passion with the expectation that their employees get some of it as if it were available in the local market. Having passion is quite wonderful and necessary in order to achieve our goals, and it's necessary for us as coaches to have passion in order to help our clients achieve their own passions. But developing passion requires an authentic connection to our values. And passion without focus is pointless. What is the most important thing you or your client is working on? You might ask: Are you clear about your priorities and purpose? Are you communicating these effectively to others so that they, too, can move about in a truly productive way? What is the message you want to communicate with your energy? How can you balance your passion with concern and meaningful direction?

"We all have the capacity to inspire and empower others. But we must first be willing to devote ourselves to our personal growth and development as leaders" (George et al. 2007). Jung understood that we need to live our lives – to be in the messiness of it and to accept the noise... sometimes even multiplying our problems before being able to make changes. He knew we often need to lose our soul in order to learn that we want to find it. He knew that if he were going to be of any use to others, he had to take the journey with all of its ups and downs. Playing it safe or just studying intellectually wouldn't do. He describes his path in *The Red Book*. My individuation journey has brought me here, to writing about it. And with all its challenges and difficulties, it's invigorating beyond belief. It pushes, prods and evolves authenticity – real, honest living of life and real, honest work with clients. I highly recommend it.

Your Notes

Jot down anything that has come to mind for you personally at this time:

_____

_____

_____

_____

_____

_____

_____

_____

_____

_____

_____

_____

_____

_____

_____

_____

_____

_____

_____

_____

What are you feeling right now? What surprises you from your notes? What insights did you get about yourself? Any other thoughts right now? Anything you want to do, communicate or absorb because of this reflection?

Additional Resources and Reading

Poems

- » *Sonnets to Orpheus, Part Two, XII,* by Rainer Maria Rilke
- » *The Man In The Glass,* by Dale Wimbrow

Read

- » *Andragogy in Action* by Malcolm Knowles
- » *Applied EI: The Importance of Attitudes in Developing Emotional Intelligence* by Tim Sparrow and Amanda Knight
- » *A Quick Guide to the 16 Personality Types in Organizations* by Linda Berens
- » *Barack, Lance, Oprah, and Rudy: Exploring Joseph Campbell's Hero's Journey in Contemporary American Society* by Joe Guse
- » *Caffeine Blues: Wake up to the Hidden Dangers of America's #1 Drug* by Stephen Cherniski
- » *Deep Change: Discovering the Leader Within* by Robert Quinn
- » *Discovering Your Authentic Self* by George, et. al., HBR
- » *Female Leadership: Management, Jungian Psychology, Spirituality and the Global Journey Through Purgatory* by Karin Jironet
- » *He,* and *She* by Robert Johnson
- » *Integrity in Depth* by John Beebe and David H. Rosen
- » *Iron John* by Robert Bly
- » *King, Warrior, Magician, Lover: Rediscovering the Archetypes of the Mature Masculine* by Robert Moore and Douglas Gillette
- » *The 13 Clan Mothers* by Jamie Sams
- » *The Three Marriages* by David Whyte
- » *What Did You Say: The Art of Giving and Receiving Feedback* by Seashore, Seashore and Weinberg

Songs

- » *Human Touch* by Bruce Springstein
- » *Where is the Love?* by The Black Eyed Peas

Movies

- » *The Citizen* (2012)
- » *Le Concert* (2009)
- » *The Illusionist* (2006)
- » *The Imposter* (2012)
- » *Mandela: Long Walk to Freedom* (2014)
- » *Whiplash* (2014)

TED Talks

- » *Measuring What Makes Life Worthwhile* Chip Conley

PART III

The Price of Admission:
One Gold Key

Leaders in Search of Insight

My fingers emit sparks of fire with expectation of
my future labours.

William Blake

Chapter 1

Going to the Depths: Finding Your Treasure Chest

The shadow is a tight passage, a narrow door,
whose painful constriction no one is spared who goes down
to the deep well. But one must learn to know
oneself in order to know who one is.

Jung (CW 9.1, p. 21)

[Guided Imagery]

There you stand now, conscious of the one large gold key in hand. It's heavy and reminds you of a fairytale. You suddenly realize that you've not only been carrying, but also discovering, the aspects to this key all along this journey. You now notice that it has four spaces like the large old keys from ancient days. And, of course, it would have four since four represents wholeness, and that is what we've been after.

Suddenly, you notice a large, heavy, wooden door ajar just in front of you. You don't quite remember at which point along the journey you slipped the key into the hole. But after some hesitation, the mustering of your courage, and the allowance of curiosity, you turned the key and began to tug open the door, which had been shut tight for some time. Had you been inside? You're not sure. But now feeling the confidence of knowing yourself to a greater degree and feeling more connected and equipped for the next part of the journey – you step toward the door with apparent ease. You're surprised that you feel lightness in your feet and legs because earlier, they felt like cement appendages.

You whisk the door open and step into a room that was formerly dark, but the light now streams in with all of the dust particles sailing on the currents you created. These particles are much like the energy you feel leaping from your formerly contained body. There is no tightness now, only openness and curiosity. You find yourself wondering, "What next?" like the young child you were in years gone by. You look around and begin to see parts of yourself forming out of the dust particles – all of those parts that you lost along the way. These characters are now welcoming you home and disappearing into your physical body. You've now integrated a lot of what you left behind over the years.

Like the Bly boys (see p. 205), you've been tossing parts of yourself in the sack behind you – aspects that were unwelcome in your world. But they have matured, too, and you have matured so that they no longer feel separate. You feel a bit like Scrooge after the last visit of the spirits when he danced around the room and dressed quickly to get out into the world and let people see that he wasn't such a tight, mean, old, miserly, miserable curmudgeon. He had found himself! And your experience is similar to what Jung described – "Suddenly, I feel I've emerged from a deep cloud and realize I am me, I am myself!" (Pause and breathe that in.)

The Individuation Journey Requires Making What is Unconscious Conscious

You've been involved in a psycho-social dance during these six chapters – going into psyche and coming back out to connect with the world of your work and your life. This is what the key allows you to do. You've been in the process of making the unconscious conscious, and you didn't even know it. This is the work of analytical coaching. You've met psyche, and you saw the aspects of psyche in the characters that formed in the semi-light room – the complexes, the archetypes (remember that archetypes form the core of our complexes). These archetypes include the masculine and feminine, warrior, charlatan, angel, martyr, mother, father, survivor, imposter, etc. And you've brought them out into the light, making subject object and subject again. And you are the wiser for it. One of the great books says, "Don't hide your light under a bushel basket." Or as you might understand much better at this point, the words of Marianne Williamson (expressing our light shadow) – "Our deepest fear is not that we are inadequate. Our deepest fear is that we are powerful beyond measure…. Your playing small does not serve the world."

You have met these other parts of yourself, and you have engaged with your psyche. Now, another turning of the key enables you to see that psyche is soul.

Yeats painted a very clear picture for us in his poem, "Sailing to Byzantium," when he wrote, "An aged man is but a paltry thing, a tattered coat upon a stick, unless Soul clap its hands and sing…." I hope that through this process, your soul has clapped its hands and gotten your attention, introducing your ego to the Self. This is the attention that draws you to live your unique and authentic life for your own sake, but also for the sake of all humanity. It doesn't serve any of us for you to play small in this world. Williamson goes on to say, **"It takes courage…to endure the sharp pains of self-discovery rather than choose to take the dull pain of unconsciousness that would last the rest of our lives."** I meet so many people with the dull ache of living small while making it look like they're living large. When you feel into that, it has to hurt.

The Real Dorothy

Dr. Cliff Smith, a brilliant psychologist and therapist in Delaware where I make my home, does a fabulous retelling of both *The Wizard of Oz* and *A*

Christmas Carol.[1] I have pondered his lessons and allowed them to evolve and make sense in me. I want to share some of the real Dorothy with you.

Dorothy's story is the quintessential individuation story. It is a psychospiritual adventure of growth toward completeness, toward wholeness, toward Self. This is a transformation story. The Dorothy you meet at the beginning, living in a very gray world and dreaming of rainbows and lemon drops, is not the Dorothy who emerges at the end – wiser for her explorations, interactions, and experiences.

> "The great myths no longer come to life in vast amphitheaters. Fairy tales are no longer recited at the hearth in flickering firelight. But inside darkened theaters and cinemas, the archetypal realities which inform our lives and prefigure our collective future are projected nightly."
>
> RICHARD E. MESSER, PhD,
> Professor of Contemporary
> Literature & Creative Writing,
> Bowling Green State University

Let's review the main characters, but not without the understanding that all of the characters are an aspect of the main character, they are just not yet related to in a conscious ego way. These are split-off personalities that need to be recognized and brought back to the central character. There's Toto of course, the wonderful companion to Dorothy, who is the instinctual aspect that is playful and carefree. In Greek, Toto means "total" or "entire." Toto embodies the *totality* of life. He is a part of the Self that is not under conscious control of the ego, and therefore, can be truly joyful and autonomous, living in the moment. Our instinctual Self pushes us toward our ever-growing, ever-expanding ego self...that which is being called into our individual journey towards our unique wholeness.

---

1   Cliff Smith, Ph.D., has had a longstanding career in psychotherapy in Delaware. He partnered in establishing the Tressler Centers of DE and served for 25 years as Director of Clinical Training & Director of Psycho-education. His approach is an integration of Existential/Gestalt therapy and the psychology of CG Jung. Cliff has researched the story of Dorothy (The Wonderful Wizard of Oz, by L. Frank Baum 1900) for years and mine is a summarizing and retelling of the amalgam of what he has researched.

But Toto with his carefree attitude toward life runs into a problem with Miss Gulch. I can hear the eerie music that plays behind the picture of Miss Gulch in the film as she rides her bicycle to the farm where Dorothy lives with her aunt and uncle. It's like a preemptive strike of the cyclone yet to come. She is furious with Dorothy because "that dog" was once again digging in her garden. (Don't we all get annoyed when those instinctual aspects come digging in our gardens, turning up all sorts of things?)

Miss Gulch is the opposing force. She represents our "evil sides" in the sense of self-limiting and self-defeating attitudes. This aspect kills off vitality, it is soul-murdering. She is the "negative mother." She has laws and rules and intends to hold everyone to them by appealing to the collective authority – the sheriff. Is there a Miss Gulch in your psyche? She stands in opposition of development, individuality, integrity, and authenticity. The positive aspect of this dynamic (Miss Gulch) is that it drives us to take the journey of development.

We must take notice of the landscape, as it, too, plays an important role in the psyche. It is set in gray, gray Kansas. It is described as *gray* many times in the opening scenes – bleak, arid, and dry. It depicts physical and emotional bleakness. In fact, the film starts out in shades of gray. These are all aspects of depression that often set in when our inner vitality and aliveness is threatened to be crushed into the confinement of the rigid expectation of convention. This depression is the driver for Dorothy to undertake the important journey of consciousness.

Auntie Em, although firm, plays the role of the positive mother complex, having taken Dorothy in and provided for her. Dorothy loves Auntie Em but finds her incessant need to do chores a little boring.

Dorothy goes off exploring one day, thinking she will run away and find that "somewhere over the rainbow" fairy land. It is an idealized place where there are no worries, no chores, no struggles, no dis-ease. But what she finds is an old man, a crystal ball, and a cyclone! This twisting, ravenous windstorm shows the powerful forces at work in the psyche. They are very upsetting to the waking ego, causing disruption and angst.

When we are moved by something from the unconscious realm, it often brings disequilibrium. This is an introduction to a *dark night of the soul* experience. Dorothy is about to be transported to Oz. Her first encounter is with munchkins, Glinda, the good witch of the North, and a great celebration. At this point the scenes go from gray to very colorful.

The munchkins are those awakened inner resources – liberated and alive! They show up to support Dorothy on her journey. These lively aspects of the Self appear in order to motivate, energize, and provide aid. They are the embodiment of unleashed creative powers that have been locked up inside.

The Wicked Witch of the West energy depicts the evil inner voices – those introjects that hold us back. We give our wicked witches too much power over us. When we determine to strategize with them, our frozen-in-fear ego gets unstuck. Through the wrestling and struggle, we realize that something must die off for us to move on. The Wicked Witch of the East holds the power in the mesmerizing ruby slippers – the Holy Grail – a golden key. They are given to Dorothy for her good deed, and they represent undeveloped and unutilized powers. The color of these shoes is the color of blood – the life-force, passion. Just what is needed on this journey to finding Self.

Glinda is Dorothy's inner wisdom guide. She is the inner ideal parent. She is the voice of possibility and insight, noting that "it is always good to start at the beginning." When we listen to our inner ideal parent, we are able to see our greatness, the possibilities for our future. And we are encouraged onward.

"Follow the yellow brick road." Yellow is the color of brightness and light – elucidation and illumination! The munchkins and Glinda launch Dorothy on her heroine's journey with great joy and delight. Along the way, Dorothy has many encounters. Her journey might be seen as a road of trials. Each leads her deeper and deeper into her Self to discover who she is and what she is meant to do. As coaches, we hear people's stories and the requisite comments all the time: "I don't know why I didn't figure it out earlier;" "I don't know why I spent so much time on X when I wanted to be doing Y;" "I don't know why I didn't have the courage to make the next move...." But, like Dorothy, we all need those forces and guides and helpers to appear in due time to teach us something, to make us stronger, and to prepare us for what we are to become.

Dorothy's goal or key aspiration is to get to the Emerald City and meet the Wizard because he is "the most powerful of all." She meets three masculine companions along the way, and with Dorothy, they make four. As I have said, four is the number of wholeness. She connects with these split-off aspects – these inner resources she didn't realize she had, in order to make herself whole through integration.

Toward the end of the story, Dorothy is given the task to get the witch's broom. She needs to "de-potentiate" the negative mother complex, to take her power back, and to conquer the inner demons that haunt her (and that haunt us all). She bursts this inflation of the powerful Wicked Witch when she dissolves her by dousing her with water. Of course, when the foursome returns to the Emerald City to debrief their escapades to the Wizard, Dorothy learns that he is just a man, and "not a bad man, just a bad wizard." And she bursts yet another inflation. She had been projecting her own power onto some idealized vision of

> "Our physician is within us and everything we need is within our nature."
>
> Paracelsus, Opus Paramirum 6.13 (as quoted in *Care of the Soul in Medicine*)

greatness that deflated when she saw clearly behind the curtain. From our beginnings of being parented, we believe we need someone else to tell us what to do. However, the reality is that the answers are within us. This is not to be confused with the ego-bound self – we must understand the "within us" to be that inner aspect we come to know when our small ego self is opened to being informed and led by the Self.

Dorothy learns that the man acting as wizard also wants to return to Kansas, and they plan their departure. They are to take off in a hot air balloon, but hasn't there been enough hot air between them and not enough of her *own* inner voice? Dorothy starts out in the balloon's basket with Toto at her side when he suddenly jumps out and scampers off. Toto, the instinctual aspect, knows that the balloon is full of hot air and that Dorothy must take the journey under her own power. She has to awaken her wisdom source because the Wizard (representing the wisdom source) went unconscious when the balloon took off suddenly. Dorothy leaps out to reconnect with her instinctual self (the archetype of the Self/ wholeness). She soon finds that she has had the power all the time (the red shoes), but she had to learn about that power for herself.

No one can really tell us what we have to do to find our way back home, but finding a good guide, companion, or helper along the way can move us into action. "Just click your heals three times," Glinda tells Dorothy. "Glinda" is the strong, confident, optimistic inner aspect that Dorothy needed to integrate and actualize.

Certainly, I have skipped many more metaphors and insights, but you get the idea. And, like most people, I'll bet that you are surprised by this version of the story. When Dorothy wakes from her "dream" brought on by a knock on the head (she went "unconscious"), she has a new perspective on her life. She sees herself and her companions differently, and she has renewed energy and vigor that are truly her own. They come from within and she has claimed them.

Jolande Jacobi, a Jungian analyst, has a paragraph in her book, *The Way of Individuation*, which I have found to be a simple, yet poignant, description of both the human condition and what is involved in consciously trying to live this process of meaningful and personal development. She writes:

Like a seed growing into a tree, life unfolds stage by stage. Triumphant ascent, collapse, crises, failures, and new beginnings strew the way. It is the path trodden by the great majority of mankind, as a rule unreflectingly, unconsciously, unsuspectingly, following its labyrinthine windings from birth to death in hope and longing. It is hedged about with struggle and suffering, joy and sorrow, guilt and error, and nowhere is there security from catastrophe. For as soon as a man tries to escape every risk and prefers to experience life only in his head, in the form of ideas and fantasies, as soon as he surrenders to opinions of 'how it ought to be' and, in order not to make a false step, imitates others whenever possible, he forfeits the chance of his own independent development. Only if he treads the path bravely and flings himself into life, fearing no struggle and no exertion and fighting shy of no experience, will he mature his personality more fully than the man who is ever trying to keep to the safe side of the road. (Jacobi, 1965)

Some of us are naturally more fearless and curious than others, while some of us are inclined to caution and tradition. Some have a proclivity for learning and others for knowing. No matter our personalities and tendencies, we must push forth, for as Socrates declared, "the unexamined life is not worth living." These words have been echoed by millions since. The pace at which we move in today's society threatens to drown out such wisdom, and we have to be steadfast and vigilant to hear the calls and follow the ambiguous path forward. Our inclination is to want things to go back to "normal." But normal is typically an unconscious state. It means numbing out, dumbing down, and "pie in the sky" living. So, with golden key in hand, we find a way to persist and march forth.

[Guided Imagery]

Back in the room you entered at the beginning of the chapter, settling down after the initial buoyancy and burst of joy from reunion and integration, you see something in the shadow (of course, it would be in the shadow) of the far corner. You walk closer and find a small opening and a set of steps descending into a very small room. You hesitate a moment and then decide to make the descent. Lucky you do, because there at the bottom of the steps in another shadowy corner off to the left is a treasure chest. There is nothing else in the closet-sized space. The chest glistens even though it is quite dark. It is encased with gold and adorned in gemstones. You step toward it with your key and quickly realize that it is not going to be that easy to open because it has a combination lock! You search your mind for numbers that might solve the challenge staring you in the face.

After a sense of disbelief and a feeling of numbness, you begin to laugh convulsively. How silly to think the process is over! You know you must continue the journey, for there is much more to be discovered. With some good fortune, you see a piece of paper sticking out from one side of the box and carefully tug at it, shimmying left and right, until it slides out fully intact. Ah, what a relief! You open the page, which is folded in three, and you're reminded that this work of Self-development is an unfolding and dynamic process. You lose your attention to this folding and unfolding of the page, seeing before you the road you have just traveled. And after some time, you are brought back to the present moment and decide to read the letter. It is the deed to your house. (In dreams, the house typically represents the psyche.) You seem to be in rightful ownership of your psychic space. You set the paper aside, grateful for all that has occurred to deliver you here to this place with your new perspective. Again, you turn to the treasure chest that you know is an aspect of yourself, and you begin to work on the combination lock, turning it ever so slowly and listening ever so carefully with full attention for a click or a sticking point.

"But the adventure is successful only when the descent into the unconscious changes from passive exposure into active participation. By taking up an attitude towards it, consciousness delimits itself from the unconscious, broadens its scope so that the personality can unfold."

ANIELE JAFFÉ,
The Myth of Meaning.
(Jaffé, 1971)

So, there is more to come, more to envisage, more to experience, and more purifying of the instrument that is *you*. Just like Dorothy when she arrived at the Emerald City to meet The Wizard of Oz, it still isn't over. She was tasked with killing the Wicked Witch of the West. There is a witch inside us all. Along the journey, our eyes are opened. We see with new perspective, and we redeem some of our true power.

Befriending our complexes instead of shunning them and keeping them locked away is germane to the analytical approach. The scarecrow thinks he has no brain, but he makes many decisions to effectively get the odd little group to the Emerald City. We do have all that we need inside of us; it just needs to ripen and be called forth. You have worked hard through these chapters to find more of your true Self, but there is much more treasure within. It might require that you go to such territory as "the land of the Winkies" and use the various powers heretofore locked up tight inside of you to fight off wolves, crows, bees, monkeys, and whatever else comes your way. You can melt the bad witches within with good intention or you can manage them in ways that are of much greater use to you.

"It is not the critic who counts; not the man who points out how the strong man stumbles...The credit belongs to the man in the arena, whose face is marred by dust and sweat and blood; who strives valiantly; who at his worst, if he fails, at least fails while daring greatly, so that his place shall never be with those cold and timid souls who neither know victory nor defeat."

THEODORE ROOSEVELT,
from a speech made at the Sorbonne (Paris, 1910)

When you commit to analytical coaching or just to your own deep development, you take time out from your busy life for reflection, for paying attention to the metaphors and symbols around you, for giving the Self a new level of respect, and for building your emotional strength and effectiveness. Remembering the past, seeing the present for what it truly is, and considering a future that includes a more authentic you are all germane to the process.

With greater appreciation for archetypes like that of the charlatan, you are ready to move on with greater intention and integrity. I'm reminded of a conversation I recently had about Dr. Phil with a woman who thought he was providing a great service. I was surprised to hear this, and she was equally surprised by my surprise. She thought I would have high regard for his efforts. I have high regard for his humanity and his place on the path, but I can't help but think that he might be stuck in the charlatan archetype – an opportunist taking advantage of the naïveté of his guests for the sake of entertainment and ratings. This, of course, does not mean that he doesn't also want to do good for people.

I am also aware that to know the charlatan in others, you must know something of that energy personally, and I am once again returned to a self-reflection and personal growth opportunity. This is the process of circumambulation – the spiraling around and around until we see more clearly.

> ""I'm halfway to heaven and a mile out of hell, but I feel like I'm coming home...These are better days...."
>
> BRUCE SPRINGSTEIN

Thousands of years ago, the Delphi Oracle proclaimed: "Know thyself." Since then, the same sentiment has been echoed by countless psychologists and development specialists. Jung's work is centered on making the unconscious conscious. Our key insights come from recognizing this aspect of living and growing.

Again, our quality of coaching is so much more about what we do for ourselves than what we do for our clients. You cannot have more to give outwardly than you have earned on the inward journey. As you work on the ego-Self axis and develop your consciousness, you enable continuously greater effectiveness with others. When your lens opens a little further, you have insight into more of life and living, and you are, therefore, more understanding of the world views of others.

The Coach's Role

Deepening rapport, seeking patterns, and gaining insight is an hermeneutical approach to our work as analytical coaches. We do it for ourselves, and we guide others in the process. We do our work of understanding aspirations and inspirations on a surface level, and we see some patterns and feedback that information to the client.

The client says, for example, "Ah, yes, that's true," and you learn something about him/her that deepens the rapport between you. Then, you go back to listening and observing, waiting for the next potential insight. Or the client says, "No, I don't think so," which takes you in another direction. You might think that the client isn't ready for this information, so you hold onto it (put it in the container), waiting to see if there is another opportunity to call it forth. Sometimes, the client will say at some later point, "Remember when you said 'X,' I didn't see what you were saying. Now, I get it, and I think you were right."

In some cases, of course, you may be wrong. "It" may not exist in the client; "it" may exist in you instead. This is a good time to consider your projections and call them back, if necessary. In the process of assisting others in their learning processes, you always learn about yourself – if you're open and attentive, that is. As Whyte relays in his poem, *Working Together,* "We shape ourselves to fit this world and by the world are shaped again."

The Jungian analytical approach takes you to the enduring core of the issues at hand – to the very essence. You cannot help but to mature to some degree in this process and become more Self-aware – the bud of change. This is why it's important that the clients you work with have adequate ego functioning for the questions you pursue, and this is why it's necessary to be attentive in the process. Sometimes, it means your work is just to strengthen the ego – taking a person from fragile to agile. Your efforts to do no harm are, of course, first and foremost.

> "Most of us would further agree that it matters that we bring no harm, or at least less harm, to others. This noble desire asks that we become progressively aware of, explore, take responsibility for our personal shadow. The shadow includes those parts of ourselves that make us uncomfortable with ourselves, whether it be our capacity for evil; our insurgent, narcissistic agendas; or our most spontaneous, healing, instinctually grounded selves." (Hollis, 2009)

Being a coach is powerful. As with all of the "helping professions," it is easy to get caught up in one side of the "healer/patient" archetype. If we can span this polarity, we can realize the help a "patient" can provide us in our own healing. If we can't face our own ills and demons, we err on the side of thinking we're omnipotent, with total lack of knowledge of our own complexes. In this state, we often create a dependency model for clients who come to see us as gods and goddesses. Sometimes, our pat phrase in coaching is that "my client has all of the answers within, and it's just my job to ask the right questions to unleash his/her own knowledge." This sounds very good, but our walk has to match our talk. So, we have to be willing to ask ourselves some tough questions as well.

> "The solution to this split archetype is to face yourself, acknowledge your arrogance, and make a genuine effort to do something about it. Notice your defensiveness when people give you hints about it. Face your anxieties, your attitude toward your work, and your fears."
>
> THOMAS MOORE on the Patient-Healer archetype. (Moore, 2010)

It's easy to develop an arrogance or Self-righteous quality in the work of helping others. I read an article depicting this attitude in the 1990s when coaching was still very new. The coach who was interviewed was pictured on her boat, boasting of an extravagant lifestyle and the ability to coach her clients from anywhere.

Then, there are the "guru" coaches who become the "teacher" of their clients, and the "best friend" coaches, who become enmeshed with their clients, building up their clients' egos and speaking badly about the inferior "others" in the client's life. It's easy to fall into any or all of these patterns. If we don't look for patterns, we won't see them because it's our nature to rationalize why we do what we do and forget that we, too, have blind spots.

The Coach's Toolkit

There are many tools in the toolkit for a coach, and each has to have a purpose. But none can be overused. One tool we are very attached to today is the phone. Some coaches choose to have phone or Skype sessions in order to reach clients more conveniently. I am not a strong proponent of phone (or Facetime or Skype) coaching, although I see how it could make life easier to manage. I believe this is a good option for in-between meetings or meetings that need to be drawn together quickly. I would have to respect the 80-20 rule here and say that 80% of a coaching engagement should take place in person. If 80% or more of your coaching engagement is over the phone, I suspect that you are getting much lower results than would be possible in person.

So much of our ability to read another person is what we see and feel, not what they say (remember the communication model), and I question the real ROI if you're spending 50-80% of your time over the phone. Those small nuances of subtle body language such as the tapping or kicking of feet under a desk, a slight grimace, a recurring itch, are all easily picked up in person but get lost through a monitor. Regular scanning of these movements in one's self and the other is very important for determining the next questions. I suppose at times that the phone might make for better listening because it eliminates distractions, but we should be seeking the greatest amount of clarity and consciousness, not comfort and convenience.

Careful listening and a high level of consciousness are what help coaches discern the right next step. You may feel that you have an amazing insight, and the ego wants to burst forth with it. Yet, you have to hold off until the right moment. This takes self-control and grounding. There have been times when I wanted to point out self-deception to a client right away, knowing how important it would be to the quality of his/her life, but I've had to restrain myself until the person's confidence and self-worth were built, as well as our relationship with one another. Sometimes, the amazing insight and the need to revisit self-deception are actually for me and not for the client, and I must be able to recognize that.

Often, clients will note that our meetings, individually or in small groups, were "therapeutic." I believe that is solely a result of "being heard." Real listening to another – what Jung referred to as the "attentive entering into the personality of the patient," (Jaffé 1989) has an amazing and lasting effect. It enables significant rapport-building. To really *hear* another person is quite an amazing thing, and all sorts of insights arise as a result.

Imagine someone listening, not only to your words, but also to what's behind them – who even listens to the spaces between the words. Someone in tune with the nuances of your voice, your emotion, your energy – who is intent on receiving everything you communicate. Someone who listens to the very best in you, even when you can't hear it in yourself. (Whitworth, Kimsey-House, and Sandahl, 1998)

At various points, we have to ask the tough questions that can move a person, that can shift the energy, and that can provide the drive that enables change to happen. I once heard a speaker say, "It's not about what it's about," meaning that what is presented as the issue is not the issue. The onion needs to be peeled back a few layers to reveal its true nature. Of course, it's important that we know how far to go. Sometimes, we must refer someone to a more qualified expert like an analyst or therapist.

As we move someone deeper, it's like a dance. We suggest an idea, we present a possibility, and we must be ready to take it away if the client is not ready. Perhaps we present it at a later time; perhaps not. If we become so identified with our own ideas that we can't let go and take them back when appropriate, we risk the relationship and the stability of the client, as well as our own.

The Patriarchy vs. Conscious Mature Leadership

In this analytical approach, I'm looking for sustainable change, not short-term behavioral change that enables me to check off the ROI box. Short-term ROI soon becomes a lie. In fact, it can make a situation worse. Those who beat the drum of ROI without insight are part of the old, blind patriarchy.

The patriarchy is one-sided, often narcissistic, and blind to self-awareness and personal development for self and others. It lacks understanding of diversity and inclusion. Nevertheless, it is the patriarchy that laid the foundations of our organizations, their systems, and hierarchical structures. These systems include how we hire, how we communicate, and how we measure work. So, is it any wonder that a 6-9-month coaching engagement might not bring about what management was hoping for? The culture (or some sub-culture) might have too great a stronghold for change to thrive, or one system might support it and another not. A new president or division head may come in and want more control. Managing performance and gaining efficiencies can trump development and employee engagement. The patriarchy is short-sighted, outdated, and yet, ubiquitous.

When I first came to coaching, I was not aware of my own wedded bliss to the patriarchy. I didn't see how many of my efforts fed the old rituals and perspectives that kept people in line and relatively powerless – myself included. I was part of the Conference Board's first Council on Executive Coaching, representing AstraZeneca. I worked with smart, creative and enthusiastic individuals like Colleen Gentry of Wachovia Bank, Monica Molina Austin of *The Boston Globe*, Bill Hodgetts from Fidelity Investments, Nina Mikelsen of the World Bank, and many others under the organized leadership of council representative, Gisele Garcia (The Glenbrook Group, Inc). We all wanted to positively impact this fledgling discipline. We learned a lot from one another and from challenging the questions and perspectives that surfaced. We felt compelled to draw up the rules and expectations of how coaching should get managed in the corporate world. For example, one of the ideas was that coaches should not work with employees of a leader they had coached or were in the midst of coaching. It was about managing confidentialities. I, for one, did not take into consideration at that time that there could be positive gains and increased possibilities from such alliances. The rule seems to suggest that coaches cannot be trusted to manage such an alliance and they need some clear stipulation to keep them honest.

As I continued my PhD work and systems thinking in particular, I started to question this ethical stance. It may be useful for the person who doesn't develop an awareness and understanding of triangulation and transference. However, the coach who is working from a systems frame and values the work of family systems is likely to add value to a team when coaching individuals, as well as the team and its leader. When you're doing your own analytical work or other reflective work, you have the capacity to see where mistakes can happen. The first rule of thumb, of course, is to do good contracting – to be clear, to communicate, and to regularly discuss and question what is confidential, as well as potential issues and concerns.

Part of the *Aspiration* phase is to discuss together what you hope for and how you expect the work to move forward and honor the individuals. Then, to commit to continuous contracting and clarification is critical to success.

> When faced with a failed conversation, most of us are quick to blame others. If others would only change, then we'd all live happily ever after. If others weren't so screwed up, we wouldn't have to resort to silly games....Although it's true that there are times when we are merely bystanders in life's never-ending stream of head-on collisions, rarely are we completely innocent. More often than not we do something to contribute to the problems we're experiencing. ....[T]he only person we can continually inspire, prod, and shape – with any degree of success – is the person in the mirror. (Patterson et al., 2002)

Some organizations are more curious, they are filled with people eager to learn. Others are more focused on maintaining the status quo and defending the patriarchy and turf. They think they know all that they need to know.

Over the years, I have found it very useful to be curious. Coworkers and clients who have incorporated a curiosity into their working style and in relating to others seem to do well. David Whyte proclaims that the part of us that does the most work is the curious part of us. He says that to keep our work alive we must keep curiosity alive. We must be curious about ourself, other people and the world. He posits that once we lose that curiosity, we lose the conversation, and we lose our edge. He suggests that happiness lies in our ability to be innocent again. This resonates very strongly with me and my experiences in life.[2] Any time I've been down about a situation, whether in my work or personal life, if I can get back to my curious nature, I learn something. I emerge with new understanding and a new attitude.

Often in my work with clients, I try to move them toward curiosity and away from anger or judgment. It's amazing how much new energy this stimulates. Take a moment to think about what you've learned from simply wondering about something. When you decide to make a shift or try a new lens on an issue, you challenge your own *knowing* and connect with your *unknowing*, opening the opportunity to learn something new. To look with a child's eyes and regain some innocence, to care more universally than just about the ego, is refreshing and germane to personal evolution and well-being.

Curiosity keeps us on the frontier of our lives, questioning what's next, what might that mean, and where could that take me/us? Choosing curiosity over stubbornness does not take away agency and goal-directedness. Innocence is also related to the issue of listening. One of my professors once chided that we can't hope to influence without the willingness to be influenced. We have to be able to truly hear someone else's point of view if we are to consider changing our perspective. One of my clients called it "generous listening." The easy answer takes no thought, no adjustment of our viewpoint, and no creativity. It drives little innovation. Yes, to be more generous with our time, effort, and faith in one another is to the benefit of our communities and ourselves.

Non-Linear Living

As I have grown, I have found myself shifting my point of view and feeling in the space of "in-betweens." Neil Diamond expresses it with great emotion in his song, "I Am...I Said:"

> But now a days I'm lost between two shores, LA's fine but it ain't home, New York's home but it ain't mine no more, I am, I cried, I am said I, I am lost and I can't even say why.

---

2   Sounds True CD – What to Remember When Waking (2010).

These lyrics certainly capture the discomfort of uncertainty. Organizations, as the name implies, tend to attract those who like planful, directed, decisive approaches. I work with more SJ's (Sensing, Judging Types) than any other Temperament group. Most of which don't like ambiguous situations. They tend to like things nailed down, divided into clear rights and wrongs, and outlined into steps from one to five. But life just isn't that simple and clean if we are really stepping into it rather than looking from the sidelines. As we endeavor to live robust lives of integrity and meaning, we might do well to consider this non-linear thought stream:

[have] **Integrity**

        [use] **Intuition   &   Inquiry**

    [get] **Insight**   **Metanoia:** Resulting in a new level and an opportunity to pick it up and continue on the growth path again.

The late Gabriel Garcia Marquez said, "...human beings are not born once and for all on the day their mothers give birth to them, but life obliges them over and over again to give birth to themselves." This is how we make for a fulfilling life.

Mindfulness is also important to success. It can be subtle to pay attention as an observer of yourself, letting go of judgment while attending to your emotions. Or it can be pure meditation and emptying of the mind.

This attempt to experience your own reality increases your compassion and ensures your growth. Having patience with your meanderings and what may seem like failures and foibles will pay off in your ability to see with new eyes. Maturing is germane to your aspirations and inspirations, your work on behalf of others, and your individuation journey.

There are other issues as well. It has taken me years to figure out how to eat to maintain my energy and alertness, for example. I struggle with my commitment to regular exercise as it gets in the way of all of the other things I *really* want to do. And I revisit these issues continuously so that I can be at my best. A goal of healthy and whole living sets me up for much greater success than a goal of perfection. Slowing things down and incorporating some meditation into my activities enables me to see the symptoms of getting off track that rise up in my body and behaviors. What are you doing for your physical body? What are you doing for your clarity of mind?

When you begin to work towards Self, you must be prepared to work and think differently, to step out of the box, and to consider new ways of being and doing. Taking time to let your defenses down is a must if you want to live an authentic life and do the work that is yours alone to do.

"The great calling is to true individuation, and individuation is awkward, it's messy, there's no script for it and it's unpredictable, but it's the only game in town." (O'Donohue, 2006)

Over a decade ago, at one of those times when I realized that I needed greater insight into my real feelings about my work, this was the path I took: I wanted to know how I would respond most authentically to the big questions in my life and the driving question for my career. It was then that I took on a specific new practice while taking part in a year-long leadership program for the parent company of the organization I worked for. The philosopher, author, and leadership consultant, Peter Koestenbaum,[3] who had been working with us in one particular session, told me that I "must go through the dark night of the soul"[4] and listen to my unconscious. "Pay attention to your dreams," he ordered. Finally, he said, you must "eat your enemies – integrate them with who you are." I'd been hearing more and more about dream work and while it seemed a little "out there" for this rather traditional professional, I decided I would give it a try. The "eating my enemies" directive made no clear sense in that

---

3   Peter Koestenbaum, author of Leadership, The Inner Side of Greatness. I worked with the 1st edition. The 2nd edition reflects his evolving Self, having the experience and shock of the 9/11/01 terrorist attacks in NYC. It is interesting to note the development of an individual who gets clearer about what is important to them.
4   "Dark night of the soul" is a popularized phrase relating to a personal crisis, which has its origins in a poem by St. John of the Cross.

moment, but the next morning I awoke with a dream of eating a hoagie. The filling was a snake.[5] At first, you might say that it was just the power of suggestion and the result of my conversation with Peter. Yes, that was true, *and* the beginning of much more. It was the data point from which my unconscious chose to work from the tens of thousands of data points that came up in 24 hours. While it was just a fragment of a dream, it was very meaningful for me at a time when I was going through a transition in my work life. In hindsight, I would say it was a time of "transformation."

> "Nothing happens…but first a dream."
>
> CARL SANDBERG

Consider a new practice that might stimulate a transformation in you. How can you empathize with and care for yourself while responding to the call to grow?

Two years ago, I redesigned my office for ergonomic correctness to help me with some back issues. I was aware that aesthetically, I wanted it to represent me and be a space in which I could flourish. Choosing and designing spaces where you spend a lot of time is very important. Consider the items that you have brought from one office to another. What is the projection on that item that makes it so important to have around? Why do you give up certain pictures, books, or relics from the past? What has changed in you? How have you moved on?

I have often noticed over the period of engagement with a client that his/her office changes shape over the time we've worked together. That old collection of cynical cartoons, for example, had to go in order to support the emerging of new ideas, transformation, and individuation. This can be a profound or subtle shift.

Mental and physical availability is also very important. If you cannot commit the necessary time for your development – whether coach or client – you may be doing too much.

---

5   Jeremy Taylor – Early in my decision to take up dream work and writing my dreams on a regular basis Jeremy provided a lot of enthusiastic support and guidance. He was the first to teach me how to do dream work. His books and workshops have been extremely helpful. (www.jeremytaylor.com).

There will be times in your life when doing "too much" is okay – short-term. A new promotion or project, having a child, or helping care for an aged parent are all things that might legitimately make your life unusually full. When I decided to start writing, I realized that something would have to be eliminated from my already full plate, and it couldn't be my own development. I decided that I could be more efficient if I took a couple of years off from golf and bike riding, both of which require a huge commitment of time. Walks in my neighborhood and a one-hour workout at a nearby gym were a good healthy trade-off, allowing me to keep a fair amount of balance. Two years ago, I decided I wanted to play golf regularly again, so I had to make other trade-offs.

With some regularity, therapists ask me how they can transition into coaching. It is much the same answer as anyone else coming to this work. However, there is a difference of context that needs to be learned. To have worked with people who are in the corporate world is not enough. Networking and asking questions, as well as staying curious and open, are still necessary. Aligning with someone who really understands the corporate environment is very helpful. Having "supervision" of some sort so that you can debrief your experiences and discuss client work makes a big difference. This exploration also allows for a courtship to discover whether this is the right work for you. One therapist told me he wanted to go into coaching, but he didn't want to go to people. He wanted them to come to him. In the end, he confessed that he really just wanted to earn more money. Then, we were able to get on to the real work of analyzing how he could make that happen.

The secret of the golden key lies in bringing life to the ego-Self axis, making conscious that which is unconscious, developing emotionally, and maturing to the challenges of the day in a way that supports your purpose, your work, your being. As a coach, you must discover your own treasures and gifts and find an authentic leadership and coaching style that capitalizes on these abilities.

The study of the nature and structure of "the unconscious" is almost certainly the most important and potentially productive area of inquiry available to us at the close of the 20th century.... I would argue that one important way of formulating the dire crisis of global ecology, world culture, and planetary survival that we face today is that it is the direct result of the disparity between the tremendously sophisticated knowledge we possess about how to manipulate the physical world to gratify our needs and desires, and the crude-to-non-existent knowledge we possess about our own unconscious depths — the place where those contradictory, self-destructive "needs and desires" arise in the first place.... The crisis we face in the world today is a crisis of evolving consciousness.

> "When life itself seems lunatic, who knows where madness lies? Perhaps to be too practical is madness. To surrender dreams — this may be madness. To seek treasure where there is only trash. Too much sanity may be madness — and maddest of all: to see life as it is, and not as it should be!"
>
> From *Man of La Mancha* (book by Dale Wasserman, lyrics by Joe Darion and music by Mitch Leigh)

Freud is correct to this extent: the dreams we remember from sleep are, indeed, "the royal road to the unconscious." Dreams are by far the most universally available, most compelling, and most potentially useful indications of the workings of the unconscious that we have. Sandor Ferenczi is also correct: "Dreams are the workshop of evolution." If we are to evolve our individual and collective self-awareness with sufficient speed and clarity to avoid the disasters we are creating for ourselves out of our partial consciousness, then paying close attention to dreams and learning to understand more about their multiple messages and gifts of increased awareness is a very important activity.

(Taylor, 1997)

This book delves into themes of authenticity and individuation that are explored on both theoretical and clinical fronts, themes which I had the benefit of exploring with Dr. Steinwedel as a student in a group leadership course, as well as when I was a client in one on one coaching. While the objective of the book is to teach professionals about executive coaching, it is also valuable for individuals pursuing self-actualization, as well as for those who manage or lead others. The concluding chapter is bound together by the story of a golden key, a key that may unlock hidden recesses on a journey of developing the Self. The story is reminiscent of a Hasidic parable, recounted by Martin Buber, in which Isaac, son of Yekel, from Cracow, has a dream of a treasure under a bridge in Prague. He wakes up, then undergoes an arduous journey to Prague to try to dig up the treasure under the bridge that he saw in his dream. When a police officer asks him why he is digging under a bridge, he mentions his dream. The police officer scoffs at him, and the officer tells him that he had a dream about someone named Isaac, son of Yekel, who had a treasure buried under his home in Cracow. While we often search for treasure in terms of material goods, the true treasure is buried within our psyche. The journey to find that treasure can be dark, and it can be illuminating. It is often a journey that can only be travelled alone. Yet, we are aided in this quest by relationships with others; a manager, a friend, a loved one, a therapist, or an executive coach. Dr. Steinwedel has provided a welcome map for this journey.

JONATHAN RUBIN, MD, MBA
Chief Medical Officer
Alcobra, Inc

The Golden Key

In the Grimm's fairy tale of The Golden Key, a boy is made to go outside into the frozen night to fetch wood. Isn't that so like our tasks in life – while still quite immature we have big responsibilities? We push through all that is frozen and impenetrable hoping for the resources that will warm us and sometimes to our amazement we find a golden key of some sort or another.

There are several silver keys – those important pieces of information, experiences and ways of being that help us to be successful in our work as coaches. We have covered many: Self-awareness, courage, curiosity, empathy, humility, vulnerability, wholeness, quieting the mind and challenging the soul. Metaphorically these are silver because while germane to our work and success with others there is something more rare and precious. The boy in the fairy tale doesn't find a silver key, he finds a golden key and it is this golden key that fits the treasure chest that he finds at yet a deeper level.

At the deeper level of our own exploration we too find the golden key and treasure chest. When the key and lock are engaged all of our knowing and hearing and being unites with that of the other and we have insight – clarity of understanding, connection. There is attunement. You will recall the communication model (p. 93). When we listen deeply we are listening for the unconscious messages to and from the Self and the other. We're aware that we are sending these unconscious messages as well as getting them and we pay close, deep attention for some new understanding that builds the relationship – the trust and the mutual interest that enables effective support on the journey each of us is on. Being in relationship entangles us with the other in ways we can't fully comprehend...but we can start the unfolding and enable the intimate dialogue that is critical to individuation.

"Coaching takes a holistic view of the individual: work, corporate values, personal needs and career development are made to work in synergy, not against one another."
British Journal of Administrative Management

The golden key gives access to having this attunement with your client, with the Self and with the organization simultaneously. The golden key opens you to hearing beyond the words – mission statements and aspirations; beyond the body language – frustration, annoyance, happiness; and engages one with the subtleties. It involves being able to orchestrate, or guide the best outcome through inquiry, intuition, integrity and insight. It is a bit like the orchestra leader who can hear the need for more brass or more subtlety, a longer stretch, an *adagio* or a *crescendo*. You set the tempo, you cue and articulate and unify the performers – but not from the ego, from humility, from authenticity – from listening, inquiring and wondering along with the other players. And you know when to get out of the way. This deep listening, this attunement is rare and very precious indeed.

On Jung

"Man's worst sin is unconsciousness, but it is indulged in with the greatest piety, even among those who should serve mankind as teachers and examples" (Jung, 1969a).

I have learned and relearned many things on this writing journey going on eight years now, not the least of which is that I know relatively little. I have challenged my beliefs and my preferences, my interests and my potential impact. I still believe strongly in the gifts that Jung left us after a full life of commitment to learning about psyche and challenging his own conscious living. I value his warnings as to what a dangerous method psychoanalysis can be and his insights on how to prepare to be in the helping profession. In *The Undiscovered Self,* he wrote, "As with all dangers, we can guard against the risk of psychic infection only when we know what is attacking us, and how, where and when the attack will come" (Jung, 1990). In other words, we cannot guard against psychic infection. This alone should stop us in our tracks, forcing us to question our willingness to continue to practice and our commitment to being lifelong learners.

Getting in touch with your complexes and the archetypes at their core is a starting place for your ability to work with others with some level of value. Studying the meaning of archetypes and understanding the wisdom they hold for you will help ground you in the midst of working with psyche. And you are working with psyche whether or not that is your intention. In the book of his own personal life reflection, Jung posited, "The doctor who does not know from his own experience the numinosity of the archetypes will scarcely be able to escape their negative effect when he encounters it in his practice" (Jaffé, 1989).

In discussing the observer's effectiveness and the importance of not only seeing objectively, but also subjectively, Jung says, "These conditions are fulfilled only when the observer is sufficiently informed about the nature and scope of his own personality. He can, however, be sufficiently informed only when he has in large measure freed himself from the leveling influence of collective opinions and thereby arrived at a clear conception of his own individuality" (Jung, 1971).

Many people don't want to do the hard work of self-assessment and personal growth. Jung addresses his concern for a doctor who has no wish to undergo his own analysis, or, even through his passion for the work, bring himself to self-analyze through work with a patient, noting he should never "touch analysis." He elaborates by saying,

> In the last resort his whole work will be intellectual bluff – for how can he help his patient to conquer his morbid inferiority when he himself is so manifestly inferior? How can the patient learn to abandon his neurotic subterfuges when he sees the doctor playing hide-and-seek with his own personality, as though unable, for fear of being thought inferior, to drop the professional mask of authority, competence, superior knowledge, etc. (Jung, 1954)

So, while we are not all doctors and rarely psychoanalysts, we still get an important message about the Self work we must engage in so that we don't wake up some day realizing it was all "intellectual bluff."

I hope you will connect with two über insights I believe we must be clear about: First, nothing gets done without relationship; and, second, our success as people (individuation, wholeness, self-actualization) – individually and in relationship – is all about consciousness. Our effectiveness as coaches is little without developing the rapport and the vulnerability that enables intimacy.

Intimacy allows the barriers to come down and real conversation to manifest. This is when the true relationship begins. Jung said, "To find out what is truly individual in ourselves, profound reflection is needed; and suddenly we realize how uncommonly difficult the discovery of individuality in fact is" (Jung, 1966).[6]

---

6   Originally from "The Relations between the Ego and the Unconscious," 1928, in 1953 it was included as part of the Collected Works, Volume 7.

It is in the examination, the analysis, the observing that we can become the person we want to be, with integrity and credibility. So I feel I am back to the beginning where I noted Shamdasani's net-net for *The Red Book* is to "value your inner life." That is what it's all about in a nutshell!

I hope you embrace your life and live it fully, modeling the individuation journey as an inspiration to those with whom you work.

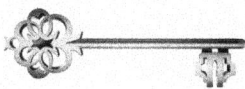

Your Notes

Jot down anything that has come to mind for you personally at this time:

What are you feeling right now? What surprises you from your notes? What insights did you get about yourself? Any other thoughts right now? Anything you want to do, communicate or absorb because of this reflection?

Additional Reading and Resources

Poems

- » *Beannacht* by John O'Donohue
- » *Start Close In* by David Whyte
- » *Wild Geese* by Mary Oliver

Read

- » *Covert Processes at Work: Managing the Five Hidden Dimensions of Organizational Change* by Robert Marshak
- » *Deciphering the Cosmic Number: The Strange Friendship of Wolfgang Pauli and Carl Jung* by Arthur I. Miller
- » *Dream Work: Techniques for Discovering the Creative Power in Dreams* by Jeremy Taylor
- » *House of Cards* by William D. Cohan
- » *A Little Book on the Human Shadow* by Robert Bly
- » *Managing Oneself* (HBR classic) by Peter F. Drucker
- » *Mountains Beyond Mountains* by Tracy Kidder
- » *Pigs Eat Wolves* by Charles Bates
- » *The Psychology of Executive Coaching* by Bruce Peltier
- » *The Razor's Edge* by W. Somerset Maugham

Songs

- » *Why do we dream in Metaphors?* by Seal
- » *Check It Out,* by John Mellencamp

Movies & Television

- » *Star Wars* (1977)
- » *Still Mine* (2012)
- » *The Visitor* (2007)
- » *The Wizard of Oz* (1939)

Where Do I Go From Here?

But the adventure is successful only when the descent
into the unconscious changes from passive exposure into
active participation. By taking up an attitude towards it,
consciousness delimits itself from the unconscious,
broadens its scope so that the personality can unfold."

Aniele Jaffé, *The Myth of Meaning*

Take a deep breath, hold it for four seconds, and let it out. Repeat.

Let go of any anxiety you feel. Start to think about what is next for you and your development, but in manageable chunks.

Take an extra three seconds to look deeply into your eyes in the mirror before you wash your face. Consider who you are and how you want to be in the world. What will it take to become that person? What one thing would allow you to feel a little more authentic, a little more joyful? What will make your life more meaningful?

What would it be like to put just a little more effort into consciousness each day? What might it be like to stop for a moment to acknowledge your family members rather than give in to the habitual grunt to your spouse and children as you pass them in the kitchen? How might it change you and open you up to greater fulfillment if you seek more awareness of who they are and what they add to your life?

There are many creative ways you can develop greater insights now that you have finished this book. For example, after each chapter you made some notes, which you might find useful to revisit at this time. Look for thoughts and ideas that might make your work more effective or that might help you to imbue more meaning in your everyday life. Here are some possibilities:

» You might story-board your ideas or create a mindmap. Use your imagination to expand on your thoughts or feelings;

» You might discuss certain ideas or insights from the book with a friend or colleague;

» You could create the website you always wanted or update a current website to capture more of the essence of who you are and the niche you wish to work within;

» You might designate one hour per week on your calendar for your own reflection, going back to areas you highlighted or made notes about;

» You might enroll in a workshop in one of your favorite topics or decide to give one in an area where you feel you have a lot of expertise;

» You might use the book in a coach's supervisory group;

» You could seek further insight or supervisory support from a therapist, analyst, or another coach;

» You could read some of the additional suggested books, even prioritizing the ones that interest you most and setting a goal of reading one book a month;

» You might write your own book, start a blog, or begin to express some of your ideas on Twitter;

» You could put together a playlist of songs that inspire you or help you reflect;

» You might start an active journal or recommit to one, making notes on your experiences, concerns, learnings, and curiosities, including pictures if you feel so inclined;

» You might like to capture many salient images in a collage – perhaps you will make a sketch or a painting of an important image or symbol or incorporate your favorite quotes, a poem, or the words of a song in your collage or journal;

» You could watch some of the films mentioned in the book – either watching alone and journaling about it after, watching with someone who could discuss it with you, or starting a movie group;

» You could reflect on some of the poems mentioned in the book or write one for yourself. You don't have to be a skilled writer – the aim is to get in touch with your authentic feelings.

Whatever you do, do something to explore who you are and the coach you wish to be. I hope you will find this book useful for some time to come.

References

Arbinger. 2002. *Leadership and self-deception*. San Francisco: Berrett-Koehler Publishers.

Barton, Michelle A., and Kathleen M. Sutcliffe. 2010. "Learning when to stop momentum." *MIT Sloan Management Review*

Beebe, John. 1992. *Integrity in depth, Number two Carolyn and Ernest Fay Series in Analytical Psychology*. College Station: Texas A&M University Press.

Beebe, John. 2013. "Approaching a patient's complexes in contemporary culture." [Workshop brochure]. Jungian Psychotherapists Association (JPA) Accessed 9/27/13.

Bly, Robert. 1990. *Iron John*. NY: Vintage Books.

Carter, Jimmy. 1975. *Why not the best?* Nashville Broadman Press.

Collins, Jim. 2001. *Good to great: why some companies make the leap...and others don't*. NY: HarperCollins.

Conforti, Michael. 2010. "Sacred" abuses in the name of God, Self and other - a call for clarity in addressing archetypal truths. (January 15, 2010).

Corbett, Lionel. 2013. Psychotherapy based on depth psychology is a superior approach. e-jungian.

Drago-Severson, Ellie. 2008. "4 practices serve as pillars for adult learning." *National Staff Development Council* 29 (4):4.

George, Bill, Peter Sims, Andrew McLean, and Diana Mayer. 2007. "Discovering Your Authentic Leadership." *Harvard Business Review*.

Goleman, Daniel. 1998. *Working with emotional intelligence*. NY: Bantam Books.

Hall, Calvin S., and Vernon J. Nordby. 1973. *A primer of Jungian psychology*: Meridian.

Henderson, Robert, and Janis Henderson. 2006. *Living with Jung: "enterviews" with Jungian analysts*. Vol. 1. New Orleans: Spring Journal Books.

Hill, Linda A., Greg Brandeau, Emily Truelove, Kent Lineback. 2014. *Collective Genius: The art and practice of leading innovation*. Boston: Harvard Business Review Press.

Hillman, James. 1975. *Re-Visioning Psychology*. New York: Harper & Row, Publishers.

Hollis, James. 2005. *Finding meaning in the second half of life*. New York: Gotham Books.

Hollis, James. 2009. *What matters most: living a more considered life*. NY: Gotham Books.

Hollis, James. 2013. *Hauntings: dispelling the ghosts that run our lives*. Asheville: Chiron.

Honigmann, David. 2009. *Vison in verse from boardroom bard*. Accessed January 11, 2014.

Hopcke, Robert. 1990. *Men's dreams, men's healing.* Boston: Shambhala.

Intrator, Sam M., and Megan Scribner. 2007. *Leading from within: poetry that sustains the courage to lead.* San Francisco: Jossey-Bass. Leadership, poetry

Jacobi, Jolande 1965. *The way of individuation.* Translated by R.F.C. Hull. New York: New American Library. Original edition, Der Weg zur Individuation.

Jaffé, Aniela. 1971. *The myth of meaning.* Translated by R.F.C. Hull. NY: G. P. Putnam's Sons.

Jaffé, Aniela, ed. 1989. *Memories, dreams, reflections.* Fourth ed. NY: Vintage Books. Original edition, Erinnerungen Traume Gedanken, 1961.

Johnson, Robert A. 1974. *HE: understanding masculine psychology.* King of Prussia, PA.: Religious Publishing Co.

Jung, C.G. 1954. *The practice of psychotherapy.* Translated by R.F.C. Hull. 18 vols. Vol. 16, *Bollingen Series XX.* New York: Pantheon Books The Collected Works of C.G. Jung

Jung, C.G. 1956. *Symbols of transformation.* Translated by R.F.C. Hull. Edited by Herbert Read, Michael Fordham, Gerhard Adler and William McGuire. Second ed, *Bollingen Series XX.* Princeton: Princeton University Press.

Jung, C.G. 1989. *The symbolic life.* Translated by R.F.C. Hull. Edited by Herbert Read, Michael Fordham, Gerhard Adler and William McGuire, *Bollingen Series XX.* Princeton: Princeton University Press. Reprint, 3.

Jung, C.G. 1990. *The undiscovered self; with symbols and the interpretation of dreams.* Translated by R.F.C. Hull. NJ: Princeton University Press. Translated and revised, excerpted from the Collected Works #10, Civilization in Transition. Original edition, Gegenwart und Zukunft.

Jung, C.G. 1960. *The structure and dynamics of the psyche.* Translated by R.F.C. Hull. Edited by executive editor William McGuire, Sir Herbert Read, M.D. Michael Fordham, M.R.C.P. and Ph.D. Gerhard Adler. second ed. 18 vols. Vol. 8, *Bollingen Series XX.* Princeton: Princeton University Press. Collected Works. Original edition, "The Stages of Life" (1930).

Jung, C.G. 1967. *Alchemical studies.* Translated by R.F.C. Hull. Edited by executive editor William McGuire, Sir Herbert Read, M.D. Michael Fordham, M.R.C.P. and Ph.D. Gerhard Adler. 18 vols. Vol. 13, *Bollingen Series XX.* Princeton: Princeton University Press. Collected Works.

Jung, C.G. 1969a. *The archetypes and the collective unconscious.* Translated by R.F.C. Hull. Edited by executive editor William McGuire, Sir Herbert Read, M.D. Michael Fordham, M.R.C.P. and Ph.D. Gerhard Adler. Second ed. 18 vols. Vol. 9.1, *Bollingen Series XX.* Princeton: Princeton University Press. Collected Works of C.G. Jung.

Jung, C.G. 1971. *Psychological types*. Translated by H.G. Baynes (with revision by R.F.C. Hull). Edited by executive editor William McGuire, Sir Herbert Read, M.D. Michael Fordham, M.R.C.P. and Ph.D. Gerhard Adler. 18 vols. Vol. 6, *Bollingen Series XX*. Princeton: Princeton University Press.

Jung, C.G. 1969b. *Aion: researches into the phenomenology of the self*. Translated by R.F.C. Hull. Edited by executive editor William McGuire, Sir Herbert Read, M.D. Michael Fordham, M.R.C.P. and Ph.D. Gerhard Adler. Second ed. Vol. 9 (part 2), *Bollingen Series XX*. Princeton: Princeton University Press. Collected Works.

Kegan, Robert. 1994. *In over our heads: the mental demands of modern life*. Cambridge, Mass: Harvard University Press.

Lombardo, Michael, and Robert Eichinger. 2002. Development Matrix. Minneapolis: Lominger Limited.

Maslow, A.H. 1971. *The farther reaches of human nature*. N.Y.: Penguin Books.

McCord, Patty 2014. "How Netflix Reinvented HR." *Harvard Business Review*.

Miller, Arthur I. 2009. *Deciphering the cosmic number: The strange relationship of Wolfgang Pauli and Carl Jung*. New York: W W Norton and Company.

Moore, Thomas. 2010. *Care of the soul in medicine*. USA: Hay House, Inc.

NetMBA.com. 2002-2010. *McClelland's theory of needs*. Accessed 10/01/11.

O'Donohue, John. 2006. *The therapist's task*. Psychotherapy Networker Symposium.

Ouchi, William. 1981. *Theory Z: how American business can meet the Japanese challenge*. 283 vols. London: Addison-Wesley Publishing, Inc.

Patterson, Kerry, Joseph Grenny, Ron McMillan, and Al Switzler. 2002. *Crucial conversations: tools for talking when the stakes are high*. NY: McGraw-Hill.

Phipps, Carter. 2008. "The cosmos, the psyche & YOU." *What is Enlightenment?* 50-68.

Quenk, Naomi. 2000. *In the grip: understanding type, stress and the inferior function*. 2 ed. Palo Alto: CPP, Inc.

Rock, David, and Jeffrey Schwartz. 2006. "The Neuroscience of Leadership." *Strategy + Business* (43):9.

Rogers, Carl. 1961. *On becoming a person: a therapist's view of psychotherapy*. Boston: Houghton Mifflin.

Rosen, Robert H. 2008. *Just enough anxiety: the hidden drivers of business success*. London: Portfolio, Penguin Books Ltd.

Samuels, Andrew, Bani Shorter, and Fred Plaut. 1986. *A Critical Dictionary of Jungian Analysis*. London: Routledge, Taylor & Francis Group.

Schein, Edgar. 1988. *Process consultation: its role in organization development*. 2 ed. Vol. 1. NY: Addison-Wesley.

Schott, Richard L. 1992. "Abraham Maslow, Humanistic Psychology, and Organization Leadership: A Jungian Approach." *Journal of Humanistic Psychology* 32 (1):106-120.

Schwartz-Salant, Nathan. 1991. "Vision, Interpretation, and the Interactive Field." *Journal of Analytical Psychology* 36:343-365.

Sedgwick, David. 1994. *The wounded healer: countertransference from a Jungian perspective.* London Routledge.

Shamdasani, Sonu, ed. 2009. *The red book, Philemon.* London: W. W. Norton & Company.

Steinwedel, Janet S. 2005. "Dream work in leadership coaching: an exploratory study." Ph.D. Case Study, Human and Organizational Systems, Fielding Graduate University.

Taylor, Jeremy. 1997. [Website] Accessed January 5. http://www.jeremytaylor.com.

Von Franz, Marie Louise 1978. *Projection and re-collection in Jungian Psychology.* London: Open Court

Warner, Brad. 2011. *Disrobing Genpo Roshi.* (February 9, 2011). Accessed November 2014.

Whitworth, Laura, Henry Kimsey-House, and Phil Sandahl. 1998. *Co-active coaching: new skills for coaching people toward success in work and life.* Palo Alto, CA: Davies-Black Publishing.

Whyte, David. 1994. *The heart aroused: poetry and the preservation of the soul in corporate America.* New York: Currency/Doubleday.

Wikipedia. 2013. "Andrea Jung." Answers.com. (http://www.answers.com/topic/andrea-jung.)

Woodman, Marion. 1982. *Addiction to perfection: the still unravished bride.* Toronto: Inner City Books.

Young, Jeffrey E., Janet S. Klosko, and Marjorie E. Weishaar. 2003. *Schema Therapy: a practitioner's guide.* London: The Guilford Press.

Zoja, Luigi. 2007. *Ethics and analysis: philosophical perspectives and their application in therapy.* Edited by David H. Rosen, *Carolyn and Ernest Fay Series in Analytical Psychology.* College Station: Texas A&M University Press.

Index

A

Active imagination 81, 179, 201, 202

Analysis 24, 26, 31, 39, 43, 59, 77, 78, 81, 104, 122, 187, 218, 256, 257, 268, 269

Analytical Communication Model 93

Analytical frame 15, 24, 36, 39, 41, 76, 90, 104, 130, 133, 135, 178, 200, 211

Analytical psychology 7, 19, 24, 43, 138, 191, 265, 268, 269

Anima, animus 144

Appiah, Kwame Anthony 217

Archetype 20, 31, 68, 69, 70, 120, 131, 138, 139, 140, 145, 149, 181, 182, 184, 185, 186, 218, 219, 224, 231, 236, 239, 241, 242, 255, 267

Argyris, Chris 97, 168

Aspiration, inspiration 5, 19, 33, 52, 53, 59, 60, 61, 62, 63, 64, 65, 66, 68, 77, 79, 80, 90, 97, 105, 115, 117, 124, 125, 126, 156, 200, 202, 209, 212, 216, 235, 240, 246, 248, 254, 257

Authenticity 5, 11, 19, 24, 69, 95, 111, 113, 114, 125, 126, 136, 138, 143, 145, 170, 175, 176, 177, 180, 181, 186, 187, 193, 205, 210, 212, 216, 218, 222, 233, 253, 254

B

Behaviorism 153, 154

Bly, Robert 224, 259

C

Campbell, Joseph 128, 130, 132, 224

CAPT (Center for Applications of Psychological Type) 115

Charlatan 138, 139, 140, 142, 143, 231, 239, 240

Coaching 3, 4, 6, 7, 115, 118, 121, 122, 123, 132, 133, 135, 136, 137, 139, 140, 141, 144, 151, 154, 155, 157, 159, 164, 165, 167, 169, 177, 185, 188, 190, 200, 201, 205, 209, 212, 217, 219, 230, 239, 240, 242, 243, 245, 251, 253, 254, 259, 268, 269

Coaching Model and Framework 31, 76, 77, 82, 84, 87, 88, 89, 90, 130, 135

Cognitive School or Cognitive Development 15, 41, 105, 158

Collective unconscious 44, 69, 84, 131, 267

Complex 31, 38, 43, 57, 58, 59, 81, 82, 85, 98, 99, 100, 103, 118, 119, 120, 122, 124, 136, 143, 145, 168, 176, 178, 179, 184, 189, 215, 216, 220, 231, 233, 235, 238, 242, 255, 265

Conforti, Michael 215, 216, 265

Corbett, Lionel 45, 141, 265

Theory X, Theory Y 159

Teilhard de Chardin, Pierre 43

Tillich, Paul 175

U

Unconscious 14, 16, 18, 24, 25, 26, 30, 37, 38, 44, 45, 53, 57, 58, 69, 80, 81, 82, 84, 92, 94, 95, 97, 99, 100, 101, 121, 122, 128, 131, 133, 134, 144, 145, 146, 168, 169, 170, 183, 199, 200, 201, 202, 204, 205, 216, 217, 219, 230, 231, 234, 236, 237, 238, 240, 249, 250, 251, 252, 254, 256, 261, 267

V

VAL 82, 91, 99, 116, 117

Values 9, 37, 40, 58, 63, 79, 82, 91, 99, 101, 102, 113, 116, 117, 118, 128, 129, 133, 137, 141, 151, 159, 160, 173, 176, 177, 180, 186, 194, 195, 196, 200, 220, 221, 245, 254

Von Franz, Marie Louise 214, 268

W

Whyte, David 14, 27, 47, 176, 180, 186, 206, 224, 241, 246, 259, 269

Wilber, Ken 96, 102, 103, 109, 163

Winnicott, Donald 53, 134

Wizard of Oz 132, 231, 232, 238, 259

Wordsworth, William 47, 212

Wounded Healer 65, 90, 268

Z

Zoja, Luigi 24, 39, 40, 269

About Janet S. Steinwedel, PhD

As President of Leader's Insight, an Executive Coaching and Leadership Effectiveness consultancy, Dr. Steinwedel provides thought leadership as a consultant and executive coach. She assists leaders in clarifying their goals and objectives and becoming more aware of themselves and their behaviors in service to their aspirations and business results.

With 25 years of experience working in such industries as pharmaceuticals, health care, financial services, insurance, communications, retail, and hospitality, Janet works effectively with a broad range of leaders. She uses an analytical framework which provides a foundational understanding of personality and human behavior—conscious and unconscious processes. In addition to her own work with corporate executives, Janet devotes time to a "coaching for coaches" process in which she helps other executive coaches with their personal and professional development.

www.LeadersInsight.com
Twitter: SteinwedelJanet